†HE SACRED BLOOD

MICHAEL BYRNES

SIMON &
SCHUSTER

London · New York · Sydney · Toronto

A CBS COMPANY

First published in the United States of America by
HarperCollins Publishers Inc., 2009
First published in Great Britain by Simon & Schuster UK Ltd, 2009
A CBS COMPANY

1 3 5 7 9 10 8 6 4 2

Simon & Schuster UK Ltd
1st Floor
222 Gray's Inn Road
London WC1X 8HB

www.simonsays.co.uk

Simon & Schuster Australia
Sydney

A CIP catalogue record for this book
is available from the British Library

ISBN 978-1-84737-238-3

Typeset in Janson by M Rules
Printed in the UK by CPI Mackays, Chatham, ME5 8TD

For Caroline, Vivian, and Camille

For God has chosen him of all your tribes to stand and serve with the name of God, he and his sons forever.

– DEUTERONOMY 18:5

†HE SACRED BLOOD

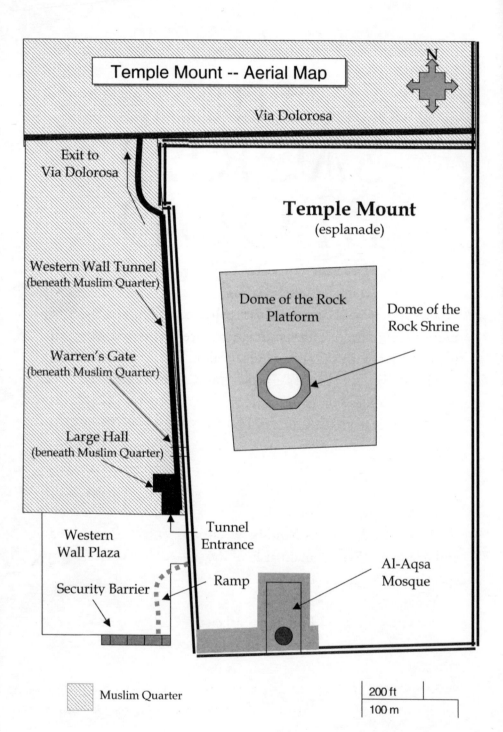

Temple Mount -- Aerial Map

N

Via Dolorosa

Exit to
Via Dolorosa

Temple Mount
(esplanade)

Western Wall Tunnel
(beneath Muslim Quarter)

Dome of the Rock
Platform

Dome of the
Rock Shrine

Warren's Gate
(beneath Muslim Quarter)

Large Hall
(beneath Muslim Quarter)

Western
Wall Plaza

Tunnel
Entrance

Security Barrier

Ramp

Al-Aqsa
Mosque

Muslim Quarter

200 ft

100 m

'Today you come with me, Aaron,' Mordecai Cohen whispered, motioning for his son to stand. He gestured at the arched opening of a corridor leading behind the altar.

The thirteen-year-old's gangly limbs froze. Glancing back over his shoulder, Aaron saw the last of the women coming down from the balcony and funneling out the synagogue's front door. A hand tugged at his arm.

'Come,' his father repeated. 'There's nothing to fear, I assure you.'

'I'm not afraid,' Aaron lied.

Mordecai splayed his hand between his son's shoulder blades and urged him up the main aisle of the sanctuary. 'This is a very special day for you, Aaron.'

'You are bringing me inside?'

'That's right. Grandfather has asked to speak with you.'

Aaron slid his trembling hands into the pockets of his black trousers.

For as long as he could remember, following Saturday's Shabbat services, the ritual had always been the same. Father would send Aaron's mother and four sisters home to prepare the fish and meats for the traditional Sabbath meal *shalosh seudot*, and then he'd disappear into a locked room situated behind the main altar. Meanwhile, Aaron would wait in the sanctuary and climb the steps to the balcony, even daringly approach the magnificent walnut cabinet, the Aron Ha-Kodesh, that housed the Torah scrolls and run his fingers along the cabinet's intricate rosette carvings, stroke the smooth *parokhet* draped over its doors. An hour later, Father would emerge from the room and they'd discuss the Torah readings during their walk home.

But today, Aaron found himself being guided around the altar's elevated pulpit, or bema, and entering a previously forbidden corridor that was long and painted with shadows. Deep in the darkness, a formidable oak door with a heavy brass dead bolt secured the synagogue's most secret place.

Never had Father spoken of what lay beyond this door.

Never had Aaron asked why.

Mordecai placed a hand on the knob, hesitated, and turned to his son. 'Ready?'

Aaron looked up at him. At this moment, Father appeared much younger than before, his graying beard and earlocks darkened by the shadows, the hard creases round his blue-green eyes seemingly smoothed away. And his expression was one that Aaron would never forget: pride and solidarity intermingled with trepidation. They were two men about to embark on a journey.

'Ready,' Aaron tremulously replied, the thumping in his chest so fierce it resonated in his ears.

Mordecai rapped twice with his knuckles, then turned the doorknob. He eased the door open and held out his hand. 'Inside, son.'

The sweet smell of incense rushed into Aaron's nostrils as he stepped over the threshold. The space that lay beyond the door was more mystifying than he'd ever imagined.

The room was cubical and humble in size. A sunbeam lanced the haze through a single arched window set high in the rear wall. Beneath the window, Aaron's grandfather knelt in front of a second Aron Ha-Kodesh even more magnificent than the one in the sanctuary. Bluish smoke wisped heavenward from a golden censer set before it.

Grandfather bobbed in prayer, a white prayer shawl called a *tallit katan* draped over his stooped shoulders, its *tzitzit* tassels swaying with his incantations.

Silently, Aaron swept his curious gaze around the room and studied an impressive collection of framed oil paintings that covered the wall to his left. Each depicted a scene from the Torah – a storyboard of images, from Moses and the Israelites to the Tabernacle and the lost temple. The wall to his right was dedicated to tall bookshelves packed tight with volumes, spines embossed in Hebrew. Was this a place meant to store sacred texts and vessels – a *genizah*? Aaron tried to imagine what his father had been doing in here every Saturday. Praying? Studying?

The old man eased off the kneeler, then took a few moments to tenderly fold the prayer shawl and tuck it away in one of the scroll cabinet's drawers. When he finally turned to them, Aaron straightened and directed his gaze to his grandfather's amazing aquamarine eyes, which brought tranquility to an otherwise fearsome façade. The family resemblance was unmistakable, to the point where Aaron felt he was looking at his own future visage. Beneath his prayer cap, or *kippah*, Grandfather's earlocks curled in tight twists around his ears to a flowing gray beard.

'*Shabbat shalom*,' Grandfather greeted them.

'*Shabbat shalom*,' Aaron replied.

3

'Hands out of your pockets, my boy,' he instructed Aaron.

Blushing, Aaron liberated his hands and let them fall to his sides.

'Better,' Grandfather said approvingly, stepping closer. 'We cover the tops of our heads to show humility to God as He watches over us,' he said, placing his hand on Aaron's *kippah*, 'but we praise Him with our hands. So be sure He can see them.' Pointing up, Grandfather winked – a small gesture that put Aaron more at ease. 'Mordecai,' he said, addressing the boy's father without taking his eyes off Aaron, 'I ask if Mr. Aaron Cohen and I might have some time alone.'

'Certainly,' Mordecai replied.

Aaron watched his father leave the room, the door closing quietly behind him. The role-switching made the boy feel special, and when he glanced back at Grandfather, he could tell the old man intended it to do so. The electric silence was pierced by a fire truck screaming down Coney Island Avenue. Aaron's eyes darted toward the window as the siren quickly faded.

'Now, Aaron,' Grandfather began, drawing his attention back from the street noise. 'When I was a young boy – the same age as you are now – my father brought me to see *my* grandfather so that I could be told about my family's legacy. First, do you under-stand what I mean by "legacy"?'

They remained standing, and it wasn't until then that Aaron realized the room lacked any chairs. Aaron nodded, though it wasn't too clear to him what his grandfather really meant.

'It is through our children that we leave behind or pass for-ward, if you will, our family history – and more precisely, its genealogy. Something you'll learn much more about in the coming years. And through each of us, God transfers His gift across generations.'

'You mean . . . babies?' Now Aaron feared this was a prelude to a discussion on puberty. After all, he'd only read from the Torah during his bar mitzvah a week earlier. Though Jewish law now considered him a man, he had yet to feel like one.

This made Grandfather chuckle. 'Not exactly. Though we can find God's gift inside our progeny.'

Aaron blushed, fighting the compulsion to put his hands in his pockets again. Grandfather's expression suddenly turned severe.

'You see, Aaron, there is something very unique about our ancestors. Something quite different than most families. In fact, it can be traced back thousands of years to a man who shares your honorable name. You see him there in the white robe?' He pointed to one of the framed scenes on the wall and the boy's curious eyes followed.

The painting depicted events from Exodus; it showed a bearded man in a white robe and ceremonial headdress sacrificing a young lamb on a magnificent golden altar. Aaron was momentarily transfixed by the blood gushing forth from the animal's slit neck.

'Your great ancestor Aaron was a very blessed man. You know him from the Torah, yes?'

Knowing his Saturday discussions with Father had paid off, he said in a proud tone, 'The first high priest of the Hebrews, the *kohen gadol* . . . from the tribe of Levi.'

Grandfather paced over to admire the painting, hands behind his back. 'That's right. And Aaron had a very special brother whom his parents had given away to protect him.'

'*Moshe,*' Aaron confidently replied. Moses.

Pride showed in Grandfather's eyes as he nodded and encouraged the boy to elaborate.

'In Egypt' – Aaron's voice trembled slightly – 'Pharaoh had

commanded the killing of all newborn Israelite males. So Moses's mother placed him in a basket and floated him down the river Nile. Moses was found by Pharaoh's daughter when she went to bathe in the river. She adopted him.'

'And raised him in Pharaoh's court,' Grandfather added. 'Very good. As you know, Moses and Aaron were later reunited. Almost thirty-three hundred years ago, God sent Moses to free his brother, his family, and his people from bondage. The Israelites escaped the Egyptian army' – he pointed to the painting showing Moses with his sacred staff set low to release the seas onto the soldiers and chariots – 'and fought for forty years to conquer the tribal lands promised to them by God. Moses was the first true messiah. The founder of a new nation. Legacy meant everything to Moses.'

'And we're his family?'

'Thirty-three centuries later, Levite blood flows in my veins, your father's veins . . .'

'And mine?'

'That's right.'

Aaron was speechless.

'Your legacy, Aaron, is a priestly legacy we desperately need to preserve.' He held up his left hand, clenched it into a fist, and shook it to emphasize the importance of his message. 'But our bloodline hasn't remained pure, as God intended. Centuries have corrupted us.'

'The Diaspora?'

Grandfather nodded. 'And other things too,' he said in a low tone, and paused. 'Some of our ancestors have not been mindful of God's plan. But one day, very soon, I am certain, we will make the bloodline pure again. And when that happens, a new covenant will be made between God and our people. After much tragedy . . .'

He stammered as he thought mournfully about his over one million brethren who'd suffered – most fatally – alongside him in Auschwitz. 'Israel is struggling to be a nation once more – to reclaim its lost lands. The tribes are still scattered. Much turmoil remains . . . an unclear future that only God knows.'

Only days earlier, Aaron's father had told him that Israel's air force had bombed Egyptian airfields to preempt a strike. Now Egyptian, Jordanian, and Syrian troops were amassing around Israel's borders. Father had not stopped praying since it all began.

'A nation, I'm afraid, that still does not abide by God's covenant,' the old man lamented, casting his eyes to the floor. 'Only when the bloodline is restored can the covenant be restored. Then Israel will truly rise up like a phoenix.'

'But how will it be restored?'

Grandfather smiled once more. 'You're not ready for that yet, my ambitious grandson. But soon, when the time is right, you'll learn the secrets entrusted to my father, me, my son' – reaching out, he gently pressed two fingers over the boy's pounding heart – 'and you. In the meantime, there is much you will need to learn,' he said, sweeping his hand across the brimming bookcases. 'You will come here with your father every Saturday following service. From now on, it will be the three of us.'

Aaron grinned.

'Three generations,' he said, patting the boy's cheek. A thought suddenly came to him. 'Ah,' he said, holding up a finger. 'Which means there is something I must give to you.'

Aaron watched as Grandfather paced to the scroll cabinet, slid open its smallest drawer, and rummaged through the contents. Finding what he was looking for, he held it tight in his hand, closed the drawer, and made his way back.

As he stared at the old man's closed fist, Aaron's face glowed with anticipation.

'For many, many centuries, our family has used a symbol to represent our ancestors. See here . . .'

Grandfather turned over his hand and opened his fingers to reveal a round object resembling a silver dollar. When Aaron pressed closer to examine its details, he realized it wasn't a coin at all.

'Tell me what you see on this talisman.'

It was the strangest symbol. Certainly nothing that looked Judaic. In fact, the occultist images seemed to go against Jewish teachings concerning iconography. 'A fish . . . wrapped around' – his brow crinkled – 'a fork?'

'Yes, but not a fish, a dolphin. And not exactly a fork, but a trident.' Seeing the boy's muddled expression, he sternly said, 'You are never to speak about anything that you are taught in this room unless it is to someone who possesses this same talisman. And you must promise that you will never show this to anyone else. Not even your best friend in the yeshiva. Do you understand?'

'I understand, Grandfather.'

'*Yasher koach.*' And the boy would certainly need strong will, thought Grandfather. The world was fast changing. Snatching the boy's left hand, he placed the talisman in Aaron's palm and wrapped the boy's fingers around it. 'Protect this.' He clasped both hands around Aaron's fist.

The cold metal disk pressed hard into Aaron's sweaty palm, sending a shiver up his arm.

'Because from this moment forward,' Grandfather warned him, 'you will dedicate your life to preserving everything this symbol stands for.'

1.

ROME, ITALY

PRESENT DAY

A flock of pigeons took flight as Father James Martin moved swiftly around Caligula's obelisk, which rose up from the center of Piazza San Pietro like a colossal dagger against the steel-gray sky. Its mid-September shadow would normally have let him know that it was just past five o'clock. But for the third consecutive day, the sun remained hidden behind a shroud of lifeless clouds. Glancing over at St. Peter's Basilica, he saw the faithful pilgrims queued for the last tour. *Even a typhoon couldn't scare them away*, he thought.

He pulled his raincoat tighter to fight off a damp chill. He'd need to move quickly to beat the imminent downpour.

Near the end of Via della Conciliazione, he heard a voice calling to him over the sounds of the traffic.

'Padre Martin?'

Stopping, Martin turned. A man waved to him, splashing through the shallow puddles in quick strides. Of medium height and build, he was ordinary looking – clean-shaven with dark hair and unreadable dark eyes. '*Si?*' Martin replied.

9

'Sorry to bother you on your way home,' he said, planting himself at arm's length.

A laminated Vatican ID badge was prominently displayed on the lapel of his raincoat, just below his white priest collar. The unfamiliar face was forgettable. Italian? Lebanese? Maybe thirty-something, or perhaps a youthful fifty, Martin guessed. 'Have we met?'

The man shook his head. 'Not yet.'

'What can I do for you, Father . . . ?'

'Fabrizio Orlando.' He extended his right hand.

Italian. When Martin reciprocated, he noticed that the priest's skin was rough. Unusual for a cleric. Perhaps the man had spent time as a missionary? *The Lord's call doesn't place everyone behind a desk*, Martin reminded himself.

'I've just been appointed to the secretariat's office.'

Why hadn't he been notified? 'I see. Welcome to Vatican City.'

'*Grazie*. Mind if I walk with you for a minute?'

Suspicion showed in Martin's eyes. 'Not at all.'

The two men proceeded down the sidewalk past the cafés and souvenir shops.

'I was told you'd been Cardinal Antonio Santelli's secretary?'

'That's right.' Martin's gait quickened and the man kept pace beside him.

'Very unfortunate, His Eminence's death. A deep loss for the Holy See.' He tightened his lips in a show of solemnity. 'He was a visionary.' As they approached Piazza Pia's busy thoroughfare, his pitch rose to compete with the bus and scooter traffic. 'Many had said he would be the Holy Father's successor.'

'Yes, well . . .' Attempting to echo the priest's fond words, Martin stalled, knowing that his own remembrances wouldn't be nearly as complimentary. The fact remained that regardless of Santelli's unsullied public image as having been a last great defender of Catholic dogma, the late cardinal had been merciless to his subordinates – a bulldog. Martin chose to bow his head in prayer.

'May God rest his soul,' Orlando said loudly as a whining Vespa sped past.

At the busy intersection, they remained silent to negotiate the crosswalk.

Martin resumed the conversation as he led the way down the cobbled walkway in front of Castel Sant'Angelo's outer rampart. 'So how can I assist you, Father?'

The priest's chin tipped up. 'Yes, about business then.' A momentary stare down at the roiling Tiber helped him collect his thoughts. 'The secretariat has retained my services to assist in ongoing inquiries concerning the death of Dr. Giovanni Bersei.'

Martin stiffened. 'I see.'

They angled onto Ponte Sant'Angelo.

The man went on to convey what his fact-finding mission had yielded thus far. Back in June, Italian anthropologist Giovanni Bersei had been commissioned by Cardinal Santelli to assist in a highly secretive project inside the Vatican. Only days later, Bersei had been found dead in the catacombs beneath Villa Torlonia. An elderly docent was also found dead on the premises and a routine autopsy showed he had been injected with heart-arresting toxins. Roman authorities had investigated the foul play. Santelli, too, Orlando conspiratorially reminded him, had succumbed to heart failure only a day later, though the Holy See had refused an autopsy.

By the time the Italian had finished, he'd trailed Martin to within a block of his apartment building.

There was no doubt Orlando was well informed. But Martin wasn't looking to rehash the exhaustive questioning he'd endured in the weeks that followed the cardinal's death. 'I trust you have been informed that the carabinieri have completed their investigations?'

The man's lips pulled tight. 'Mine is an internal investigation,' he repeated.

Approaching the narrow alley that was the shortcut to his apartment building, Martin stopped. 'I don't mean to be rude, but I think it would be best for us to speak about this during business hours. After I've obtained permission from the sec-retariat's office.'

Orlando forced a placated smile. 'I understand.'

'A pleasure to meet you, Father Orlando.' Martin nodded.

'Likewise.'

Martin stuffed his hands into his pockets and turned down the alley. As he was about to pass a stocky deliveryman unloading produce boxes from an idling van, he heard the priest calling after him again, quick footsteps tapping along the ancient cob-blestones.

'Father.'

Stopping in his tracks, Martin's shoulders slumped. Before he could turn to address Orlando, the anxious priest had circled in front of him.

'If I could just have another moment.'

'What is it?'

Later, Martin would recall no answer. Just the priest's eyes turning cold, slipping back to the sidewalk, then up to the win-dows overlooking the alleyway, and finally over Martin's shoulder to the deliveryman.

Without warning, two strong hands grabbed at Martin's coat,

yanking hard, forcing his body into an uncontrolled spin, directly toward the van's open cargo hold.

What in God's name?!

A sharp blow to the knees forced him down onto the cold metal floor. '*Aiuto!*' he screamed out to anyone who might hear. '*Aiu—*'

2.

The deliveryman responded instantly, crowding into the van and clamping his enormous hand over Martin's mouth and nose. Orlando jumped in right behind him and slid shut the side door. Martin barely glimpsed the bald scalp and jagged profile of a third accomplice slumped low in the driver's seat.

The transmission ground into gear. The van lurched forward, thumping its way over the cobblestones.

Martin's terrified eyes met the deliveryman's disturbingly calm gaze. As he struggled for breath, the smell of leeks and basil invaded his nostrils. The deliveryman straddled him and grabbed him in a powerful hold that demanded complete submission.

'I let go, we talk. You fight or scream, he shoots you.' His free hand pointed toward the man crouched near the windowless rear doors gripping a black handgun trained on Martin's head.

Desperation flooded Martin's gaze as he moved his head up and down. The deliveryman eased off and sat across from him with his thick arms crossed over a propped-up knee.

Martin almost retched as he gasped for air.

'Sit up, Father,' Orlando instructed him, motioning with the gun.

After a few steady breaths, Martin eased himself up against the metal sidewall and threw down his hands as the van slowed abruptly and made a right turn. The thumping cobblestones gave way to smooth pavement. 'What do you want?'

'We have questions for you. Details concerning Bersei's death.'

'I told you . . . I've answered all the carabinieri's questions. I—'

'Only hours before he went into the catacomb,' the Italian said, overriding him, 'Bersei had contacted the carabinieri . . .'

The imposter's accent had changed to something completely different, suggesting he wasn't from Italy. And the detached manner in which the man referred to the Italian authorities suggested to Martin that he wasn't one of them either.

'He left a message for a Detective Perardi, stating that he had information concerning a Roman link to an artifact stolen from Jerusalem. And only days later, that artifact was miraculously returned to Israel in a shipping crate originating out of Rome.'

'The . . .' Martin's brow crinkled. 'The stone box? Is that what you're referring to?' He remembered seeing the news reports on CNN International.

'The ossuary,' the imposter corrected. 'The bone box.'

Bone box? The van made another turn and rocked Martin sideways as it sharply accelerated, then settled into a cruising speed. Where were they taking him? Confused and frustrated, Martin shook his head and said, 'What does this have to do with me?'

'Patience, Father. Dr. Bersei was murdered in that catacomb. And multiple eyewitnesses saw a suspicious man leaving Villa Torlonia shortly thereafter.'

'So why don't you find *him*?'

The deliveryman leaned forward and brandished a massive fist that made Martin flinch. Orlando held up a hand for the man to stand down. The muscles in the deliveryman's jaws clenched as he slunk back to a sitting position.

'We did find him, Father Martin – in the Italian countryside with a bullet in his head.'

Martin cringed.

He dipped into his breast pocket, pulled out a photo, and handed it to Martin. 'Recognize him?'

The face in the color photo – set against the stainless steel of a gurney – was ghost white, the eyes murky with death. Above the right ear, the skull was blown apart – a ragged mess of purple flesh and bone. Yet the features were unmistakable. Martin's reaction signaled he'd indeed met the deceased. When he looked up, he could tell that the gunman was pleased by this.

The gunman snatched the picture back and gave it a glance. 'Israeli authorities also believe this man was involved in a heist that took place at Jerusalem's Temple Mount in June.'

Martin couldn't recall hearing this in any news report.

He slipped the photo back into his pocket. 'Many innocent people died because of this man. Soldiers. Police. Now, please. I want you to think very hard and tell me his name, please.'

Unlike that of the imposter waving a gun in his face, the mercenary's first impression had been lasting. And Martin wasn't about to cover for him. After all, the man's only link to the Vatican was the late Cardinal Santelli. 'Salvatore Conte.'

The deliveryman pulled a notepad and pen from his pocket, verified the spelling, and jotted down the name.

Salvatore Conte. Orlando regarded the picture once more to match the name with the face. 'Now let me connect the dots for you, Father. Salvatore Conte stole that ossuary from the Temple Mount and brought it to Rome. He was involved in the death of Giovanni Bersei, who, at that time, was commissioned for a project inside Vatican City. The study of a yet undetermined artifact, as coincidence would have it. A project of which the Vatican denies all knowledge.'

Martin stared at the floor. How could Orlando know these things? Following Santelli's death, the secretariat's office had collected the cardinal's computer, files, and personal effects. He could only guess that any sensitive information had been destroyed or locked away in the Secret Archive. As far as the Italian authorities were concerned, the Vatican had never seen or heard of Salvatore Conte, and Dr. Bersei had merely consulted on restoration work taking place inside the Vatican Museums' Pio Christian Museum.

'Look at me, Father,' Orlando insisted.

The priest complied.

'Bersei was found broken to pieces at the bottom of a pit, Salvatore Conte assassinated in the Italian wine country. All within days of Conte's theft in Jerusalem. Leads one to think that the Vatican is the common thread. Like many times in the past, the Vatican, with its – how would you say? – infallible influences, has persuaded the carabinieri to disregard these matters. We, however, cannot be bought.'

'Who are you?' Martin asked again.

The gunman merely gave a smug smile before resuming the interrogation. 'Much of these formalities are of no concern to us. There is one matter, however, that is of grave concern. So I have only one simple request to make of you, Father.'

He swallowed hard. 'What is it?'

Orlando leaned close, saying in a low voice, 'The ossuary was returned empty. I need you to tell me what happened to its contents.'

'Contents?'

He shook his head, cocked the Glock's trigger, and pressed the barrel against Martin's forehead.

The priest's eyes snapped closed as his face reflexively turned sideways. The cold steel bit his skin. 'I don't . . . don't know what you're talking about!'

'The *bones*, Father Martin. That ossuary contained a skeleton. Where are the bones?' He pressed the gun barrel harder against the priest's temple.

At first, Martin was dumbfounded. *Bones?* The idea that these men had abducted him for such a thing seemed preposterous. The gun rocked his head back against the van's wall, sending crushing pain through his skull.

'Father Martin!' the man spat. 'I don't think you're listening to me! Dr. Bersei was a forensic anthropologist. Forensic anthropologists don't study paintings or sculptures. They study bones.'

'I don't know! I swear!'

Holding the gun in place, the man reached into his pocket again to produce a second photo. 'I want you to look at this very closely,' he said, holding it out for the priest.

As he trembled, Martin's eyes went wide when he saw the family in the portrait – a handsome couple, early forties, a young boy and his slightly older sister.

'The most efficient path to truth comes from the blood of loved ones. Your sister is very beautiful. Her daughter looks very much like her, though the boy is his father's son.'

'God save you,' Martin contemptuously replied.

'Insurance, Father,' he said. 'Help us and I assure you that their lives will be spared. Now, once again . . . Where are the bones?'

A sour taste came into the priest's mouth, and his limbs quaked uncontrollably. 'I'm telling you the truth. I don't know!'

A pause as the gunman studied the priest's eyes and body language.

'Then tell me who does.'

Martin's brain went into hyperdrive as he recalled the events. At Cardinal Santelli's behest, he'd indeed arranged Dr. Bersei's June visit to the Vatican Museums to examine and authenticate an 'important acquisition.' Confidentiality agreements had been signed too. But Santelli had never disclosed to Martin what the artifact was. This ossuary, perhaps? Bones? Another scientist had been summoned as well. An American geneticist – though her name now escaped him.

Nonetheless, there was one man who he was certain had the answers these men were seeking. And with frightened eyes glued to the picture, Martin gave them his name.

3.

QUMRAN, ISRAEL

Stepping out from beneath the blue origami canopy that sheltered the team's provisions, Amit Mizrachi's glum gaze shot halfway up the sheer sandstone cliff to a lanky twenty-year-old Israeli harnessed to a rappelling line. Dangling directly beside the student was a boxlike device on wheels that resembled a high-tech lawn mower.

'Anything?' Amit yelled, his deep baritone echoing along the chasm.

The student planted his feet on a craggy outcropping and pushed himself closer to the ground-penetrating radar unit. Pressing his face close to its LCD, he paused for a three-count to inspect the radargram. Zero undulation in the line pattern. 'Nothing yet.'

Amit had grown somewhat accustomed to this response, yet he couldn't help but curse under his breath. He made a futile attempt at swatting away the tiny desert flies swarming about his face.

'Keep going to the bottom?' the student called down.

Going to the bottom. Just like Amit's career if something meaningful wasn't soon found. With excavations at Qumran approaching the two-year mark, the team's findings thus far were unremarkable: broken clay shards from Hasmonean oil lamps and amphorae, clichéd Roman and Herodian coins, a first-century grave site with male skeletal remains that replicated earlier discoveries found nearby.

'Go to the bottom,' he instructed. 'Then take a break before you move to the next column. And stay hydrated. You won't be much good to me if you get heatstroke.'

The kid snatched the water bottle from his utility belt and held it up in a mock toast.

'Mazel tov,' he grumbled. 'Now get moving.'

The burly, goateed Israeli pulled off his aviator sunglasses and used a handkerchief to blot the sweat from his brow. Even in September, the Judean Desert's dry heat was unrelenting and could easily drive a man mad. But Amit wasn't going to let Qumran beat him. After all, patience and resolve were paramount for any archaeologist worth his chisel and brush.

The project's benefactors, on the other hand, followed a much different clock. Their purse strings were drawing tighter by the month.

As he watched the student holster the water bottle, then lower the GPR unit two meters for the next scan, he felt a sudden compulsion to swap places with him. Maybe the rookie was missing something, misinterpreting the radargrams. But Amit's forty-two-year-old oversize frame didn't take well to rock climbing – particularly the harness, which crushed his manhood in unspeakable ways. No doubt those of slight stature were best suited to archaeology. So Amit approached things the pragmatic way: delegate, delegate, delegate.

Glaring at the cliff – the wily seductress who'd stolen away his want or need for anything else – he grumbled, 'Come on. Give it up. *Something.*' This project had single-handedly accounted for his most recent marital casualty – Amit's second wife, Sarah. At least this time there weren't kids being played like pawns.

A second later, he heard someone screaming from a distance. 'Professor! Professor!'

He turned around and spotted a lithe form moving through the gulch with athletic agility – the most recent addition to his team, Ariel. When she reached him, she planted herself close.

'Everything all right?'

Ariel used an index finger to push back her glasses, which had slid down her sweaty nose, and reported between heaving breaths, 'In the tunnel . . . we . . . the radar is picking up something . . . behind a wall . . .'

'Okay, let's slow it down,' he said soothingly. New interns were prone to overreacting at the slightest blip on the radar, and no one was greener than nineteen-year-old Ariel. 'What exactly did you see?' He fought to keep his frustrated tone on an even keel.

'The hyperbolic deflections . . . they were *deep.*'

Reading a radargram was more art than science. One had to be careful with interpretation. 'How deep?'

'Deep.'

Amit squared his shoulders and his barrel chest puffed out against his drenched T-shirt. The creases on his overly tanned cheeks deepened as he considered this. *Don't get too excited*, he told himself. *It's probably nothing.* Though radar was quite effective in penetrating dry sandstone, subterranean scans were temperamental due to excessive moisture that choked the UHF/UVF radio waves. A deep deflection suggested a considerable hollow in the earth.

She sucked in more air and went on. 'And this wall – it's not stone . . . well, not exactly. We began to clear away the clay—'

'You *what*?'

'I know, I know.' She raised her palms up as if to tame a lion. 'We were going to come get you, but we needed to be sure about – Anyway, we found something. *Bricks.*'

A rush of cold ran up his spine. 'Show me. Now.'

These days, when Amit pushed his body to anything beyond a light trot, he felt like a rhinoceros on a treadmill. But as he trailed close behind Ariel, there was a fluidity in his stride that he hadn't felt since he was dodging hostile gunfire in Gaza over twenty years earlier. As *seren*, or company commander, he could easily have pursued a military career with the Israel Defense Forces, but by then he'd had enough of Israel's gummy politics concerning the occupied Palestinian territories. So Amit set his sights on a much different pursuit at Tel Aviv University that swapped a Ph.D. in biblical archaeology for his three-olive-branched epaulets.

A hundred yards from the tent, Ariel led him through a ravine, into a cool wash of shade. Ahead, the crevasse narrowed and dipped over the cliff where winter flash floods would rage down to the sapphire-blue Dead Sea. Just over the rise, she stopped at the foot of a tall ladder propped at an angle against the vertical rock.

Catching his breath, Amit glanced at the cave opening – a good four meters up.

His mind rewound four weeks, when the GPR registered this subsurface anomaly buried behind what amounted to almost two meters of rubble, clay, and silt. It had taken ten days to clear it all out; every ounce of soil was thoroughly screen-sifted for the slightest commingled artifacts. Nothing found. What lay beyond, however, wasn't a cave per se, but a tunnel that rose sharply into the cliff's belly.

Ariel went up the ladder first – an effortless ascent. At the top, she pulled herself into the darkened opening.

Drawing breath, Amit clutched the sides of the ladder with his meaty paws. His heartbeat quickened. Keeping his eyes on the opening, he started cautiously upward, the aluminum rungs groaning. Feeling suddenly vulnerable – it happened any time his feet left earth – he fought the urge to look down. *Keep moving. Eyes on the prize.*

At the top, he clawed the opening's stone rim and heaved himself up and in.

'Show me.'

'It's far in . . . at the end, actually,' she said, waving for him to follow. Snatching a flashlight off the floor, she flicked it on, then made her way up the tight passage in short steps.

Amit trailed close behind her, bending slightly at the waist to avoid the low ceiling while twisting his torso to prevent jamming his broad shoulders in the narrow channel. Within seconds, what little sunlight penetrated the tunnel had dissipated. The subterranean air chilled his damp neck and the redolence of minerals stirred up into his nose – what he liked to call 'Bible smell.'

A few meters up the grade, the glow from work lights pierced the darkness. Amit could hear echoing voices and the dry sound of gravel being scooped into buckets. He detected a *swish swish swish* – a brush dusting stone. 'Stop what you're doing!' His scream rippled along the tunnel.

The outburst made Ariel flinch and hit her head on the ceiling. She stopped, cupped her hand over the tender spot, then checked it under the light. Only dirt.

'It'll only be a bruise,' Amit said, noting the lack of blood on her hand.

Shaking her head, Ariel proceeded upward. The sounds of

work had stopped, but the mumbling had just begun, mixed with some giggles.

The tunnel reached its high point and flattened out, yielding to a wide hollow. Amit straightened with half a meter to spare overhead. Immediately his eyes found the cleared section in the chamber's rear, a square meter, he guessed, crisply lit by two pole lights. Three more eager students stood in silence around the spot, buckets and tools at their feet, looking like they'd just been called to the principal's office.

Huffing, he made his way closer. He fumed, 'I can't tell you again how *critical* it is to—' But the words were lost as his eyes took in the remarkable sight set before him. Moving forward and dropping to his knees, he pressed his face close to a neat patchwork of angular bricks the students had mindfully exposed. His heart seemed to skip a beat. Early on, Amit had given Mother Nature full credit for this chamber, since its interior surfaces displayed no telltale scarring from tools. Now that hypothesis had to be completely discounted. 'Oh my,' he gasped.

4.

A radargram was a far cry from a Polaroid. But as Amit studied the wild undulations in the GPR's frequency patterns, he concurred with young Ariel. These deflections were definitely *deep*. He rolled the scanner away from the bricks and patted his fingers against his lips in rapid motion.

'What do you think, Professor?' Ariel finally said.

Mind racing, Amit stared at the brickwork a few seconds before answering. 'This wall isn't very dense. Probably less than half a meter.' For scale, he propped a ruler and a chisel against the bricks, then proceeded to snap some digitals with his trusty Nikon. After twice reviewing the images on the camera's display, he was pleased. He turned to Ariel and said, 'I need a detailed diagram of this space, with laser measurements all around.'

'I can do it,' she confidently replied.

'I know you can.' The kid not only had a knack for academia, but she was an excellent artist. Extremely useful for field study and precisely why she'd been handpicked to join his team. 'Take some video too. Use plenty of light.'

Beaming, Ariel nodded in fast motion.

Then he addressed the others. 'The rest of you start tagging the bricks. Then we'll see what they were looking to hide.'

'They,' the students immediately understood, were the Essenes – the reclusive Jewish sect that had inhabited these hills for two centuries beginning in the second century B.C.E., until their mass genocide by the Romans in 68 C.E. Their primary settlement was set along the shore of the Dead Sea, a cluster of crude clay brick dwellings that included sleeping quarters, a refectory, and ritual bathing pits called *mikvah*s. But the site's dominant building had been a long hall furnished with drafting tables – a scriptorium where multiple copies of the Hebrew Bible, the Tanakh, as well as a plethora of apocryphal texts, had been fastidiously transcribed. The Essenes had been the scribes, librarians, and custodians of the Dead Sea Scrolls.

'Think we'll find scrolls, Professor?'

Irritated by the ask-it-and-kiss-your-fortunes-good-bye query, Amit turned to the nineteen-year-old Galilean named Eli, who was all nose and ears beneath a tight knit of black curls topped off by a brightly embroidered *kippah*. A spasm rippled Amit's lower left eyelid as he agitatedly replied, 'Anything's possible.'

An hour later, when Amit nudged free the brick pin-tagged 'C027,' he saw a black space open up behind the wall's final layer. Grinning ear to ear, he carefully handed the block to the Galilean kid, who used it to start a new column in the ordered matrix of bricks laid neatly on the chamber floor.

Amit held a tape measure along the top of the recess. The radargram had been right on the shekels. 'Half a meter.'

'Exciting stuff,' Eli said, rubbing his hands together and crouching to peek through the hole.

'You getting all this?'

'Every brick,' he assured Amit as he grabbed his clipboard and wrote 'C027' on the inventory sheet.

Grabbing a flashlight, Amit shone the beam through the gap, moving it side to side, up and down. The light clung to two meters of tight walls and ceiling – another passage? – before being swallowed by a much larger void. A second chamber? His knees popped as he stood. 'Let's get the rest of this cleared away,' he instructed the interns.

5.

After another two hours, under Amit's close supervision, the ancient wall had been completely dismantled.

He reclaimed his kneeling spot.

'Let's have a look.' Crouching, he shone the flashlight into the rocky gullet while trying not to inhale the stagnant air spilling out of the breach. Just beyond the opening, he studied the angular passage and ran his fingers over its scooped chisel hashes. Definitely quarried. A tap on his shoulder made him turn. It was Ariel, holding out a silver-cased Zippo lighter.

'To check for oxygen,' she explained.

'Right,' Amit said, taking it from her. She'd obviously noticed that he'd left his fancy digital oxygen sensor back at the tent. So the crude method would have to suffice. Flicking the top open with a small *ting*, he lit it up. The tang of butane filled his nostrils as he extended the Zippo into the passage. The robust flame held steady. All clear. 'Here goes.'

Crawling through the short passage, flashlight in his left hand, Zippo in his right, Amit hesitated when he quickly reached the end. A large void opened up in front of him.

Craning his neck, he swung the light in wide arcs through the black soup. The light melted deep into the space – a sizable angular chamber hewn from the mountain's innards.

Confusion came fast. The space seemed to be empty. But there was lots of Bible smell here.

Working his way inside, Amit stood and rolled his neck. Though the Zippo's quivering taper suggested questionable air quality, he wasn't about to vacate the chamber. He hadn't felt this exhilarated in years. Pulling in shallow breaths, he paced the level floor and examined the symmetrical walls and ceiling – a ten-meter cube, he guesstimated, every surface blank. Why would the Essenes brick up an empty cubicle?

'Speak to me,' he muttered.

On cue, his Doc Martens scuffed across an uneven surface in the center of the floor – a variation so slight he could easily have dismissed it. Then the ground seemed to shift slightly beneath his weight. He dipped the flashlight onto the spot and eased onto his knees. Flicking the Zippo shut, he slid it into his shirt pocket. He trailed his fingers through a dust layer blanketing the floor and detected a ridge. Pressing his face close to the floor, he gently blew away the dust to reveal a tight seam that cut a hard angle. He repeated the process until he'd uncovered a sizable rectangle cut into the floor.

A stone slab?

He tried working his meaty fingers into the seam. Nothing. Snapping to his feet, he paced to the passage opening, crouched down, and called to Ariel. 'Bring in the tools . . . a pry bar too. And let's get some lights in here. Quickly!'

'I'm on it,' she called back.

Once the interns funneled in with the gear, Amit had them set up battery-operated pole lights around the chamber's center. He momentarily mused on their lit faces, their untamed excitement. It brought back pleasant memories of his first student excavation at Masada.

Working a pry bar into the seam, Amit instructed Eli to mirror the action on the slab's opposite side. He could see that the gangly kid was a bundle of nerves. 'On three,' he said. Eli nodded. 'One . . . two . . .'

The first attempt was sloppy but managed to unseat the slab. The second pinched Amit's fingers when he prematurely slipped them beneath the stone – hard enough to take some skin and elicit what he considered a rather girlish yelp. A third tandem try levered the stone up enough for Ariel to wedge a pry bar into the opening, enabling Amit to fully grip the thing and drag it off to the side.

Catching his breath, Amit knelt along the edge, where carved steps dropped down into the hollow they'd uncovered. 'Now we're getting somewhere.'

Ariel immediately handed over his flashlight. Then the video camera was back in her hand and she started humming the theme to the Indiana Jones movies. 'Da da da-dah, da da dah . . .'

The other students laughed, and Amit allowed himself a chuckle too as he clicked on the light and aimed it down the steps. He counted twelve treads cascading to a stone floor. 'All right. Let me get a look down there, see what we've got.' These were the moments that defined the quest, he thought. He stood, dropped his left foot onto the first carved tread, and began his steady descent.

It was another tight fit for the Israeli as he folded and tucked himself against the hewn walls, the light playing shadow dances along the chisel-scarred rock.

When Roman legions had swarmed over Qumran, they'd

torched the village and slaughtered its inhabitants. Though there'd been little warning, the Essenes had managed to stash their most vital scrolls in these desert hills – a time capsule to preserve their heritage. But none of Qumran's caves contained excavated rooms like this one. And why so purposely sealed away? *What could the Essenes have been doing here?* he wondered.

Adrenaline pumped through him as he negotiated the last three steps and touched down onto the floor. He deliberately closed his eyes for a three-count as he brought the light to waist level. Then he opened them.

What he saw made him gasp.

6.

BELFAST, NORTHERN IRELAND

It had been nearly three months since Father Patrick Donovan had taken a sabbatical from the Vatican and returned to his childhood neighborhood in Belfast. Yet not a day passed that he didn't think about the events leading up to his hasty departure.

And it was no wonder why.

Back in June he'd presented to the Vatican secretary of state, Cardinal Antonio Santelli, an authentic first-century codex containing eyewitness testament to Christ's ministry, crucifixion, and secret burial beneath Jerusalem's Temple Mount. To preempt the discovery of Christ's mortal remains by Israeli engineers who were set to study the Mount's structural integrity, the cardinal had employed a master thief named Salvatore Conte to forcefully extract the relic. Conte and his mercenary team had succeeded, but only after engaging in a sloppy firefight that left thirteen Israeli soldiers and police dead.

Conte had safely brought the procurement to Vatican City, where Donovan had arranged for its confidential authentication by two prominent scientists: Italian forensic anthropologist Dr. Giovanni Bersei and American geneticist Dr. Charlotte Hennesey.

The scientists' findings had been astounding.

Upon the project's completion, Cardinal Santelli ordered Conte to eliminate any trace of the relics, *and* those who'd studied it. Conte cleverly murdered Dr. Bersei in a Roman catacomb, but Dr. Hennesey managed to flee Vatican City before he could get to her. When Donovan had accompanied the killer to the Italian countryside on a mission to destroy the ossuary, the bones, and relics, Conte had made it known that Charlotte was to be marked for death in the United States. After a nasty struggle with fists and guns, however, Donovan had managed to put an end to Conte first.

Yes, with all that had happened, he was glad to be home.

There was a certain comfort here: a familiar damp chill to the air, the quilted gray clouds that washed away the lush peaks of Cavehill, the steely swells of the river Lagan.

But his homecoming had been bittersweet.

Following the Irish Republican Army's voluntary disarmament in 2005, Donovan had been told, the last of his old schoolmates had uprooted their families to seek better opportunities in cities like Dublin, London, and New York. He'd also learned that in 2001, his best friend, Sean, had been imprisoned in Lisburn's HMP Maghaberry for stabbing to death a prominent Protestant businessman during the Troubles – a fate Donovan himself had barely escaped when he was just a young man.

Donovan had moved in with his ailing eighty-one-year-old father, James, in the rebuilt two-bedroom redbrick row house off Crumlin Road standing on the footprint of his childhood home, which had been burned to the ground by rioting Unionists in 1969.

Most days were spent watching over the old man's quaint luncheonette on Donegall Street, aptly named Donovan's. As a young boy, Donovan had spent many hours in the store making change at the register, refreshing coffee, buttering rolls, sorting the newspapers, and restocking the refrigerated cases. So the routine brought a sense of comfort and familiarity.

However, it'd also been here where a smooth-talking patron named Michael had exploited fifteen-year-old Patrick Donovan's naïveté and recruited him as an errand boy for the IRA. Prior to Donovan's entering the seminary at eighteen, Da had considered renaming the establishment Donovan and Son. But like Abraham himself, Da couldn't have been more pleased to lose his son to serve the Lord, especially after learning how Michael had so dangerously manipulated his only child.

It had taken a solid month for Donovan to get back up to speed: to learn how to run credit cards through the machine, work the new coffeemakers, and deal with the latest generation of vendors. The first two weeks, Da sat behind the counter coaching him, wearing a continuous smile beneath the rubber tubes running down from his nostrils to a portable oxygen tank. Then Da's condition abruptly worsened to the point that he was homebound. So Donovan would tend the store during the day and spend quiet nights sipping whiskey and playing cards with him, making some small talk about politics and the day's happenings at the store.

Never had the events that transpired in Vatican City been discussed. Donovan simply explained that he needed some time to sort things out.

In mid-August, the old man lost his decade-long battle with emphysema. The service at Holy Cross Church had drawn a few neighbors, some old acquaintances, and dozens of store patrons. On that day, Donovan buried his father at Milltown Cemetery in a reserved plot alongside his loving wife, Claire, who had passed on ten years earlier.

So it seemed that here Donovan's recent past had been buried as well.

Until today.

The store was empty when the two men arrived just before noon, each claiming a stool at the end of the counter, close to the door.

Donovan folded the *Eire Post* and made his way over to greet them. He could tell immediately they weren't locals. Tourists, most likely. One was of medium height and build, the second tall and broad.

'*Dia duit*,' he said in Gaelic, followed up quickly with, 'Top o' the morn'.' Though twelve years with the Vatican had suppressed his brogue, Belfast had slackened his tongue. 'Coffee, lads?'

'That would be wonderful,' the smaller one said.

'Coming right up.' Donovan grabbed two mugs and set them on the counter. As he retrieved the coffeepot from the burner, the pair removed their rain-dampened overcoats in tandem. Turning back to them, he immediately noticed that each wore a black shirt with a white square covering the collar button. Priests.

As he filled the mugs, Donovan tried to place the smaller man's plain face, but conjured no recollection. The accent, too, certainly wasn't local. 'Cream, sugar?'

'No, thank you, Patrick.'

The taller priest simply shook his head.

'*Sláinte*,' Donovan said with a friendly nod and another glance at the man's priest collar. 'Forgive me, but' – he backed up a few steps to return the pot to the burner – 'have we met?'

'No,' the smaller one said. He sipped the coffee, steam wafting over his dark eyes. 'But we come on behalf of the Holy See.' Orlando made his introductions, referring to his colleague as 'Father Piotr Kwiatkowski.'

'I see,' Donovan said.

'It wasn't easy finding you,' he said, embellishing the truth. Passport tracking had indicated Donovan's entry into Northern Ireland on July seventh. And though he hadn't used credit cards, a recent obituary for his father, as well as the deceased's estate transference records – including a deed for a family home in Ardoyne and ownership of this establishment – had been easily found in their search of public records.

Donovan gave him a stiff stare.

'Seems you left in quite a hurry after Cardinal Santelli's, shall we say, sudden demise.'

'The reasons for my departure are no one's business,' Donovan dourly replied, snatching up a rag and buffing the counter. 'Best for you to state *your* business, Father.'

'We'll waste no time then.' Clawing his mug with sinewy fingers, the man slurped another mouthful of coffee before going on. 'We've been informed about your involvement with Dr. Giovanni Bersei . . . and the ossuary he'd been studying in the Vatican Museums.' He paused to gauge the Irishman's reaction. But the man didn't react or even look over. 'I'm sure you take great comfort in knowing that the carabinieri have closed their investigation into Dr. Bersei's *accidental* death.' Father Martin certainly had.

Uneasy, Donovan glanced over as the man reached into his pocket and produced a photo.

'I'm certain you will recognize this man, though he's a bit pale in this photograph,' he said, flattening Salvatore Conte's morgue shot onto the counter. As Donovan cautiously stepped closer and looked down at it, Orlando could see a reaction – a subtle twist in the jaw, apprehension pulling at the eyelids. Orlando unabashedly laid out the connections for Donovan – the ossuary, Bersei's death in the catacombs, Santelli's timely passing, Conte's murder. 'All of this within days of a theft that took place in Jerusalem.'

'I'm afraid the only man who has the answers you are looking for,' Donovan replied, 'is Cardinal Santelli. And as you've stated, he's taken those answers to his grave.' Moving back to the coffeemaker, he moved the rag fast along the stainless steel, polishing it to a soft glow.

'His Eminence appreciates your dedication, Patrick. Our intention is not to levy accusations.'

'Then what might your intention be?' Donovan said with a note of challenge.

Orlando's face tightened. 'First, we need to determine why the ossuary had been brought inside Vatican City. There's also a matter of locating relics that supposedly had been contained inside the box.'

'And Cardinal Lungero requests this information?'

Without diverting his firm gaze, Orlando faltered for a split second. 'That's correct.'

Donovan calmly set down the rag. Lungero was the name of someone in Vatican City, but certainly no cardinal. If these men weren't envoys from the Vatican, then who could have sent them? Perhaps they'd aided Conte in Jerusalem and failed to receive their cut prior to his demise? 'What relics might he be questioning?' his asked, his brogue thickening.

'You know better than most that an ossuary is a bone box. As such, it stands to reason that there had been bones inside it. Other relics too.'

Would mercenaries be at all interested in the bones? Donovan won-dered. 'I'm not sure if I'll be able to assist you. But there is something . . .'

'Yes?'

He shook his head dismissively. 'I was asked to sign confiden-tiality agreements prior to my leaving the Vatican. I'm not supposed to—'

'Those agreements are meant for those outside the Holy See.'

Strike two. Donovan had signed no such agreements prior to his departure. The fact remained that the Holy See still wasn't aware of what had truly transpired and thought it best not to pursue such inquiries. There wouldn't be a strike three.

At that moment, the front door opened and a man wearing mud-stained yellow coveralls came strolling in. 'Patrick-me-boy!' he said cheerily.

Donovan straightened and conjured a smile. '*Conas tá tú,* Kevin?'

'Eh,' the man responded with a tired shrug. He eyed the priests as he lumbered past. 'Mornin', fathers.' His grin revealed a mouthful of tobacco-stained, crooked teeth.

'Good morning,' the short one tersely replied. He watched as the man trudged to the farthest stool at the end of the counter.

'A moment, please,' Donovan said apologetically, then went to tend to the patron.

Orlando monitored the ensuing exchange. The man in cover-alls was animatedly talking with his hands, most likely about his mundane morning digging a trench somewhere. Then he finally placed an order with Donovan. All somewhat garbled, but spoken very loudly. The conversation, however, was happening in Gaelic.

'What's he saying?' Kwiatkowski asked inconspicuously.

'No idea.' He cursed under his breath. Had Donovan sought refuge in any other country in the EU or anywhere in the Middle East, he could have easily deciphered the local dialect, even read their lips if the volume was insufficient.

Then Donovan slipped through a doorway, as if to get something for the patron.

Kwiatkowski immediately reacted, making to get up from his stool.

Orlando grabbed his arm. 'Give it a moment.'

Moments went by. No Donovan.

'My heavens! What did you order, my son?' Orlando called with playful sarcasm to the laborer.

'Coffee, just like you, Father.' The scraggly man gave another toothy grin. 'If it's good for your soul, it can only help the fire in *me*.'

This caused both men to push back their stools and spring into action.

The laborer's eyes widened as he saw them darting his way – particularly the tall one, a giant of a man. He coiled into himself. 'I'll drink tea if it'll make ya 'appy!' he said, cowering.

But the two paid him no mind as they whisked by, rounded the corner of the counter, and disappeared through the door.

7.

It was easy for Orlando to see that the rear room was meant for storage: it was filled with dried goods and cans lined neatly on shelves, and stock glassware. There was a large walk-in refrigerator to one side, its door open wide. 'Check it,' he said.

Kwiatkowski reached it in three strides and poked his head in. Lining the floor and shelves were crates of milk and eggs, cases of soda and beer, bins of cheeses, wrapped meats, and butter. No Donovan. 'Not here.'

Then just outside a solid metal door in the room's rear, they both heard the muffled sounds of an engine coming to life.

Donovan had considered blocking the door with something, but in the narrow alley, there was only a large Dumpster that wasn't budging. Hopping onto his motorcycle, he jammed the key into its ignition and started it up, forgoing the helmet in the rear stow box. He pulled back on the throttle just as the door swung open behind him.

The cold V-twin sputtered before yanking the Kawasaki Vulcan forward with a squeal of rubber. Donovan shot a glimpse over his shoulder and spotted the two men dressed as priests scrambling out the doorway and into the alley – each brandishing a handgun.

Donovan's eyes shot forward, sharpening on the opening ahead – a good fifty meters, nothing but brick wall corralling him on both sides.

An easy target for a straight shot.

Pressing his chest down against the fuel tank, he cranked the throttle to the max and serpentined the bike as best he could, trying to avoid skidding out on the rain-slicked pavement. The first shot ricocheted low off the wall in front of him. A second punctured the exhaust pipe and made the bike produce an ear-numbing grumble. Clearly the men could shoot. But they didn't seem to be aiming directly at him. Were they attempting to blow out a tire?

In a panic, Donovan made a split-second correction to maneuver around a pothole that caught the rear tire. The Kawasaki jerked hard and forced him close to the wall just as a third shot nearly grazed his calf and pinged off the chrome engine block. Another five meters and he gripped the brakes and skidded out into the roadway, leaning right to force a wide turn. In the process, he clipped the bumper of an oncoming truck, whose horn was blaring.

The bike slid hard to the opposing curb, forcing Donovan to throw out his leg to keep from rolling into an older woman who was walking her poodle. The muffler's throaty rumbling covered her shouted obscenities as he pulled the bike upright and raced away.

8.

JERUSALEM, ISRAEL

Descending the precipitous steps from the Old City's Jewish Quarter, Rabbi Aaron Cohen gazed over at the fortified Temple Mount complex, which covered thirty-five acres of Mount Moriah's summit like an artificial mesa with its huge filled rectangle of retaining walls, parapets, and embankments. A second, lesser platform rose up from the Temple Mount's center to support the shrine that had dominated the site since the late seventh century – an elaborate building with a massive gold cupola perched upon an octagonal base of marble and colorful Arabian tiles.

The Dome of the Rock, Islam's third-most-holy shrine.

And when Cohen's eyes defied him and caught a glimpse of it, he cringed severely. He muttered a prayer to suppress the deep-rooted emotions that surged every time he thought of the grand Jewish temple that once graced the world's most hallowed hilltop. The feelings of loss and insult came in equal measure.

At the bottom of the steps, he made his way to the security checkpoint for the Western Wall Plaza. As always, he set off the metal detector. Casually stepping aside, he held up his arms. The young IDF soldier, dressed in olive fatigues and beret with an Uzi slung casually over his left shoulder, shook his head as he got up from his stool. He grabbed a black security wand off the bag scanner. '*Shalom*, Rabbi.'

'*Shalom*, Yakob.'

The soldier lackadaisically ran the handheld metal detector over the Hasid's limbs and torso. As always, it let out a high-pitched screech along the left thigh and hip. Sighing, the guard discreetly patted the area to confirm nothing was there. 'No way to get rid of that stuff, Rabbi?' he asked with a polite smile as he rounded back to his stool.

'Not if I want to keep walking.' Cohen shook his head. 'Better get used to it.'

The deeply embedded shrapnel was a physical reminder of the suicide bombings at Jerusalem's Mahane Yehuda market that left sixteen dead and dozens more wounded, including Cohen, who'd stood mere meters away from the *shaheed*'s detonation. Despite four surgeries and five months at Hadassah Medical Center, nails and pellet-shaped metal remained where surgical extraction would guarantee paralysis. For two years following the incident, he'd relied on a cane for walking.

Normally, Cohen would present a medical badge prior to triggering metal detectors. But that badge wasn't required here. Everyone here knew Rabbi Aaron Cohen – very well. Over the past two decades the fifty-three-year-old Brooklyn-born Haredi had become one of Israel's most influential religious and political voices – a staunch proponent of ultra-Orthodox Judaism, the return of Zion, and the official state adoption of the Halakha – Jewish laws of the Torah – to govern public life. As a younger man, he'd served two terms in the

Knesset's leftist National Religious Party, whose credo had been 'The land of Israel, for the people of Israel, according to the Torah of Israel.' And his teachings at Israel's most prestigious yeshivas had earned him much acclaim. Jewish and secular Israelis considered him the next contender for Chief Rabbi.

'Have a great day,' the soldier said.

Cohen tipped his wide-brimmed *zayen* to him, then strolled outside with a slight hobble, the white tassels of a prayer scarf worn under his black vest swinging in rhythm with his quick shuffle. The strands of his long black beard and tightly twisted payess danced against a gentle breeze.

The spacious open plaza led up to an exposed section of the Temple Mount's western retaining wall that was fifty-seven meters wide and nineteen meters high – the Kotel. Normally the place would be full of Jews chanting prayers, rending their garments, and shedding tears for the lost temple – all of it exemplifying how the place had earned its most famous nickname: the Wailing Wall. And for good fortune, tourists would stuff prayer notes into the razor-thin seams between the wall's enormous Herodian stone blocks.

But for the past month, the scene here had been much different.

Barricades zigzagged through the plaza. Backhoes ferried debris out to dump trucks parked outside the Dung Gate, where tour buses typically queued. Judaism's most holy site now looked like a construction zone.

Cohen headed to a tall arched entry on the plaza's north end that accessed the Western Wall Tunnel – an underground network of ancient roadways, cisterns, and water passages running deep beneath the buildings of the Muslim Quarter along the

Temple Mount's western foundation. Prior to its recent closure, tourists could've walked the subterranean passage from the Western Wall Plaza all the way to steps leading up and out onto Via Dolorosa beneath the Temple Mount's northwest corner. An archaeological marvel. *But more important*, Cohen thought, *a direct link to first-century Jerusalem.*

He greeted half a dozen IDF soldiers chatting in a loose circle. He'd insisted on the added security detail prior to his agreeing to assist overseeing the sensitive and highly secretive project now under way here. Death threats from Muslim fanatics had already been received, with many more to follow, he was certain.

Inside, the cool air refreshed him. Wilson's Arch swept high overhead – the remnant of a grand first-century bridge connecting the Upper City to the Temple Mount courtyards. A series of connected vaults formed a spacious hall normally used as a synagogue. Near where the Torah Ark had been only four weeks ago, Cohen maneuvered around heaps of limestone brick and mounds of cement aggregate. He descended a metal staircase that accessed the next level of the tunnel.

Emotions came quick in this mystical place – a gateway to an ancient world his grandfather had taught him so much about in a secret room in Brooklyn.

Swapping his *zayen* for a bright yellow hard hat, he entered a massive subterranean chamber – the Large Hall – where tour groups would normally assemble for an orientation about the Temple Mount's first-century construction by Roman and Egyptian architects employed under the visionary architect King Herod the Great.

Cohen stayed close to the massive, beveled Herodian blocks that formed the mount's base – one was the largest stone in Israel and weighed over six hundred metric tons.

Work lamps flooded white light over dozens of men working atop tall scaffolds who were repairing heavy fractures in the hall's four lofty interlocking vaults. In many spots, massive gaps remained where whole sections of the thirteenth-century-B.C.E. arches had forcefully dislodged.

The earthquake that caused the damage had happened almost six weeks ago. Part of the Lord's plan, Cohen was certain. Another sign that the prophecy was being fulfilled.

His eyes fell to the tiered seating in the rear of the hall, set in front of a miniature model of the mount and the temple precincts atop it circa 70 C.E., now crushed beneath three massive stones. Amazingly, the tourists who'd been present when the tremor hit had not been injured, or anything worse.

'Good morning, Rabbi!' a worker yelled over the clanging jackhammers.

Cohen waved to him.

The 5.3-magnitude quake, which had originated in the Great Rift Valley and cut through the Dead Sea to the east, paled in comparison to 1927's 6.3 quake fifteen miles north in Jericho, which had claimed over two hundred casualties. Jerusalem's Old City, however, built predominantly from unreinforced ancient limestone, sat upon layers of debris left behind by centuries of destruction and rebuilding. Seismic waves, therefore, came with amplified effect.

And so did the political aftershocks.

For over a decade, the tunnel's ongoing excavation had been a flashpoint for Jewish and Muslim dissension over control of the Temple Mount – the world's most coveted religious ground. And the unilateral restoration now under way here had drawn much protest from all Muslim and Palestinian groups – the Waqf, Hamas, the PLO . . .

Cohen gazed woefully up at the vaults once more. What sat above them contributed hugely to the controversy – the residential Muslim Quarter.

Over the centuries, the Muslims had constructed the stone vaults to raise their dwellings up to the level of the Temple Mount's esplanade and facilitate easy access to the mosques. Over the centuries, the tunnel hollows had filled with mud and debris, which helped stabilize the superstructure. Therefore, Muslims contended that the recent Israeli excavations threatened the integrity of the structures above. Which was why it was so critical that no Muslim or Palestinian witness the extent of the damage that had truly taken place – because the riots and death that marked the 1996 opening of the tunnel would be nothing compared to the violence that could stem from this. As such, the Israeli government was funding this project while actively spinning its purpose.

Cohen proceeded to a temporary door painted in red letters: AUTHORIZED PERSONNEL ONLY. He punched a code into its digital keypad and the lock opened. Pushing through, he closed the door behind him.

Poured cement slabs paralleled the Temple Mount's bare foundation wall to form a narrow corridor, crisscrossed overhead by steel stabilizer girders. Underfoot, the ground sloped steadily upward.

He moved fast through the passage and up some steps leading to the approximate midpoint of the Temple Mount's western wall. The ceiling opened up high above and the foundation stones gave way to a massive sealed archway that crested at six meters – Warren's Gate, discovered by British archaeologist Charles Warren in 1867.

Shortly after Saladin's twelfth-century recapturing of

Jerusalem, this opening to the lower structure of the Temple Mount platform had been blocked off. But now, a sizable breach had been made in its center, and light spilled out from the burrow.

He crouched down and peeked inside, where a second crew was busy clearing debris. Though the men wore the same uniforms as the crew in the main hall, they were not under the employ of Israelis. These men were one of Cohen's many teams.

He couldn't help but smile when he saw how far they'd already penetrated beneath the Mount.

Deep beneath the Temple Mount esplanade, their ear-pounding jackhammers still had Cohen concerned about what might be heard above. This secret dig, however, was in close proximity to the Large Hall, so he was certain that the noises would be easily confused with the sounds of the renovations taking place there.

A vibration against his chest startled him. He dipped into his breast pocket, pulled out his cell phone, and checked the display's caller ID: an inside line at the Rockefeller Museum. Fortunately, the Israeli crews had installed signal-relay boosters throughout the tunnel to make outside communications more efficient. Flipping it open, he loudly said, 'Hold a moment.'

He moved away from the archway and further up the tunnel. 'Yes, what is it?' he finally asked.

Through the static, he listened to what the man on the other end had to say. News of a remarkable discovery in Qumran.

'Is it . . . authentic?' he asked, a slight tremor running over his fingers .

The caller said he believed it was.

'And who found it?'

The caller told him, and his hand shook even harder.
'Who did Mizrachi ask to handle the transcription?'
Cohen didn't like this answer either.
'I'll be there in an hour.'

9.

JEZREEL VALLEY, ISRAEL

Cresting the massive earthen mound crowned by fortified ruins, Amit parked his Land Rover and hopped out onto the dusty trail. He took a moment to admire the lush expanse of the Jezreel Valley spreading for kilometers around the tell until it broke like waves against the distant rolling mountains. The unassuming plain had hosted countless battles in antiquity as empires had fought to control this busy interchange where trade and communications were channeled between the East and the Mediterranean.

For centuries, the mound had been used as a strategic stronghold. Its sinister name derived from the Hebrew Har Megedon, or 'hill of Megiddo.'

Armageddon.

Designated in Revelation as ground zero for an apocalyptic showdown between the forces of good and evil.

Armageddon's past tenants included a host of Old Testament kings, among them Solomon and Josiah. All had left their mark somewhere within Megiddo's summit, the tell's visible foundations a mere veneer covering over twenty successive settlements hidden beneath.

Winding through the maze of ancient foundations, Amit stopped beneath a cluster of fragrant palms and peered down into a deep, neatly cut excavation trench staked along the rim with yellow flags. Below, a small team of archaeologists was busily working their way deeper with trowels and brushes, one micro-thin layer at a time.

On hands and knees, sporting a wide-brimmed pink sun hat, he spotted world-renowned Egyptologist Julie LeRoux. It was the imprint of the Egyptian pharaohs that had brought her here – Thutmose III, to be precise, he recalled. Recent digs had uncovered a treasure trove of relics left behind during the king's occupation in the late fifteenth century B.C.E. Julie had flown in from Cairo the very next day. It had been almost four months since her arrival.

'Hey, Jules. Reach China yet?'

Without diverting her attention from dusting a partially exposed, orblike artifact lodged in the earth, she called out with a fine-tuned French accent, 'Monsieur Amit? That you?'

'The one and only.'

'*Zut alors!*' Setting down the brush, she stood and looked up at him, silver-blue eyes squinting tight against the imposing sun.

Something about Jules had always managed to make Amit swoon. Three kids and forty-three years had done little to affect her athletic, trim form. Her face – wide-eyed, cheeky, and insolently youthful – was arguably not her best physical asset. But the radiance it emanated was infectious. Funny that she seemed so content, so happy, seeing as her marital record bore a striking similarity to his own – though the number of her failed attempts to substitute a spouse for archaeological mysteries had only reached one.

'Where is your shovel?' she said.

A jab only an archaeologist could appreciate. Jules considered shovels sacrilege – a tool relegated to only the impatient and the irreverent. He shrugged with a boyish grin. 'Seem to have forgotten it.'

'Pity. Why don't you come on down here and let me teach you a thing or two?' She motioned to a tall aluminum ladder leaning against the rim of the pit.

'So what brings you to Armageddon?' Jules asked.

Helping her dust the artifact, Amit was now able to decipher the orb – a clay decanter covered in hieroglyphs. The coincidence tickled him. 'Egypt, actually.'

The words caressed her ears. 'You don't say,' she seductively replied.

He glanced over his shoulder at her understudies, none of whom seemed interested in listening in on the conversation. 'A hieroglyph, more precisely.'

'Ahh. Looks like the gods have anticipated your visit to the oracle,' she teased, eyeing the jug. 'Best be gentle with this one,' she instructed him, pointing at the amphora. 'She's flaking.'

Grinning, Amit treated it more tenderly.

'A glyph, you say. I suppose you've brought it with you?' Jules eased back on her knees. Amit nodded. 'Then let's have a look,' she said.

Amit set down his brush. He reached into his vest pocket, pulled out a photo, and handed it to her.

'I found this etching, you see, and . . .' He pointed to it, realizing it pretty much spoke for itself.

She bit her lip, her head tilted to one side as she studied it for only a moment. 'Clear enough.' She refolded the paper and gave it back to him with a taunting smile.

'Well?' He pocketed the print.

'Why didn't you tell me you were in Egypt?'

'I wasn't.'

'Oh,' she said, confused. 'Just seems like the only place you'd be able to take pictures of something like that.'

'What does it mean?'

'It represents a nome.'

A nome was ancient Egypt's equivalent of a province. 'Are you going to make me beg for the name?'

'Maybe I'll just have you work for it. Now let me think of clues.'

Jules's trademark trivia caught the attention of one of her students. The attractive young woman made eye contact with Amit, smiled, and shook her head in a sympathetic gesture.

Jules's eyes scrunched, pinching subtle crow's-feet at the corners. 'Okay, it's probably the most famous of ancient Egypt's forty-two nomes, and today it exists only by name, though the place to which it applies is not its original location.' She glanced at him with anticipation. After ten seconds, she correctly assumed that he needed some help. 'Hints: Book of the Dead, Atum, Horus, Ra—'

'Heliopolis?'

'*Parfait!*' she exclaimed, giving him a pat on the knee. 'Yes, the legendary City of the Sun.'

He exchanged a victorious glance with the student, who bestowed her solidarity with a thumbs-up. Then, briefly falling into a trance, he tried to determine what purpose the glyph could possibly serve among the seemingly unrelated discoveries he'd unearthed at Qumran.

'Something wrong?' she asked.

Rousing, he said, 'No . . . It's nothing.' He waved it all away. 'I knew I could count on you to figure this one out. Would have taken me hours of sifting through books.'

'You're welcome.' She smiled. 'Care to tell me what this is all about?'

'I'd love to, Jules, but it's not something I'm at liberty to discuss,' he softly replied, motioning with his eyes to her nearby crew.

'Oooh . . . mysterious.' Her eyebrows flitted up and down and she poked his large belly with a stiff index finger, making him laugh out loud. 'You know, it's okay to ask for help if you need it. If you found that glyph here in Israel, there's no one better than me to help you decipher its context. So why don't you show me what you've found?' she challenged him.

How feisty could this woman possibly be? He scowled and shook his head. 'Not sure if I'm ready to—'

'Jezza,' she called to the student, cutting him off.

'Yes?' the young woman responded.

'Think you can watch over things for the rest of the day?'

'Of course.'

'Excellent.' She turned back to Amit. 'Then it's settled.' Springing to her feet, she grabbed a towel and wiped her hands.

He groaned as he got up.

She tossed the towel to him, then stepped over to the ladder. 'Off we go.'

10.

Another call went to voice mail as Charlotte Hennesey pored over the genoscan data again. Finally pushing aside the reports, she swiveled her leather chair and gazed out the floor-to-ceiling windows of her sleek sixteenth-floor corner office. BioMedical Solutions had spent lavishly on its corporate headquarters: an expanded state-of-the-art genetics lab, refurbished offices, and a cavernous mahogany paneled conference room. Times were good. BMS was growing like wildfire. And she was the second in command – executive vice president of genetic research.

Seeing as she'd recently cheated bone cancer, by all measures, things couldn't be better.

Just beyond the glass, the city's panorama spread wide before the serrated peaks of the Phoenix Mountains. The desert's perfect blue sky offered tranquility. Nowadays, she still needed to remind herself to take stock of life's more simple beauty. A fancy job title and stock options were fleeting novelties that she likened to new-car smell. A new lease on life, however? That was a transformative event that left a permanent, humbling impression. And it was an impression that she was anxious to share with the world.

Rubbing her eyes, she swiveled back to the computer monitor, where two images were paneled side by side.

'Just makes no sense,' she muttered.

The image on the left was a spectral karyotype plotting twenty-four fluoresced chromosome pairs in a grid. The image on the right was virtually identical, except for the label on the last pair – XX instead of XY. Nothing wrong there.

Sample XX had been extracted from the nucleus of her own blood cell. Female.

Sample XY had been extracted from a two-thousand-year-old skeleton found inside the ossuary she'd secretly studied at the Vatican Museums back in June. Male. Identity? . . . The possibility still sent shivers down her spine.

But the real difference – the aberration – was plainly evident in both images. It was the chromosome pair marked '23.' The strands indeed had a normal wormlike shape, but lacked the visible bands of a compressed helix. Closer study had revealed why: pair 23's genes weren't structured in tightly wound strands. In microscopic view its structure resembled . . . *rock candy*? Adding to the genetic mind-bender was the fact that the nucleobases – guanine, cytosine, adenine, and thymine – found in all other chromosomes were not present in 23. Which led to a most amazing discovery: a previously undocumented coding nucleobase she and her boss Evan Aldrich had, for the time being, simply dubbed 'chromosome 23' or just '23.'

And 23 operated like a super organic nanomachine, rebuilding and recoding damaged cells in the remaining chromosome set – a synthesis she still couldn't fathom. And when introduced into an organism – like an unsuspecting thirtysomething female geneticist with bone cancer – it swept through the bloodstream like a virus to repair damaged coding, system-wide.

She still couldn't believe Evan had been so daring as to inject her with it. For all he'd known, it could've killed her. Then again, he wasn't the type to leave things to chance. When he'd spotted the anomaly while performing a routine genome scan on the ancient bone sample she'd sent him months back, he knew what he'd stumbled upon. He just couldn't explain exactly what it was.

When they'd returned from Rome in June, that job had been delegated to her.

So far, her search to find answers had only brought bigger questions. Where had 23 come from? How could it have only existed in a two-thousand-year-old man? A chromosome that could *selectively* undo countless centuries of adverse genetic mutation? It was an epigenetic riddle of unprecedented proportion.

Charlotte sank back into her chair and sighed.

She couldn't help but contemplate an idea serious researchers considered taboo: the 'origin – unknown' variable that pointed to something bigger than scientific rationale. Irreducible complexity? *Don't think it*, she told herself. But she did anyway. *Intelligent design?* If her analysis even hinted at creationism, she could kiss her career good-bye.

'Come on,' she admonished herself. *You can find the answer. You can do this.*

But even if she could, what about the commercial aspects of the research? This thing would be the Pandora's box of medicine. Eradicating every disease could have daunting implications – like the complete collapse of the medical-industrial complex.

'Just breathe,' she muttered to herself.

'Take a breath for me too,' a voice called from the door.

She turned. It was Evan, looking like a billboard ad in his Armani navy double-breasted suit and a tasteful periwinkle and white striped tie that made his blue eyes flash – a more serious corporate image (adopted not by his own volition, but at the insistence of the board of directors). She still opted for the company's standard-issue white lab coat over her 40-percent-off Ann Taylor Loft pantsuit.

'How ya doin'?' He stayed leaning against the door frame.

'Oh, you know. Trying to figure out how we trapped the Garden of Eden in a test tube,' she said with great sarcasm.

'You say that like it's a bad thing.'

She shrugged.

He tipped his chin up at the monitor. 'Your sample still stable?'

'Yes.' Enzyme levels normal, blood cell counts immaculate, no trace of cancer cells. Remission.

'Nothing wrong with that.'

'I'm not complaining,' she said with a smile. 'Still think we should keep this under lock and key?'

He nodded slowly and sharply. 'One step at a time. This little wonder has already helped BMS redesign its gene sequencers. And now those puppies can pick out just about every known disease.'

That was putting it mildly, she thought. Beta testing of the Genocodifier XMT by the country's leading genetic researchers had led to unbiased euphoric reviews in the industry's most prestigious journals and had set the entire health-care market buzzing – from pharmaceutical companies to biotech firms to fertility clinics. The orders were flooding in from all corners of

the globe, presenting Evan with a CEO's most invited dilemma –
how to keep up with production and growth. He'd been meeting
nonstop with venture capitalists to arrange funding for BMS's
global expansion. Wall Street was already whispering about 'the
next Microsoft.' Hence the spiffy suit. *What a difference a few
months had made*, she thought.

'A bit premature to follow up with a potential cure-all,' he
said, 'especially when my best researcher can't quite explain what
it is.' He folded his arms to await her rebuttal to the dig.

'Is that right?' she said, feigning offense.

He shrugged. 'There could still be side effects,' he reminded
her.

'Like what? Me growing a beard?' she quipped.

Aldrich laughed. 'We just need to be patient.'

The smile faded from her lips. He'd recently applied those
same words to their relationship. Given the circumstances, his
noble reasons had been justified – the huge corporate responsi-
bilities now commanding all his time and energy. Problem was,
those circumstances wouldn't be getting any easier going forward.

Sensing what she was thinking, he parried with 'I was going
down to Starbucks for a coffee. Want me to pick you up one of
those frappa-mocha-soy-latte Frankenbrews you like?'

She snickered. 'I've already exceeded my caffeine quota for
today, but why not. And it's *"venti,"* not "medium."'

'Right.' He made to leave, but paused to offer some encouragement. 'Remember, Charlotte: we know the world isn't flat
and the sun is the center of our solar system. The answer is
there,' he said, pointing to the monitor. 'You'll figure it out.' He
gave a wink and made his way into the corridor.

Through the clear glass partition, she watched as he got onto the elevator. 'But I'm not Copernicus,' she mumbled as the doors slid closed in front of him.

As she twirled her chair back to the computer, the desk phone chimed. She pressed the speakerphone button. 'BMS Genetic Studies Department.'

'Doc, it's Lou.'

Charlotte immediately recognized the security guard's distinct Brooklyn accent. The big voice complemented the man's impos-ing stature. 'Hey, Lou. What's up?'

'Just a sec . . .'

Through the receiver she could hear his heavy footsteps, then a door closing to block out the sound of voices in the back-ground. Then came the groaning of upholstery and some heavy breathing as Lou settled into a chair.

'Sorry 'bout that. Had to come into the office before I talked to you. Anyway, we got a guy down here – out front at the desk. Askin' for you. Told him you ain't workin' here no more. Seven freakin' times I told him.'

Charlotte straightened in the chair.

After all she'd told Evan about what had happened in Vatican City – that goon, Salvatore Conte, quite literally chasing her out the front gate – they'd agreed it would be best to leave her name off the company directory. To further limit her exposure, Aldrich had taken her off media duty too. She'd even gotten a new cell phone number and home number.

Lou continued, 'But this stubborn mother – uh, pardon my French – refuses to vacate the premises till we tell 'im where you're at. I'm gonna call the police, but—'

'Did you get a name?'

'Sure. But he sounds like a leprechaun,' he said, digressing. 'I think he's after your Lucky Charms—'

'My folks were Irish too, Lou,' she reminded him. 'Remember, I've got the reddish curly hair, green eyes?'

'Ooh. Sorry 'bout that. But you've got that great tan—'

'His *name*, Lou?' Down at the front desk, she'd overheard the ex-nightclub bouncer sizing up the female employees. Best to cut him off before he started commenting on her great 'rack.'

'Right. Just a sec.'

There was a pause, then she heard his chair creak, the crinkle of paper.

'Name's Donovan. Patrick Donovan.'

Father Donovan? Here?

'Just thought I'd tell ya before I call the black-and-whites. Case he says something and they call ya.'

'Wait, Lou,' she said, still caught up in confusion. 'Is he bald, about five-nine . . . mid, late forties maybe?'

'Bald as a baby's butt cheek. And he ain't no NBA draft pick, age or height, I can tell ya that.'

'Give him a pass and send him up.'

'You sure?' he asked, disappointed.

'He's safe. I'll vouch for him.'

'If you say so. Just give a shout if he gets fresh.'

She disconnected the call and sat back in her chair. What could possibly bring Donovan all the way from Vatican City?

11.

Each time the elevator doors opened, Charlotte reacted like a little girl waiting for her daddy to come home. She even caught herself nibbling at her unmanicured fingernails.

During her short stay in Vatican City – which Patrick Donovan had arranged with BMS – the priest had been a consummate host, looking out for her at every turn. She'd dismissed any notion that he could have been responsible for siccing Conte on her when she made to leave Vatican City unannounced. That look in Donovan's eyes when Conte first wheeled the crated ossuary into the Vatican's lab? Conte was certainly not under his control.

When the doors smoothly parted for the third time, a man in jeans and a short-sleeve plaid shirt with a white guest badge plastered across its pocket stepped off the elevator looking lost. Even without the black suit and white collar, she immediately recognized him. Rising from her chair, she smiled and waved to him through the glass, then made her way to the door.

'Can I hug a priest?' she asked.

'If you don't squeeze too hard and make all the confessions come out,' he said with a wide grin.

'It's so great to see you,' she said, bending slightly for a quick embrace. 'Quite a surprise.'

'Yes. So sorry, Charlotte. Rather rude, me showing up unannounced like this.'

His soothing voice delighted her. 'Don't be silly.' Right away she could sense something was troubling him. 'I take it this isn't a social visit?'

Smiling tightly, he said, 'We must talk for a few minutes. It's quite urgent, I'm afraid.'

Immediately she felt her stomach flutter. 'Sure. My office okay?'

He looked over her shoulder. All the walls were clear glass and he could see a young woman who appeared to be Charlotte's assistant in an adjacent glass cubicle. He seemed to think it was private enough, because he said, 'Certainly.'

Charlotte led him inside, locked the door to avoid interruptions, and motioned to the small oval conference table set by the window. She watched as he sat with hands folded on the table, his posture timid and vulnerable.

'Lovely view,' he couldn't help but comment.

'Scores high in our employee satisfaction surveys,' she replied, taking the seat across from him. He smiled genuinely for the first time – the smile she remembered from their strolls in the papal gardens. 'Speaking of which, how are things at the Vatican?'

Donovan contemplated his hands for a moment. 'Oh, you know . . . as long as there are sinners out there, business will be good, I suppose.'

'And Cardinal Santelli?'

His eyes met hers for a moment, then went back to his woven hands. 'I take it you haven't heard.' He told her about the cardinal's death, which, for now, he explained simply as unexpected heart failure. Only he and God were privy to the true nature of Santelli's demise.

'I'm sorry' was all Charlotte could muster.

'Well, I'm sure he's in good hands now.' Whether they were God's or Satan's, Donovan wasn't certain. Before proceeding, he knew he had to address something else too. 'And Dr. Bersei—'

'I read about it,' she said, her voice suddenly choked. 'I still can't believe . . .' Eyes watery, she had to stop herself. 'Was it really an accident?' she managed in a low voice.

The emptiness in Donovan's chest felt instantly larger. The Vatican could spin anything. 'About that . . .,' he said, but reconsidered. 'Later, actually. No time now. You see, I left the Vatican . . . after all that had happened. Returned to Ireland. Back to the homeland,' he said.

'Temporary leave?'

'Permanent, perhaps. Anyway, it worked out fine . . . got to spend time with my father before he passed on, God rest his soul.'

She *tsk*ed and reached out to touch his hands. 'So sorry.'

'Lived a full life. He was a good man. God will take him with open arms.' *Unlike me*, he thought, and drew a breath before going on. Leaning forward, he looked deep into her eyes. 'Something very troublesome happened to me yesterday. When I couldn't reach you by phone, I had no choice but to come find you immediately.'

Luckily, his checkered past in Belfast meant always keeping his Italian passport (the de facto standard for Vatican citizens) alongside his wallet, and a small travel bag was always at the ready in his motorcycle's stow box. After the incident at the store, he'd headed straight for Belfast International and immediately got standby seating on an Aer Lingus flight bound for New York. A second booking on Continental got him to Phoenix by late morning.

'Two men came looking for me,' he explained, 'asking about the ossuary we'd studied.' The fear this brought into her eyes pained him. Guilt came fast.

Confusion rumpled her brow. 'I saw the ossuary in the news. Tough to miss the dolphin-trident etching. They said it'd been stolen,' she said, without trying to make it sound like an accusation. 'Then it was anonymously returned to Jerusalem. Right after Dr. Bersei was found dead.' Hearing her own words made her consider the facts. Conspiracies immediately began spinning in her head. 'Was it him?'

Donovan shook his head. 'Not Bersei.'

She studied his shamefaced expression. '*You?*'

A reluctant nod.

'To set things right,' he said, trying to defend himself. 'A long story I don't have time to explain just yet. But the big problem is . . . I returned it empty. And it seems these two men were looking to get the skeleton back.'

'The bones?'

'Yes. They were very insistent. And when I chose to remove myself from the conversation' – he looked up with hard lines creasing his brow – 'they came after me with guns.'

Charlotte's face blanched. Oddly, the first thought that struck her was industrial espionage. Could it be the miraculous gene code they were after? But only she and Evan knew about that. 'Wow' was all she could say.

'Besides me, I'm afraid you are the only person left who's worked on the project. And . . .' His voice trailed off and he spread his hands to compensate for the lost words. He'd never anticipated all of this when he'd first acquired the ancient manuscript that told of the ossuary's existence beneath Jerusalem's Temple Mount.

'You don't think . . .' She looked hard at him. 'You think they might come after *me*?'

Looking down again, he nodded. 'I had to warn you.'

At that moment, he happened to divert his eyes to the corridor, where two technicians were just coming off the elevator. They were attired like Charlotte – spotless white lab coats covering business-casual clothing. But the taller man's coat wasn't buttoned because his broad shoulders pulled at it too tightly.

Donovan's eyes went wide when he spotted the fellow's companion – an ordinary, forgettable man. It took only a split second before the man made the connection too. 'Jesus save us!' Donovan yelled, jumping up from the chair.

The shorter man snarled as he went for the door and began fussing with the lock.

A second later, the elevator doors parted and Evan emerged with a to-go cup clutched in each hand.

'Oh no!' Charlotte cried. 'Evan!' But her scream was subdued by the glass partition. She watched in horror as Evan stopped in his tracks, his confused gaze bouncing from the two lab techs to Donovan, who was frantically waving his arms, shouting for Evan to move away. But Evan failed to grasp the gravity of it all.

Instead of retreating, Evan stepped up to the tall man and scrutinized the tiny photo on the security badge dangling over his chest. When he surmised that the two lab techs were imposters, his temper flared. While trying to urge the short one away from the door, Evan attempted to sidestep the tall man. But the giant blocked his advance so that Evan's face collided with his chest. Some verbal sparring ensued, all inaudible on the other side of the glass.

'We'll have to let him handle it,' Donovan implored her. 'We've got to leave right now.' But Charlotte was frozen. 'Let's go!' Donovan yanked her up from the chair.

'We can't just—'

'Get moving!' He pulled her arm even harder.

Overwhelmed, Charlotte couldn't take her eyes off the scene as the large man planted a huge hand on Evan's chest and thrust his arm like a piston, sending Evan stumbling backward. By the time Evan regained his footing, the giant had reached beneath his lab coat, produced a gun, and raised it to Evan's face. Horrified at the dire turn of events, Evan threw the two cups at the man and tried to run for the fire exit. The gunman barely reacted as the scalding coffee hit his chest and splashed up under his chin, steam swirling into his face.

With unwavering aim, he snapped off a shot that drilled a red circle through the back of Evan's head and ripped open bone and skin in a red spray as it exited his face. Evan's body catapulted forward onto the tiles.

It wasn't the crack of the gunshot that caught the assistant's attention; it was Charlotte's bloodcurdling scream. When through the glass partition she spotted the two men near the elevator and Evan's body sprawled in a pool of blood, she panicked and darted for the metal security door leading to the labs. She fumbled for the employee ID card clipped to her suit jacket and slid it through a reader on the lock.

Donovan swung open a second glass door leading into the assistant's cubicle, dragging Charlotte behind him.

'Wait!' Charlotte protested. 'Evan!' she cried.

'Stay down!'

An instant later, the door leading to the elevator let out a loud *clack* as cracks webbed out from a single hole blown through the center of its tempered glass. The round thwacked into the window-pane behind Charlotte's head, making her snap into action.

The assistant was just making her way through the metal door, and Donovan muscled Charlotte through right behind her. He stole a glimpse of the large gunman, who was throwing his shoulder against the fractured glass. A third attempt brought the door down in a thousand pieces, the man stumbling forward into the office.

'Come on!' Donovan screamed. He ducked into the doorway, Charlotte at his heels. He yanked the safety door shut just as another round thudded close to the handle. 'How do we get out of here?' he panted.

'Follow her,' Charlotte replied, her tone full of dread. She pointed to her assistant, who was already halfway down the corridor. Adrenaline was helping her to pretend that she hadn't just witnessed Evan's murder.

12.

Orlando unclipped the geneticist's ID badge from a neck strap he'd spotted on her desk and waved it in the air. 'Hey! Take this,' he called loudly. On the other side of the glass partition, his partner was trying unsuccessfully to unlock the door through which the three had escaped and was preparing to blast a hole through the lock. The facilities on this floor required higher security access than what was permitted by the badge he'd forcefully 'borrowed' from the undersize tech he'd stuffed into a utility closet in the parking garage.

Kwiatkowski – his shirt and lab coat drenched with coffee; the front of his neck blistered and red – raced in to retrieve the key card.

'I'll handle this,' Orlando said, eyeing the computer monitor. 'You go.' He waved toward the metal door. 'And put that away,' he ordered, eyeing the man's Glock.

Tucking the gun into a concealed underarm holster, Kwiatkowski rushed next door, opened the metal door with the first card swipe, and disappeared beyond.

Orlando grinned when he saw a laptop patched into the

workstation's dummy terminal. Shortly after giving up Donovan's name, the Vatican priest, Father Martin, had since called to inform him of an American geneticist's involvement in the project too. The cleric couldn't recall her name, but he'd remembered invoices paid to her Phoenix-based employer, BioMedical Solutions, Inc.

After Donovan had fled his shop, Orlando and Kwiatkowski had scoured Belfast for his motorcycle, with no results. It was while they were ransacking his home that the call came through on Orlando's cell phone – results from traces run on Donovan's passport and credit cards. By then, Donovan's Aer Lingus flight to JFK International had already lifted off Belfast International's runway.

Though the priest had been one step ahead, they hadn't been far behind.

Their employer's private Learjet had swiftly begun closing the gap. While in the air, another credit card trace came through, showing Donovan had purchased a second fare on Continental Airlines. A search of flight manifests had him en route to Phoenix – home of BioMedical Solutions, Inc. The Learjet arrived an hour ahead of Donovan's flight, plenty of time for Orlando to make a preliminary visit to BioMedical Solutions's downtown headquarters. While the guard at the security desk provided him directions to the nearest men's room, Orlando had discreetly stuck a dime-size microphone to the underside of the granite countertop. When Donovan finally arrived, the adversarial conversation he had with the guards had been crisply transmitted to Orlando's cell phone.

Next, Orlando studied the geneticist's desk.

Luckily, whatever she had been working on wasn't on the company's main server. That saved lots of time and risk in trying to decrypt passwords and navigate sophisticated firewalls. He unplugged the laptop and tucked it under his arm.

Was this woman Donovan's accomplice? Whatever the case, the fact that she was a geneticist was troublesome. Because if she'd examined the bones . . .

His eyes made a quick inventory of the framed photos on her desk. Mostly shots of an older man whose facial similarities suggested he was her father. He snatched the photo that showed her face most clearly.

Next came the desk. In the top drawer, he found some business cards among the paper clips, Post-it pads, and pens. 'Dr. Charlotte Hennesey. Executive vice president of genetic research,' he read, impressed. He slipped one into his pocket.

The bottom drawer gave up her abandoned Coach purse. He pulled it out, unzipped it, and rifled through the wallet. The bad news was her credit cards were left behind and there were no keys. The trail would be that much harder to follow. The good news was her Arizona driver's license had been left behind too, so accessing all her records would be that much easier. He tucked the wallet into his pocket.

Then he hastened through the shattered glass and into the corridor.

Luckily, no other employees had come by during the commotion – less killing, fewer complications. To his right was another solid keyed entryway marked LAB 11 – LEVEL 4 CLEARANCE ONLY. To his left, sprawled in front of the elevator, the dead executive lay in a swirled pool of blood, coffee, and brain matter.

'Nice suit,' Orlando said, staring into the man's lifeless blue eyes. Sidestepping the mess, he calmly made his way to a fire exit sign that pointed to a door at the end of the hall.

13.

In the genetics lab, Kwiatkowski was attempting to be low-key while trying to figure out where the geneticist and priest had headed. He could tell he was on the right path when one of the female techs became frightened at the sight of him. She grabbed at a phone to attempt a call to security.

Promptly, he strode over and squeezed the thin hand that held the receiver while the middle finger of his free hand pressed down on the base's disconnect button. 'Don't even think about it,' he growled.

'Don't hurt me!' the woman pleaded through quivering lips.

'Which way did they go?'

Without hesitation, she pointed across the pristine workstations to a fire door. When he scanned the room and didn't spot anyone else paying attention, he jabbed his right fist once at the woman's face, knocking her out cold onto the floor.

Then he sprinted through the stainless steel islands heaped with microscopes and gadgets and slammed through the door. In the stairwell, he paused to listen. Quick footsteps echoed, sounding close to the bottom.

Swearing, he bounded downward, taking the treads in huge leaps.

Just as he passed a placard for the fifth floor, he heard a door slam far below. He swore again and quickened his pace.

By the time he made it to the bottom he could already hear tires squealing. Pulling the Glock, he threw open the door. But the front end of the speeding car swerved to push it right back at him, knocking him down and cranking his ankle sideways. Pain shot up his calf.

He cursed, sprang to his feet, and leapt out the door, crouching for a shot. But the car was just rounding out onto the roadway.

Cursing again, he tested the ankle. Nothing broken, maybe only a slight sprain. That's when Orlando appeared on the street, spotted him, and came rushing over.

'I couldn't make out the license plates.' Kwiatkowski agitatedly shook his head. 'But it was a silver Volvo. Convertible with Arizona plates.'

'Doesn't matter; I've got plenty,' Orlando said, patting the laptop.

14.

JERUSALEM

Jozsef Dayan was no stranger to handling ancient papyri. The seventy-two-year-old had dedicated five decades to deciphering the ancient secrets buried beneath his homeland. His transcriptions and interpretations of the historical treasure trove found in the hills overlooking the Dead Sea had earned him worldwide notoriety, as well as numerous citations from the Israeli government. His most recent book on the subject, *The Essenes and Qumran: Unlocking an Ancient Mystery*, was considered mandatory reading for any biblical archaeologist worth his salt. Fluent in all the biblical languages – including Hebrew, Aramaic, and Greek dialects – he'd been instrumental in revealing a world that had been lost for centuries.

Qumran's first set of scrolls had been found accidentally by a Bedouin herder whose search for a lost sheep led to a cave filled with ancient clay jars. Shortly thereafter, when the United Nations helped Israel to raise its flag in 1948, the texts began surfacing in the underground antiquities market at a time when Israeli nationalists were paying handsomely for artifacts substantiating Jewish heritage.

Ever since, the discoveries had kept coming. To date, the Israel Antiquities Authority had cataloged over nine hundred scrolls.

But none compared to what his colleague Amit Mizrachi had brought to him only yesterday.

The sand-colored clay jar containing the papyri had been what first captured Dayan's attention. It was twenty-three centimeters in height; had a cylindrical, bulbous form; and was slightly tapered from top to bottom – just what he'd expect. But a most peculiar symbol had been traced into its side prior to the clay's firing. And its domed lid had been sealed with wax. Most unusual. So he'd known straightaway that whatever had been stored inside carried great importance and promised to be excellently preserved.

On a light box to his left, the lid rested beside the empty jar and a glass dish containing the fragments of the wax seal.

A separate light box, set to barely a glow, sharpened the Greek text on three papyri laid out beneath protective glass.

The papyri had been meticulously preserved, the best he'd yet seen, in fact. A bit brittle along the edges, but no distortions, stains, or discolorations. It was obvious that no moisture had gotten past the jar's seal.

And the text was so perfectly legible – so cleanly inked by the quill along horizontal guidelines cut superficially into the sheepskin vellum, all written by the same steady and patient hand; the characters' unique formation was undoubtedly first century. Surprisingly, careful analysis with an ultraviolet wand detected none of the alterations or overwrites typically found when scribes corrected for errors. Incredible specimens.

At an adjacent computer terminal, Dayan typed out the final lines of the transcription, backspacing numerous times to correct for the typos that resulted from his severely trembling fingers. The Hungarian couldn't shake the growing dread that had quickly overcome his initial euphoria.

The ancient message was shocking. Something so profound that Dayan knew these texts might never find their way to the scroll vaults beneath the Shrine of the Book at the Israel Museum.

He managed to type out the final line of the transcription, then saved the document. Next, he opened his e-mail account, scrolled through his extensive contact list, and selected Amit Mizrachi. After attaching the document, he began his message:

Dear Amit:

In all my years, I've never seen anything like this. So many have tried to extrapolate meanings from the Qumran texts, seeking connections to the Gospels – contradictions, perhaps. But as you know, only ambiguous interpretations exist. If these scrolls truly date to the first century, and I have no doubt they do, what you have discovered will challenge everything we know. I fear that such a controversial message might

'Yosi?' A gruff voice interrupted his typing.

The septuagenarian gave a start as his head swung to the figure dressed all in black standing in the open doorway. 'Oh, for heaven's sake,' he said in a dry voice. He coughed before getting his next words out. 'You nearly scared me to death, Rabbi.'

'Everything all right?' Cohen cautiously moved into the lab.

'Of course.' The response sounded as insincere as it felt. He quickly clicked the send button on the message window before the Hasid could get within sight range.

'Did I interrupt something?'

'No,' he said, shaking his head. 'Not at all.'

Hands folded behind his back, Cohen approached the light boxes and first scrutinized the clay jar. 'I've heard that Amit Mizrachi has come up with a most unique find,' he said, his tone almost accusatory.

'Indeed he has,' Yosi feebly replied.

'Please,' the rabbi insisted, tipping his head at the jar. 'Tell me.'

'Well, it's all very early on,' he said, getting up from the chair and joining the rabbi at the table. 'We must perform a luminescence study to validate the pottery . . . radiocarbon on the vellums too, of course.' He swept his hand over the three papyri.

'I understand. But nothing provides better validation than your gut, Yosi,' the rabbi said with an air of flattery. 'You're the best of the best. So why not tell me what you already know the tests will confirm?'

Reluctant to share, the archaeologist needed to buy more time. It was only right that he speak with Amit before discussing the remarkable transcription. 'It would be premature, I'm afraid. There are some inconsistencies here, and . . .' He let the lie fall flat. Perspiration was welling beneath the sparse white hairs of his high widow's peak.

'Is that so?' Cohen said, eyeing the pristine writings. 'Seems quite clear to me. Greek, is it?'

'That's right.'

A closer look tightened his squint. 'Koine Greek, if I'm not mistaken?'

Yosi didn't like where the rabbi was going. But if he didn't take the bait . . . 'Correct. You have a keen eye.'

He assessed the three pages, which were dense with writing. 'Only three sheets. Surely you've finished the transcription already?'

'I have,' he finally confessed.

'Perhaps you could give the museum's largest benefactor a first look?'

Yosi's timid gaze dropped to the flattened scrolls. The rabbi didn't need to remind him of his merit here – no doubt attributable to the seemingly unlimited funding his organizations had supplied Israel's museums and IAA research programs with. As far as the IAA was concerned, Rabbi Cohen was to be treated on equal footing with the organization's president. But Yosi also knew that the man's intimate work with the Ministry of Religious Affairs had caused much controversy – particularly his involvement in preserving grave sites accidentally uncovered by construction crews in and around Jerusalem. He'd personally witnessed Cohen laying his body in front of a backhoe to stop the desecration of a first-century tomb uncovered during a high-rise project in Talpiot, all in defense of the strict Jewish laws – Halakha – that demanded respect for the dead.

This discovery would surely put up the rabbi's defenses. Yosi was keenly aware that he was walking a fine line. 'Forgive me, but I don't think that would be wise, just yet.'

The rabbi cocked his head sideways in silent frustration, lips pursed. 'Then perhaps you wouldn't mind if I have a look?' He pointed to the jar.

'Of course. But if you could, please . . .' Yosi reached up to the shelf and pulled a fresh pair of latex gloves from a small box. He handed them to Cohen.

Cohen pulled the gloves over his pianist-like fingers. Then his attention went back to the jar.

It looked ordinary enough. Palming the sides, he gently lifted it from the light box. It was heavier than he'd have guessed – a robust piece. First, he checked inside to confirm that it was empty. Then he examined the outside. It was when he began rotating the jar that he spotted the symbol cleanly etched into its side. His eyes immediately went wide and his face drained. He actually had to suppress a gasp.

'Most unusual, isn't it?' Yosi noted. 'Looks to be the same symbol on the side of the ossuary we recovered in June.'

'Indeed,' Cohen said, doing his best to conceal his anxiety. As if to confirm it was real, he ran a finger over it – the imprint of a legacy. Grandfather's words echoed: '*Yes, but not a fish, a dolphin. And not exactly a fork, but a trident.*' 'Qumran, I take it?'

More hesitation. But it was no secret that Mizrachi had been sited there for some time now. Yosi nodded. 'Just when you think the well has run dry.'

Carefully, Cohen returned the jar to the light box. As he peeled off the gloves, he eyed the archaeologist's computer monitor. The screen had gone solid blue with a pop-up box in its center framing two blank fields labeled USER NAME and PASS-WORD.

'Well then,' Cohen said. 'I certainly look forward to your findings.'

'As do I,' Yosi said as he began slipping out of his lab coat. 'I must lock up now. I've got a previous engagement to attend to.' This wasn't a lie. 'A symposium at the Israel Museum,' he added for good measure. He hung the coat on a rack behind the door.

'Ah, yes. Something about the Babylonians, as I recall?'

The rabbi surely knew exactly what the topic would be. '"Relics from Babylonian Exile," to be precise.'

'Should be fascinating.'

'We shall see.' Forcing a smile, he motioned to the door. 'I must get going if I'm to make it on time.'

Eyeing the jar and papyri one last time, Cohen went out into the corridor and waited as Yosi pulled the door shut and locked it with a key.

'Good seeing you, Rabbi. *Shalom.*'

'*Shalom.*'

Cohen folded his arms tight across his chest and watched the old man disappear around the corner. Then he studied the door lock.

15.

PHOENIX

'I don't know what to say . . .,' Donovan began, shrinking in the Volvo's leather passenger seat. 'I'm so very sorry, Charlotte. If I'd known they'd—' But as he glanced over at her again – the pain that contorted her face, the tears, the trembling hands gripping white-knuckled at the steering wheel – he knew there weren't words to console her about such a thing.

Silent, with eyes staring emptily at the roadway, Charlotte was lost for words too. The moment she'd safely left the downtown high-rises in her rearview mirror, the fight-or-flight rush had given way to overwhelming shock and grief. It wasn't just the man she thought she'd loved who had been mercilessly murdered before her eyes, but a visionary genius as well. A man who'd revolutionized genetics. It was a profound loss that would affect so many.

Heading north on Squaw Peak Parkway, she had yet to consider a specific plan or destination. Escape had been the only thing on her mind. But finally, she eased off the accelerator as more tears blurred her vision. 'They're going to follow us, aren't they?' she finally said, opening the center console to pull out a tissue.

Hearing her speak was comforting. 'I'm afraid so.'

She wiped her runny nose, then her moist eyes. 'Who are they?'

He shook his head. 'Not sure. But they're definitely professionals. How they could find me so quickly . . .' He sighed and threw up his hands. 'They'd need access to all sorts of information.'

'Did Conte send them?' she sniffled. 'Is that what this is about?' Ever since the creep had chased her out of Vatican City and she'd landed a firm foot in his crotch, she'd feared his retaliation.

Donovan glanced out the window at the omnipresent freeway signboards for Paradise Valley before answering. 'Conte's dead, Charlotte,' he said with conviction. 'It couldn't have been him.'

This took Charlotte completely by surprise. 'What? How?'

A pause.

'I killed him.' His brogue grew stronger. 'I had to kill him,' he stressed. 'There was no choice.'

'My God,' she gasped in repulsion. 'How could you do such a thing? You're a *priest*.' Now she couldn't dismiss the fear that maybe Donovan was somehow baiting her.

His wounded stare remained on the approaching desert hills, dotted with cacti. 'Just before he tried to kill me, he told me he would come for you, Charlotte.' He could still hear the mercenary's words clearly in his mind: '*Did the cardinal tell you she skipped off with her laptop . . . loaded up with all the data? . . . I've got to fix that too and her blood will be on your hands . . . if a freak accident should happen to befall the lovely geneticist . . . the authorities would be none the wiser . . . Of course, I'll be sure to show her a good time before she goes.'* 'I couldn't handle another loss . . . after Dr. Bersei . . . the Israelis.'

Mute, Charlotte couldn't believe what she was hearing.

'I had a gun,' he went on. 'There was a struggle . . .'

For a moment, Donovan was back at the misty grove atop Monte Scuncole, peering down at the ossuary he and Conte had dropped into the pit they'd dug. He remembered fixating on the crack that had snapped the stone lid in two – wide enough to reveal the sacred bones beneath. Conte intended to drop Donovan's body in right behind the relic and use C-4 to finish the job.

'I managed to run from him . . . out onto the roadway. He was right behind me when the car came.' The images reeled through his mind, making his pulse drum. He needed to take a breath before continuing. 'By the grace of God, it swerved and took him down – like the Angel of Death . . . but even with that, he was still breathing.' He shook his head in disbelief. 'Only the devil himself could have kept him alive. But Conte was *breathing*. Had he somehow lived, there's no telling what—' Trembling fingers went to his lips to repress the surge of emotion. The next words came fast: 'So I took the gun and finished him.' He quickly crossed himself. *God, please have mercy and forgive me for these deeds.*

No matter what the consequences, airing the confession felt good – cleansing. The Irish way of 'stuffing it down' simply wasn't good for the soul. However, Donovan still wasn't prepared to offer up that when he'd stripped Conte's body of its personal effects, he'd found a syringe filled with clear serum, which he'd snuck past the Vatican metal detectors to eliminate what he thought had been the final threat – the Vatican's secretary of state. Otherwise Santelli would have stopped at nothing to complete what he'd set out to do: eliminate any trace of the Vatican's involvement in the church's greatest cover-up.

He allowed a few moments for the air to settle.

'Then Conte *did* kill Bersei?' She'd suspected that all along.

Donovan nodded. 'Many others too.' Though he felt he'd already said too much, Charlotte would need to know the whole story. 'There's more,' he said. 'I suppose there's nothing to lose now,' he said, and sighed.

He went on to tell her how just weeks before she'd been summoned to Vatican City, he'd been given a book by an anonymous contact ('The book I showed you during our meeting with Cardinal Santelli,' he reminded her), how it had actually included a map showing the ossuary's hidden burial vault beneath Jerusalem's Temple Mount. How when he realized the implications of what would happen if the ossuary was discovered by Israelis, he'd convinced Santelli to take action. Though he'd advocated a peaceful solution, the pragmatic cardinal immediately sent for Salvatore Conte. Upon assessing the job Conte had used untraceable Vatican funds to employ a team of men to forcefully extract the ossuary – an elaborate plan involving guns, explosives, even a stolen helicopter. Many Israelis had been killed during an ensuing firefight at the Temple Mount, Donovan explained.

She recalled hearing these things in the news. Even given Conte's ruthlessness, which she'd witnessed firsthand, his involvement in such a huge heist came as a complete surprise. Wrapped in thought, Charlotte caught herself tailgating a semi that was chugging up the steep grade. She checked the mirrors, flipped on the turn signal, and maneuvered around it.

'Then he brought the ossuary to the Vatican,' Donovan said. 'And, well . . . you know the rest.'

Trying to process the unbelievable story, Charlotte was silent for a solid minute. 'I guess I should be thanking you,' she finally managed.

He raised a hand to dismiss any idea of it. There was no glory in what he'd done. Especially since he still wasn't certain if Conte's murder had incited what had happened today.

'At first I thought these men might have known that Conte was working for the Vatican,' Donovan explained. 'Perhaps he hadn't paid them for their services in Jerusalem. But they spoke about Conte as if he were a stranger. And no mention of money . . . or the ossuary, or the nails, or the book. Just the bones,' he grimly replied. 'The *bones*,' he repeated in disbelief. 'I can't imagine why. Even if I were to give bones to them, how would they know they came from inside that ossuary? I suppose I could give them any skeleton . . .,' he said, hands cast up.

But Charlotte knew that was not the case. Those bones hid a one-of-a-kind imprint. And if these men knew what made them so special . . . A cold chill ran over Charlotte's body.

There was a more direct answer she was hoping for. So she just needed to go for it. 'That skeleton I studied . . . It belonged to *Jesus*, didn't it?' She'd thought it impossible. But Dr. Bersei had been the first to suggest this, finally convinced after deciphering the strange relief carved into the ossuary's side – a dolphin wrapped around a trident.

Charlotte's hands clamped harder on the wheel as she awaited Donovan's slow reply.

A trembling hand went loosely over his mouth while he tried to formulate a response. 'You saw the bones and the relics with your own eyes. If archaeologists had found them first, the evidence would have left little doubt—'

'Was it *him*?' she firmly insisted.

Exasperated, Donovan swallowed hard. 'Yes.'

16.

'And you have no doubts about that?' Charlotte said. After seeing the incredible genes hidden in the bones, their healing powers . . . Could there be any doubt that it had been Jesus's remains she'd studied in secret at the Vatican Museums?

'There's always room for error, but . . .' Donovan shook his head.

'You . . . a priest . . .,' she said, stalling. 'You're basically telling me that there was no resurrection or ascension?'

'Not in a physical sense.'

'Then what about the Gospels?' Charlotte bitterly replied. 'Is it all just made up?'

'The biblical accounts of events immediately following Christ's burial are highly suspect, dare I say . . . falsified.'

'How so?'

The proof was fairly complicated, but he started at the easiest point. He explained that the oldest Gospel – Mark – originally ended with the empty tomb and that verses 16:9 through 16:20, where Jesus makes His appearances to Mary and the disciples, then ascends into heaven, were an addendum, written by a completely different hand. The Vatican's oldest manuscripts from the fourth century, the Codex Vaticanus and the Codex Sinaiticus, didn't include the long ending, but by the fifth century Mark had *four* different endings that spoke about resurrection and ascension.

Charlotte could tell that Donovan was calm about all this but also felt somewhat cheated. To her, it seemed too big a conspiracy to have been kept under wraps for so long. 'And nobody figured this out?' she asked, incredulous.

'Oh, it's no secret,' Donovan insisted. 'Any good Bible will reference this omission in its footnotes. Not to mention that even if you read these added verses verbatim, Jesus's post-burial appearances are still referenced in *metaphysical* terms.'

Giovanni Bersei had told her this too. But she was interested in the priest's perspective. So she asked for examples.

Donovan went on to give a sampling from all four Gospels, noting that each read like many of the omitted apocryphal texts the Catholic Church had considered heretical. He told her that immediately following the resurrection accounts in John 20 and Mark 16, Jesus appeared to Mary Magdalene and was unrecognizable to her; she'd actually mistaken Him for a gardener. And in Luke 24, two of the disciples not only doubted His identity when he appeared to them, but then Christ literally disappeared from their sight – *vanished!*

In Donovan's opinion, however, John 20 was the most telling of a metaphysical resurrection. He said, 'John stated that the disciples were hiding in a sealed chamber and Jesus suddenly appeared in the room among them . . . from out of thin air,' he pointed out. 'So you see, all four Gospels contain specific language suggesting that the Jesus who appeared after the resurrection was not that same Jesus who was buried in the tomb. So I ask the scientist in you, Charlotte: does that sound like a physical body to you?'

'No.' There were too many things it sounded like, she thought. But disappearing from sight? Appearing out of thin air into a locked room? How else could that be explained? Another wave of mixed emotions crested over her as she came to terms with the notion that the DNA inside her could actually have been taken from Christ. She sighed. 'I suppose I'd rather be an apparition in the next life too,' she said.

To a scientist, this actually made more sense anyway, she thought. After all, the body's 'spirit' was really an electrical charge running through the nervous system. And Einstein's most basic principle maintained that in a closed system, energy could never be lost or gained – merely transferred. If one viewed a dead body as a battery that had lost its charge, then logically, the body's energy would be given back to the system. *What* system, however, was anyone's guess.

'The real question is, should this knowledge impact one's faith or discredit Christ's teachings . . . His mission?' Donovan added. 'A physical body doesn't negate the teachings found in the Gospels. Nor does it downplay that God's kingdom does promise eternal peace for the righteous. But after all these centuries, the Vatican has emphasized an archaic interpretation of Christ's physical death. So you can imagine the threat a body would pose.'

He tried his best to explain how the Vatican had for centuries speculated about a physical body and feared one might turn up. Occasionally, charlatans had attempted to blackmail the Vatican with anonymous relics lacking any provenance whatsoever. But with today's scientific methods, Donovan pointed out, had a genuine relic been excavated, in its context from beneath the Temple

Mount, the threat would then be very, *very* real. He stayed silent for a few seconds, then said, 'Now we just need to figure out why these two men want the bones so badly.'

Charlotte shifted uneasily in her seat. One thought kept repeating itself – Evan Aldrich had used those bones to save her life. Now those same bones had made him a casualty. And though Donovan was fishing for an explanation in the theological realm, there was only one thing that could logically be their true motivation.

'I think I might know what these men are after.'

17.

The Volvo idled at a scenic overlook along Camelback Mountain. The two passengers inside had just reversed roles; now Donovan was hearing Charlotte's confession. And what she had to say – had to release – was something far more astounding than anything weighing on his soul.

Far across the valley below, beyond the unnatural green swaths of golf courses set amidst suburban sprawl, Donovan's empty eyes were locked on BMS's gleaming edifice, which rose high above the buildings clustered around it – an ungodly Tower of Babel forged of glass and steel, where humans challenged God on an entirely new level.

'There's something else you need to know about what we discovered,' she said. 'I'd been very sick back in June . . .'

'I gathered that,' Donovan weakly replied. 'I was told you'd left behind things in your room. The drugs were for cancer, weren't they?'

She nodded. 'Multiple myeloma.'

It wasn't the first time he'd heard of this aggressive disease, and he couldn't hold back the grim expression that immediately came over him. How ironic that it attacked the *bones*, he thought.

Picking up on his distress, she quickly added, 'But I don't have cancer anymore.'

Amazed, he looked up at her. 'Praise God,' he said, beaming. 'That's incredible! A miracle.'

'Yes . . . and no,' she said. 'You see, that same gene I just told you about—' Her voice choked off.

'Go on,' he encouraged her. The same words he'd used countless times in the confessional.

Glancing over at him, she could tell he didn't fully comprehend. 'The DNA . . . Jesus's DNA? It has special qualities.' The genetic synthesis was fairly complicated – something she still couldn't completely decipher – so she needed to keep it simple. 'It's like a virus, but a good one. And when introduced into someone who's sick . . .' She tried to envision 23 intelligently replicating system-wide at super speed to destroy the malicious cancer cells.

Donovan slumped in his seat.

'His DNA is inside me,' she said, her voice low, reverent. 'It cured me. Probably minutes after it got into my bloodstream.'

Now Donovan was practically hyperventilating. On impulse, he crossed himself.

'So it seems we both have secrets.' He looked like he was going to have heart failure. So she reached over with a soothing hand and laid it on his forearm.

The fingers of his right hand went back to his quivering lips once more. The implications of what they'd uncovered in Jerusalem kept coming. 'What have we done?'

'Isn't everything God's plan?' she said defensively, mostly to ease her guilt.

There may have been a time when he believed that. It would

be comforting to think that God played puppeteer when Donovan killed Conte and Santelli. And it would offer great solace to know that the desecration of Christ's ossuary was divinely sanctioned. But could God possibly have intended these consequences? 'I don't know, Charlotte. I just don't know.' He looked out to the horizon. 'What I do know is that we're in this together,' Donovan grimly replied.

'Well, here's what I'm thinking: what if these men somehow found out about my genetic studies?' It seemed impossible, given the unbelievable secrecy and security protocols she and Evan had built around the study. She pulled her hand back. 'Maybe that's why they're coming for us?'

Sitting up, Donovan thought about this. At first, it actually seemed possible. Then he shook his head. 'You saw how they got into your building. It was easy for them. Why would they have wasted time trying to come for me first?'

It was a good point. 'Because I don't have the bones?' she guessed.

'But you just told me you don't need the bones. Your small sample can be replicated easily, right?'

'I see what you mean,' she said – a major hole in the hypothesis. 'So you don't think they actually know about the DNA?'

Based on the interaction he'd had with them in Belfast, he said, 'I don't think that's what they're after – at least not directly. But it's evident that they want one of us to show them where the bones are hidden.'

Her eyes flashed with curiosity. She'd forgotten all about this. 'Where *did* you hide them?'

'Best I not tell you that. For your own safety,' he insisted. He could see she was disappointed. 'But I promise that if we get through this, I'll show you.'

'Fair enough,' she said. 'So where do we go from here?'

Donovan sighed. 'We can't stay here, that's for sure. Apparently they can track us everywhere we go.'

'Why not just call the police? I mean, they murdered —' She felt her throat close off. The tears came again.

He shook his head. 'These men are professionals. We don't have names, a plausible motive. Nothing. They won't be found. The real investigation that needs to be done . . . well, I think we'd agree that they just wouldn't believe our story. Police won't matter. We'd be sitting ducks,' he soberly replied. Looking up at her watery eyes, he could see she agreed. 'Until we figure this all out, we need to be in a place where even if they know where we are, they can't get to us. Someplace with very, very tight security.'

'We'd need to hire bodyguards. Lots of bodyguards.'

'No need,' he said, grinning. 'Someone's already done that for us.'

Obviously he had an idea. 'Share, please.'

He simply replied, 'I've been on sabbatical long enough.'

18.

THE TEMPLE MOUNT, ISRAEL

Sheikh Ghalib Hamzah ibn Mu'adh al-Namair claimed the leather armchair at the head of the teak conference table. The arched window behind him had been cranked open to allow a gentle breeze to freshen the cramped meeting room, but more important, to give the Waqf's assembled council members the necessary vantage to set eyes on the brilliantly sunlit Dome of the Rock, situated across the esplanade – visual reinforcement of their duty to protect the sanctity of the Haram esh-Sharif.

To further emphasize that duty, he'd slotted the early evening meeting immediately following Asr – the fourth of the five daily prayers that preceded the setting of the sun. And Ghalib had insisted that those now present recite the silent prayer inside the Dome of the Rock. He felt it would better set the mood.

Ghalib sat back tall and rigid, with forearms aligned perfectly on the chair's armrests. Loose, wiry hands hung from the sleeves of his bright white tunic. Beneath a white prayer cap, or kufi, wisps of jet-black hair framed his wide, bony face and blended seamlessly with a patiently grown and meticulously groomed beard and mustache. An ever-present sneer favoring his right cheek gave a permanent crook to his lips. He was only thirty-eight, remarkably youthful for such a post – a testament to the fact that youth tended to preserve the fight in a man.

'*As-salaam alaikum*,' he said, greeting the dozen prominent elders and Muslim clerics gathered around him. He bowed his head, closed his eyes, and said, 'Praise to Allah, the merciful and the beneficent. May He guide us and watch over us.' Then he tipped his head back and opened his eyes. It wasn't only the stuffy room that needing airing. 'I'm well aware that some of you have voiced concerns about my appointment here.' His caramel irises swam in pure white orbs resting behind taut eyelids, passing over the innocent with no regard, tightening accusatorily on the known dissenters.

And some dissension was expected. As a star pupil of the right-wing Wahhabi brand of Islam, Ghalib was a highly vocal fundamentalist with strong ties to Islamic militant groups, a regular teacher at universities throughout the Arab region, and hailed as the next great voice in Palestinian liberation.

'So let us talk,' he said. 'Voice our concerns. Discuss our ongoing mission to preserve Islam and its sacred shrines.' His head tipped right as his accusatory stare went directly for the man who most opposed him. 'Why don't we start with you, Muhammad?' The turbaned sixty-two-year-old shifted uncomfortably in his chair and cleared his throat. 'The Israelis continue to dig beneath the Haram while the Waqf sits idly by . . . watching, waiting,' Ghalib said in a sharp tone. 'What do you suppose we are waiting for? Do you believe that your prayers will stop the bulldozers?'

'Of course not,' Muhammad said defensively. 'You know that is not the case.'

Ghalib spread his hands. 'Then defend your case.'

Another dry cough. 'Ever since the theft in June . . . since your predecessor was indicted as an accomplice,' he reminded Ghalib, 'our power has been greatly diminished.'

Ghalib's crooked lip tilted higher. His predecessor, Farouq bin Alim Abd al-Rahmaan al-Jamir, was still in custody with the Israeli authorities and facing severe charges for conspiring to commit a theft that left thirteen Israeli police and soldiers dead. Though Israel's only state-sanctioned execution had been the May 1962 hanging of Nazi SS leader Adolf Eichmann (who'd been captured hiding in Argentina by Mossad agents), many high-ranking Israelis in parliament insisted that Farouq should be put to death for treason.

Ghalib shook his head, his lips turned down. 'Your power has not changed. But your *will* has surely weakened.' He knew what made the man soft and sympathetic. Though Palestinian by blood, Muhammad was Israeli by passport. It was evident that it wasn't just the cover of his immigration documents that had changed from green to blue. And unlike his suffering brethren, Ghalib knew, righteous Muhammad lived on the prosperous side of Israel's separation fences that cut away the West Bank and Gaza with hundreds of kilometers of poured concrete, steel, and wire.

Anxiety building quickly, Muhammad was hoping someone at the table would support him. None spoke up. 'There *was* an earthquake,' he stressed. 'Mild, yes. And when it first happened we were granted permission to see what had happened. I personally viewed the tunnel . . . you too, Safwan,' he said, pointing to the gaunt Arab wearing a kaffiyeh who sat across from him. 'You saw it with your own eyes. Tell them.'

Safwan was silent; his charcoal eyes went to his hands.

Muhammad persisted, 'Considerable damage *was* done—'

Ghalib overrode him. 'Need I remind you that the damage was done long ago when you sat idly by over the past decade and allowed Jews to excavate the tunnels beneath the Muslim Quarter?'

'It was a trade-off,' he insisted. 'They got the tunnel; we were permitted to restore the Marwani Mosque.' He held his hands and balanced them like scales.

'And see where that got you? You cleared the way for thieves to blow a hole through it.'

The Marwani Mosque had been the thieves' entry point to the arched vaults beneath the mount – and a hidden chamber sealed behind its rear wall, which they'd accessed with C-4 plastic explosive.

Muhammad's face reddened. He was playing right into Ghalib's hands. And the man was certainly looking to make an example out of him. One thing was now clear: Ghalib's appointment here was indicative of a subversive political agenda playing out on a much higher level. Given the current state of affairs, he still couldn't imagine how the Israelis had even granted Ghalib entry into the country. Most likely, Ghalib had been snuck in by his Lebanese Hezbollah contacts. Ghalib had yet to step foot off the Haram, refused all media appearances, and corresponded under the assumed name Talal bin Omar. However, the Israelis weren't stupid, so Muhammad could only guess that they preferred having Ghalib within easy reach. 'The proper resolution we've always sought has been *peace*. Cooperation. Coexistence. Just as the Prophet teaches us.'

Ghalib sneered. 'Peace? Coexistence?' He mockingly held his hands out at the man and let his gaze circle the table. 'There is no *peace* in Jerusalem. Peace is a hopeless ideal that appeals only to the weak. There will never be peace in a place where Jews burrow like vermin beneath the great Prophet's sacred mosque. And coexistence is an excuse for your fear of their guns and nuclear weapons. Only victory will bring peace. And in the name of Allah, we will prevail.' The teacher in him shone through, ever ready to provide Qur'anic *tafsir* favoring jihad. 'Do you not agree?'

Scowling faces swung toward Muhammad. The Keeper's question was a loaded gun. He paused to consider an appropriate rebuttal. 'I do not condone what is now happening, but—'

'My ears have heard this digging!' another elder burst out. 'While praying in the mosque . . . below my feet . . . I hear chipping sounds!' He cupped a hand around his ear and tried to imitate it: '*Chh-chh-chh. Chh-chh-chh.* This is what I hear. It is true. The Jews seek to destroy the Haram!'

The room erupted.

Smiling, Ghalib savored the moment. A half minute later, he finally raised his hands up to silence them. 'Infestation. Like termites. That is what we are dealing with. There is a plague here that must be eliminated. We must free our house from defilement. It is not a choice. It is our sworn duty.'

The council members barked their support.

'We must avoid drastic action,' Muhammad delicately pleaded as he rose to his feet and placed a hand flat on the table. 'Hostility will only cost innocent lives,' he said, patting the hand twice. 'Has this not been proven time and time again?'

Rebuking shouts drowned him out. Ghalib once again intervened to settle them down. Then he jabbed a spindly finger toward Muhammad and commanded, 'Sit down!'

Muhammad's firm expression withered into despair. He threw his hands up in surrender. 'I cannot support this . . .' He made to leave the room.

Ghalib's right hand sliced the air like an ax blade. 'I am not finished!' he roared, nostrils flaring.

Muhammad froze and turned back to him.

'Jews have no place here!' Ghalib held up a balled fist and swung it like a hammer. 'This is a truth that cannot be questioned! Be assured that our response to recent events will be swift and concise. And our voice must be one. It is evident that your disgraceful words are solely your own and will not poison our ears. Therefore, your services are no longer required by this council. Now go, and don't come back.' His hand chopped an arc to the door. 'And let me remind you that anything you say outside these walls will have very serious consequences.' His face twisted. 'Very serious indeed.'

Glaring eyes bored into Muhammad like needles in a pincushion as he slunk out of the room.

The room erupted again, the men boisterously voicing their approval of Ghalib's fervent patriotism.

19.

QUMRAN

By the time Amit steered the Land Rover off Kaliah-Sedom (Highway 90) and up the drive leading to an empty parking lot, the sun was setting over the hills of Jordan, making the Dead Sea glow amber and sapphire. He claimed the spot closest to the planted palm grove bordering the tiny makeshift oasis that was Qumran's visitors' center.

'Isn't this romantic,' Jules said. 'We have the place all to ourselves.'

'Too bad I didn't bring some wine.'

'Always a step behind,' she teased, shaking her head.

He grinned tightly, knowing she wouldn't be saying this after he'd shown her what he'd found up in the hills.

They both hopped out.

Amit circled to the Land Rover's rear and lifted the hatch to retrieve some provisions.

Meanwhile, Jules took a few seconds to admire the picturesque sea with its white mineral-crusted shore, the stark umber hills jutting up into the amethyst glow spreading into the sky above.

The Land Rover locked with a quick flash of lights and a tiny chirp as Amit pocketed his keys. He came to her side holding flashlights and a black rucksack.

'God, it's so beautiful,' Jules said.

'Sure is. And smell that?' He breathed through his nostrils, long and steady – the distinctive aroma of clay, potash, and bromine.

She sampled it too, her thin nose flaring at the sides.

'That's history . . . the Bible; what keeps me coming back,' he said.

'Smells a bit like a swimming pool,' she said in a snooty French accent, 'but whatever floats your ark.'

'You're ruthless.' Shaking his head, he handed her a light.

He led her up some paved steps past the squat gift shop and ticket center, out back to the gravel trails leading to the sheer cliffs that formed a continuous wall to the north and south. To their left were the excavated ruins – mainly foundations – of the village the Essenes had inhabited up until the first century. Not far beyond them was a deep gorge extending from the sea to a huge mineral-coated crevasse cut into the cliffs by the winters' flash flood runoff. They were headed to a zigzag path running up it.

'How far up?' she asked, eyeing the towering cliffs.

'Pretty far,' he flatly replied.

'Fabulous,' she huffed.

Peppered around a sliver of a crescent moon, winking stars were starting to break through the darkening sky as Amit led Jules to the ladder set beneath the cave opening.

Drenched in sweat and complaining incessantly about the buzzing flies, Jules was razzing him about how they were going to make it back down the cliff in the dark. She was still upset that some spots had required them to climb over boulders.

'The hike down is much less challenging,' he said, stretching the truth. Despite her complaints, he knew the payoff was certain. He flicked on the flashlight and pointed it up at the opening.

As Jules craned her neck back, her flashlight lit up the tight curves where her sweat-soaked white T-shirt clung to her chest. The opening was another climb, but nothing like the clamber up the gorge. When her gaze snapped back to Amit, she caught him quickly diverting his bashful eyes from her raised nipples. 'I'd hate to think you dragged me up here to look at my tits.' She crossed her arms in front of her chest and squeezed her breasts together, to make matters worse for the Israeli.

His face went red. 'I was just . . . just . . .' Then he decided that his attraction didn't require an apology. 'It's hard not to stare, that's all. Take it as a compliment.'

'Compliment taken.' She actually blushed. 'Now can we get moving?' She waved for him to get up the ladder.

The episode had taken away his fear of climbing, because he stepped off the ladder and into the cave without care. He snuck another forbidden peek when he clasped her hand and helped her up.

'We're heading all the way in,' he informed her, his voice taking on a professional air. 'Watch your footing. It gets a bit dodgy in spots.'

'Lead the way so I can check out your ass,' she quipped.

'Enjoy the show,' he said, and began the steady climb up the tight passage.

'Double feature,' she said, shining the light on his rump.

The tricky tunnel forced Jules to concentrate for the

remainder of the climb. When Amit spilled out into a wide hewn chamber, she wasn't quite sensing the magic.

'You okay?' he asked, making his way to a light pole.

'*Oui.*' She ran her flashlight over a bunch of bricks arranged neatly on the floor. It was when the work light went on that she saw the wide opening in the rear wall. She moved closer.

'Hands and knees for this one. But it's only a couple meters.' He could see some agitation building in her skeptical gaze.

Amit took the lead again, shuffling along on all fours into the rear chamber. When he stood, he immediately went for a second pole light close to the opening. The room came to life as Jules clambered in and got to her feet.

For a few seconds she said nothing as she paced the perimeter of the square chamber, skipping a corner where equipment and tools were heaped, pausing in spots to run her fingers along the hash marks cut into the stone walls. 'Who *made* this?' she finally asked.

'I'm almost positive it was the Essenes.'

'Ah, the Essenes,' she incredulously replied. 'Our scroll-writing friends again. A busy bunch, weren't they?'

And he hadn't even shown her just how busy they'd been. 'Those bricks you saw on the ground out there' – he pointed to the passage – 'had sealed the opening and were covered in earth and clay so no one would ever find this place.'

'Okay. So let's say they carved this room.' Downplaying the significance, she shrugged. 'So? Why?' But she could tell by the shit-eating grin on the Israeli's face that he knew more – lots more. 'And I'm still not seeing the glyph.'

'The good stuff is down below,' he promised, pacing over to the toolboxes placed around the opening in the floor to prevent anyone from falling in. With Jules watching over his shoulder, he slid some of the stuff aside to access the steps. 'Why don't you go first?' he said to her.

A tentative pause. Then she took a step closer and angled her flashlight downward. 'Sure.'

Amit's widening grin pinched his goatee at the corners. Now she was doing a lousy job of suppressing her excitement. 'Careful on the steps.'

Jules kept her right hand on the wall as she made her way down, fingertips rising and falling over countless other hash marks. Her hiking boots squeaked on the smooth treads. At the base of the steps, she made some room for Amit to stand beside her.

While she stood frozen in place, mouth agape, Amit reached over to turn on another pole light that sucked out the darkness from the spacious, cube-shaped chamber. When he looked back to Jules, her breasts were rising and falling fast, and she wasn't paying much attention to the fact that he noticed. The cool air had only improved the show.

Her mesmerized gaze was glued to the huge painting covering the wall opposite the steps. It was a magnificent specimen – white with colorful designs – and looked like it had only been painted yesterday. She strode over to it.

'I'm sure I don't need to remind you not to touch it,' he teased.

'Ha-ha,' she said without taking her eyes off the image. 'It's amazing.'

In the center of the wall painting was a small arched niche carved into the underlying sandstone – empty. Spreading out around it, concentric circles made a sunburst, drawn upon a larger design – an equilateral cruciform, wrapped by grapevine tendrils. The ends of the cross widened into spades, each painted with Judaic symbols – two shofars, the ceremonial horns used to usher in the Jewish New Year, on the north and south axis; two lemon-shaped *etrogs* – fruits used during Sukkot, the feast of the Tabernacle – at the east and west points.

But most intriguing were the four quarter circles that curved between the arms of the cross, each containing a most unusual symbol – a dolphin entwined around a trident.

'I wonder what was here,' she said, pressing her face close to the empty niche.

'A clay jar, actually,' he knowingly replied. 'And it contained three scrolls.'

Her astounded eyes finally gave him some time. 'You're kidding! Where are they?'

'Certainly would not have been wise to leave them here,' he

reminded her. 'I brought them to the Rockefeller Museum for transcription.'

'Jesus,' she gasped. 'This is amazing.' Hands on her hips, she studied the painting a few moments longer, eyes squinting tight at the strange dolphin-trident symbol. 'This symbol . . . what's it doing here?'

He moved close to her side and took it in once again. 'Crazy, right? Seems almost pagan.'

'Exactly.' She gave it a few seconds longer, then shook her head in defeat.

'We have a sacrificial altar too,' he added, moving to an enormous raised stone commanding the room's center. It had been carved into a cube, its top scooped out like an ancient sink.

'Spooky,' she said, giving it only a cursory once-over.

'And a *mikvah*.' He pointed to the far corner, where more steps sank into a wide rectangular pit cut into the floor – once filled with water and used for ritual bathing and purification. The finding was consistent with other *mikvah*s found in the village near the sea and underscored the Essenes' strict hygienic practices.

'You'd think they were using the place as a temple,' she said with some sarcasm.

But that's precisely what Amit had thought too. 'The plot thickens,' he replied simply.

'And the glyph?'

'Right. Over here,' he said, waving her to the corner closest to the stairs.

'On the wall there.' He pointed to an etching that wasn't easy to discern until they were within a meter of it.

Jules aimed the flashlight directly at it to pull the shadows out from the lines. 'So I take it you're thinking the Essenes did this?'

'It would make the most sense. The room was sealed away. The jar was still here when we opened this chamber. If anyone else had come in, they'd at least have taken the jar, don't you think?'

Looters were looters. 'I see your point.' She ran a finger along the lines. 'And this is very clear. A clear message. Even its positioning near the steps . . . the last thing one would see when exiting the chamber.'

'So the question is,' he asked, 'why leave a glyph for Heliopolis?'

She considered this. 'A forwarding address, I suppose.'

He hadn't thought of this. 'How so?'

'Well, whatever was here, maybe upstairs in the other chamber, must have been moved to Egypt.'

Amit blanched. 'My God, Jules. That actually makes sense,' he muttered.

'Good thing you brought me here.' She patted his solid shoulder. 'Question is, what was in the chamber upstairs?'

'Maybe the scrolls have something to say about it,' he surmised, stroking his goatee. That's when he heard the first faint sounds coming from above, trickling down the steps.

'But if these symbols—'

'Shhh,' he cut her off, grabbing her wrist. 'Hear that?' he whispered.

'What?'

'Shhhhhh.'

Then Jules did hear it. Subtle scraping sounds. Feet scuffing along stone? 'Are you expecting someone?' she whispered.

He shook his head. A program started running in the back of his brain – a hardwired protocol from his IDF days, activated only during the silent infiltrations of radical Islamic safe houses in Gaza. 'Let's get up top,' he suggested, pulling her to the steps. Then, as an afterthought, he quickly unzipped the rucksack and pulled out a tiny device.

'What are you doing?'

'Keep moving. I'm right behind you.'

20.

In the front corner of the upper chamber, empty polyethylene toolboxes and storage bins were stacked three high. The clunky radar unit was parked in front of it all, next to a small generator. Behind the organized clutter, a sizable gap ensured there would be no contact with the chamber walls. But now, contact had been made – not by the gear, but by Jules and Amit as they squeezed in tight to shield themselves. Since the stack was barely a meter in height, Jules was practically flat against the cool stone floor. Amit could only fit sideways, lying on his left side.

Amit's head peeked out the side just enough to monitor the shadows playing across the floor in front of the passage opening. Thus far, it sounded like only one set of footsteps. A looter, he guessed. His fingers wrapped tighter around the handle of a hefty pickax he'd grabbed from a tool rack. It would only be a matter of time before . . .

The scuffing sounds grew louder as the dark silhouette stretched in front of the passage.

The intruder was coming.

Amit craned his head back at Jules and signaled for her to stay low. Keeping his head out of view, his ears fixed on the footsteps to monitor the movement.

Chssst, chsst.

Pause.

Chssst, chssst, . . . chssst, chsst.

The intruder was now in the chamber. Amit hoped his decoy would divert any search behind the boxes.

Then he could hear the quiet footsteps easing down the steps toward the loud voice spouting academic jargon in the lower chamber.

Waiting till he counted seven footfalls, Amit quietly got up on his haunches and crawled over to the steps, careful not to let the pickax scrape along the stone. It wouldn't take long for the looter to realize that the lower chamber was empty and that a small digital recorder was playing back Amit's dictation at high volume from the bottom of the bathing pit.

The intruder figured it out sooner than expected. Amit heard a gruff male voice curse in Hebrew, then footsteps rushing back to the steps. He dropped the pickax and scrambled for the stone slab set just beside the hole. With all his might he began pushing the slab over the opening.

The first muffled spitting sound confused Amit as something ricocheted off the edge of the slab, taking a chunk of the stone with it. It took a split second for it to sink in: the man was shooting at him! The gun was equipped with a silencer – not what he'd expect from a run-of-the-mill grave robber. 'Jules! Get out of here! He's got a gun!' he yelled.

The feet were rushing up the steps. No time to think. Amit gave another huge push and the stone fell into place.

Another obscenity came from below.

The archaeologist's eyes darted around for something to pull over the top of the slab. Nothing heavy enough to keep the man trapped for long.

The slab suddenly fractured in the middle. Once. Twice. Each time with a *thwunk*.

The guy was shooting it to pieces. Amit didn't bother with the pickax, but grabbed his flashlight and doused the lights.

Jules was already in the outer chamber as Amit began scurrying through the passage on all fours. 'Don't wait! Go!' he screamed to her.

With flashlight in hand, Jules dashed into the tunnel.

Amit killed the lights in the front chamber too, then flicked on his flashlight. From the other side of the passage, he could hear the large pieces of slab tumbling onto the floor. He raced down the tunnel.

Up ahead, Amit spotted Jules. She was regrouping from a nasty fall, blood pouring down her right knee. 'Keep moving!'

He caught up to her as she was beginning to make her way down the ladder, raw fear glinting in her eyes. 'I want you to run as fast as you can, back the way we came,' he instructed in a low voice. 'And zigzag. Don't run in a line. Turn off the flashlight when you've made it out about fifty meters.'

She nodded quickly. He liked the fact that she knew when wisecracking wasn't appropriate.

Amit was already a third of the way down the ladder when Jules hit the ground running. She looked back over her shoulder and paused when she saw that he wasn't following her.

'Go!'

Luckily, she listened.

There was a sharp bend to the cliff wall, just beneath the out-cropping that formed a rim beneath the cave. Immediately switching off his light, Amit threw his back up against the stone face behind the ladder. He hoped the intruder wouldn't see him there.

As she sprinted through the gorge, Jules's flashlight cut side to side, up and down.

Go, Jules, go. She seemed even faster than his intern Ariel.

Then the gun spat overhead.

Dread came over Amit when he saw Jules stumble . . . no, not stumble. The shot must have pinged off something in front of her, forcing her to duck and weave. Then her flashlight disappeared. And so did Jules – swallowed by the dark gorge.

Another curse echoed from above.

There was a long pause. Too long. Was the gunman trying to figure out where Amit had gone to?

But less than two minutes later, the man mounted the ladder to make his descent.

Amit made his move. He lunged forward, throwing both hands against the ladder. It took everything he had to lever the man's weight away from the wall. The gun swung as the ladder teetered sideways.

The gunman landed flat on his back against some jagged stones and let out a moan. The ladder came down right on top of him, trapping his gun hand between its rungs.

Then the dazed assassin – dressed all in black, including a mask – was scrambling beneath the ladder, trying to train the gun on the giant Israeli target. That's when the C-4 the assassin had planted throughout the chambers, tunnel, and cave opening detonated.

Amidst a pulsing rush of orange fire, rock and debris shot out from the cave opening, the blast rumbling like a thunderclap through the gorge. The powerful shock wave pulled Amit off his feet and landed him right on top of the ladder, his mass instantly snapping the gunman's protruding forearm between the rungs. The broken limb bent unnaturally to one side, a spear of bloody bone jutting through the black sleeve. The man howled in pain.

Amit covered his head with his hands. Rocks showered down on him, pounding his back. When the deluge ended, he quickly looked up to see that the gunman was struggling to use his good arm to retrieve the fumbled handgun.

Amit got to the gun first. Then came the rage.

'Stay where you are!' he shouted in Hebrew, pointing the gun at the man's face. The weapon felt very familiar. The man's dropped flashlight sat beside them, and Amit could see the blood seeping out of a tear in the mask where the man had taken a stone to the head. He reached down to pull off the man's hood. As it loosened from under his shirt the man reached to his hip for a knife.

As the blade darted quickly into the light, Amit reacted, throwing out his free hand to grab the wrist. Instinct and adrenaline told him to shoot the man. Instead, he brought the gun up high and slammed it against the man's head where the rock had started the job. He went out cold.

Amit peeled back the mask and tried to place the face. The guy was young, maybe mid-twenties – appeared to be an Israeli. A quick search of his pockets yielded no identification. Nothing but two magazines full of ammo. He pocketed them.

Amit wasn't about to pull him down the gorge. And forget about calling the authorities. Qumran was situated in the West Bank, policed by the Palestinian Authority. He knew the political kowtowing he'd endured just to get permission for these excavations. The last thing he needed was to be connected to an explosion and a rogue Israeli hit man.

He took out his cell phone, swapped the gun for the flashlight, and snapped a mediocre picture of the man's face.

Folding the phone, he slid it into his pocket and picked up the gun. Dismay came fast as he pointed the flashlight up through the heavy dust. The blast had completely collapsed the cave. He had to remind himself that the scrolls still remained – that he and Jules were still alive.

But it crushed him to see that the discovery of a lifetime had just been obliterated.

And he was determined to find out why.

21.
JERUSALEM

Despite the high-speed connection with an IP address assigned to an Internet café located in Phoenix, Arizona, the streaming data feed had taken over three hours to finish. The entirety of the data stored on the American geneticist's laptop had been transferred to a new hard drive located in Jerusalem's Old City, in an office beneath the Temple Institute's unassuming museum gallery in the Jewish Quarter.

The delay had been prolonged by the sophisticated encryption and password protection layers that had locked down the hard drive. However, highly secretive code-breaking algorithms were standard issue on the mobile phones of field operatives.

Analysis of the computer's contents had then been entrusted to the ever-capable, waiflike twenty-one-year-old computer whiz named Ziv.

'There's an awful lot to look at here. So I began by sorting the files, pulling out all the program-specific stuff. I usually look at source tags first; tells me where data is originating,' she explained to Cohen. Beside her workstation – which, with its multiple plasma screens, armada of slim drive towers, and blinking lights, looked like command central for a space mission – the surly rabbi stood with arms crossed.

Cohen let the mousy computer genius spout some technical jargon. It seemed to give her confidence. And he needed her to stay motivated.

'And all these files here' – her wiry fingers tapped the keyboard at hyperspeed and a list came up on the center monitor – 'caught my attention. Seems they all came off a server – an intranet actually.' Her eyes showed fatigue from the hours she'd spent staring into glowing plasma crystals, not to mention overt frustration at Rabbi Cohen's keeping her well after the workday ended. It was already nine P.M., and he seemed to have no intention of quitting. The rabbi looked a bit edgy too, she thought.

Get on with it, Cohen thought.

'Point is, they all originated from the same domain and country code: dot V-A.' She looked up at him with excited eyes, quickly realizing he didn't get it. 'That's the server for Vatican City. Remember, you asked me to see if I could find anything unusual?'

The rabbi's arms fell limp and his mouth dropped open. 'You're positive?'

'Oh yes. Couldn't have come from anywhere else.'

'What kind of files are they?'

'Pictures mostly. Documents too.'

He leaned close to study the file names. When he saw some of the labels, he felt light-headed. Not only were the file details imprinted from Vatican City's host server, the files were tagged with June dates – mere days after the ossuary's theft from Jerusalem, and immediately preceding the date stamped on the ossuary's shipping container when it was anonymously sent back to Jerusalem from a DHL office in Rome.

'Open this one,' he instructed, tapping the screen midway down the list.

Ziv worked the mouse and brought up the image. She made a sour face when it appeared in high resolution on the monitor. 'Yikes. That's creepy.'

The rabbi's knees felt weak as he studied a clear snapshot of a complete skeleton laid out upon a black rubber mat. He could make out the sleek edges of a stainless steel table. Just as he'd suspected. The ossuary definitely hadn't been empty. *The ancient texts of the priests are never wrong*, he thought. 'I want to see all of them,' he said, voice quivering.

'Are you okay?' Three shades paler than usual, the rabbi looked like he'd seen a ghost.

He nodded without taking his eyes off the image.

'Pull up a chair,' Ziv said. 'There's actually a PowerPoint file here that has most of the pictures in a slide show.'

22.

Ziv ran through the highly detailed PowerPoint presentation with the rabbi three times. And it was really starting to bother her. To say the images were disturbing would be an understatement.

The pictures had been marked up with a virtual pen to leave yellow highlights and circles around the areas of interest. Cohen had studied every detail: the skeleton's gouged ribs; the ground-down bones joining at the wrists and feet, and the rust marks left there; the fractured knees. He spent little time on the image of three black, jagged spikes, even less on two coins laid side by side.

Shots of the ossuary from various angles had plenty of yellow 'ink' pointing to the dolphin-and-trident relief on the side of the box. He could practically hear his grandfather screaming blasphemy from his grave.

Only minor highlights pointed to the less fascinating rosettes and hatch patterns carved into the ossuary's front face and arched lid. Cohen couldn't help but notice that the lid wasn't cracked in these photos. Perhaps it had broken during its clandestine shipment from Rome?

There were slides with bullet points that no doubt summarized the study's findings, which were detailed in the document files Ziv had pulled up. The message was clear: this first-century specimen, otherwise a picture of perfect health, had died from crucifixion. And patina tests performed on the ossuary reinforced the conclusion that he had been buried in Israel.

Beneath the Temple Mount. Where the Levites had purposely hidden his ossuary to fulfill the prophecies. Now the prophecies had been jeopardized – a centuries-old plan, maliciously interrupted. By the Vatican, nonetheless.

The bullet point that spoke to ethnic origin listed one telling word: 'UNKNOWN' – the rabbi's worst fear confirmed. They'd analyzed the DNA. He didn't even realize that he was loudly grinding his teeth.

Ziv took a two-minute break before the final viewing to stretch, pee, and refill her coffee mug. When she returned, the rabbi hadn't budged. The haunted look in his eyes had only gotten worse.

At the moment, the rabbi was stuck on a most impressive digital re-creation that used meticulous calculations of the laser-imaged skeleton to re-create what the thirtysomething man would have looked like prior to his brutal death.

The rabbi had zoomed in on the face, captivated by the man's aquamarine eyes, which mirrored his own.

'Are you sure you're going to be all right?'

His bloodshot eyes broke from the monitor. 'We will be just fine.'

'We'? Who else is he answering for? she thought.

Sighing, he sat back and wove his hands behind his head. 'I'm very much interested in how they came up with this image,' he said, pointing with his chin to the monitor. Having spent plenty of time in genetics labs, he was certain that the equipment was far too sophisticated to bring into Vatican City. Most likely, a sample would have been sent off-site. God willing, the geneticist's laptop would have some record of it. 'So I want you to search every file for anything pertaining to genetic studies.' The request seemed to overwhelm Ziv.

'I'm not exactly a scientist.'

'You don't need to be *geneticist*,' he corrected. *You don't need to be Dr. Charlotte Hennesey*, he bitterly thought – the name the field operative had found on the geneticist's business card and driver's license. A search of her passport activity would certainly show that she'd been in Rome back in June. Though it seemed unnecessary, he made a mental note to have his contact at Immigration Control run the query.

Looking apologetically at Ziv, Cohen realized he'd be better suited for this task. 'Just get me a list of all the files. I'll select the ones for you to look at.'

'Of course.' Lightning-fast fingers back at the keyboard, she stripped out unneeded information, filtered, refined.

In the quest to reclaim the purity of his family's sacred bloodline, Aaron Cohen had become proficient in human genome studies – specifically the genetic research pioneered by Israeli professor Karl Skorecki in 1997, which traced unique gene markers in the patrilineal Y-chromosomes of Ashkenazi (European) and Sephardic (Spanish, North African, and Middle Eastern) Jews claiming to be *Kohanim* – the priestly descendants traced back over 3,300 years directly to Aaron and Moses. The Cohens. Of the world's seven million male Jews, less than 5 percent bore the unique genetic markers passed down by Moses's brother, Aaron. And since the mutations were preserved exclusively in the male Y-chromosome, intermarriages resulting from intercontinental Diaspora had virtually no effect.

Not surprisingly, the study's expansive database showed that Cohen's own Cohen Modal Haplotype had been the most pure to date, just as his late grandfather had promised – now vindicated by genome analysis. The problem with his own DNA was that countless mutations, or polymorphisms, had corrupted God's original perfection. Genetic distortions had been passed down from generation to generation. No doubt it underscored God's scorn.

The whittled-down list took almost fifteen minutes.

'Not too bad,' she said. 'Looks like there wasn't much here – at least important stuff, that is.' She clicked a command on the screen and the printer came to life, spitting out a seven-page directory of files sorted alphabetically and grouped by file type. Scooping the sheets up, Ziv passed them to the rabbi. 'Just let me know what you want to see.'

23.

In the Land Rover's fully reclined passenger seat, Jules was fast asleep, snoring like a barnyard animal, hands crossed over her chest.

A new sun was rising over Jerusalem as Amit put the truck in drive with a scab-knuckled hand. He was bleary eyed, exhausted to the bone. The falling rocks had pounded his back, bringing a physical pain that was oddly reminiscent of the automatic gunfire he'd once taken to his Kevlar vest in Gaza – nothing broken, but definitely some deep bruising. Even if he tried, he wouldn't be able to sleep – not without something to numb the pain . . . and his growing paranoia.

For the time being, he felt they needed to keep moving. Call it instinct. And for good measure, the flat black Jericho 941F pistol he'd recovered from the assassin rested on his lap, its two spare magazines weighing down the deep pocket of his cargo pants.

As the Rover lurched forward, Jules stirred and her bandaged knee touched up against the dash, making her flinch. Amit glanced down to verify that the bleeding had stopped. He'd done a good job cleaning the wound with the iodine from the truck's first aid kit. The cuts beneath the second tight wrap of gauze were deep, but nothing that required stitches. All things considered, last night could have ended much worse.

He checked the mirrors to make certain that no suspicious vehicle was tailing them.

A few hours earlier, when she'd first spotted him from her hiding place in the ruins of the Essenes' scriptorium down near Qumran's visitors' center, she ran up and threw her arms around him. *'What the hell just happened back there?!'* she'd cried, squeezing too tight around his tender ribs. But he liked it nonetheless. It'd been a while since Amit felt like any kind of hero.

Now he was still searching for an answer to Jules's question.

Why would a professional assassin try to kill them? Was what he'd uncovered at Qumran so shocking that its complete destruction was warranted? It made no sense. Sure, the wall painting was highly unusual and the unique chambers brought to mind all sorts of possibilities. And the glyph? Well, the glyph for Heliopolis could mean just about anything.

Then there was the matter of tactics. The assassin came with gun in hand, precisely when he and Jules had been seemingly trapped inside. The run-in, therefore, had been no coincidence. Amit wondered how long the man had been waiting to make his move, because there'd been no other vehicle in the parking lot last night. What had his plan been?

The jar. At least the jar was safely locked away at the Rockefeller Museum. The jar and its scrolls.

The scrolls?

Gears were turning in Amit's busy mind. Maybe his dear friend Jozsef Dayan could shed some light on matters. No doubt he'd finished the translations already. The man was a machine. The IAA would never get him to leave his post. And why should they? Age had only improved him. And years had only added to the trust Amit shared with the old man.

'Morning.'

It was Jules. He hadn't even noticed she'd stopped snoring. With hands folded behind her head, she was arced in a stretch.

'Hey.' Out of the corner of his eye, Amit couldn't help but notice that her shirt had hiked up to expose her lovely flat stomach. And her puckered navel was an innie. Nice. 'Sleep okay?'

'Not too bad. Been a while since I've been laid out on a guy's car seat.' She yawned. 'So what's the plan?'

He shrugged. 'Tough to say. I'll need to make some calls. I've got a friend who can probably help us.'

'A *friend*? How about the police?'

He shook his head. 'Not an option yet.'

'What? You told me that *dément* is still alive. How is going to the police *not* an option?'

'Because of this,' he said, holding up the pistol. 'Standard issue for the IDF. Also used by Israeli intelligence field agents.' He set the pistol back in his lap.

The mere suggestion of it had her smiling. 'So what?' She cranked the seat-back upright. 'You think he's one of them?'

'Too early to say. But look here,' he said, reaching into his breast pocket and flipping open his cell phone. 'That's him.'

Jules closely scrutinized the grainy picture. He liked the fact that she wasn't panicking. Most people would fall apart if someone had just tried to off them. 'As I was saying. I've got a friend, a contact inside Israeli intelligence. I'm going to forward this to him, see if he can figure out who this guy is – who he works for, perhaps. You never know. We might get lucky.'

'How would that be lucky? Someone obviously wants you dead.'

'If he wanted me dead, he would have shot me on the spot.'

'Too suspicious,' she said. 'If you were killed in a cave collapse in Qumran, no one would suspect a thing.'

He glanced at her and grinned. 'Not bad.' Maybe the gun in his lap had only been the guy's insurance. The real plan was probably a lot simpler, just like Jules was suggesting. Clever. 'Sounds like you may have done this yourself a time or two.'

'When you go through a shitty divorce, you can come up with all sorts of ways to pull off the perfect crime.'

She had a point. His second breakup, with Sarah, hadn't gone too badly – dare he say, amicably. But the first . . . The fierce custody battle for his two girls, and the fallout from Jasmina having forfeited her professorship to stay home and raise them? Brutal. Could have driven a lesser man to fantasize about unspeakable remedies.

'Sorry about this,' he said. 'I had no idea . . .'

She reached out and gave his thick, dusty arm a gentle squeeze. 'It's an adventure. And I'm a sucker for a good thrill. No need for apologies.'

Her words were sincere. But she'd once told him that her eye color changed with her moods. And the silver in her irises seemed more pronounced. 'Glad I could entertain,' he said with a half smile. 'Thanks, Jules.'

The Land Rover climbed Hanoch Albeck into downtown Jerusalem. The city was still waking up, so the sidewalks were empty.

Amit pulled over so Jules could run into a café to use the facilities and get some coffee and pastries. As she got out of the truck, he reminded her that it was imperative that she pay only with cash.

He kept the truck running, his wary gaze scouting for anyone who looked shady.

Ten minutes went by before she came scurrying out the door with a carrying tray holding two Styrofoam cups cradled in her left hand. In her right hand, she victoriously held up a white paper bag and made a dramatic face as if she were just crossing the finish line at a marathon. Chuckling, Amit reached across and threw open the passenger door for her. She handed him one of the cups, then hopped in.

Taking a sip of the slightly bitter coffee, Amit checked his watch. It was almost seven A.M. 'In a little while, I'll make some calls. Need to get some petrol, too,' he said, checking the fuel gauge. 'Don't worry, we're going to get some answers.'

'Worry?' she mocked, eyeing the Jericho. 'With you packing a pistol on top of your crotch? A girl couldn't feel more secure.'

24.

After topping off the tank, Amit pulled the Land Rover away from the pump and idled near the petrol station's pay phone. He hopped out to place a call from the anonymous landline. His contact picked up in two rings.

'*Boker tov!*' Amit said cheerily.

'Good morning to you, Commander,' Enoch Blum replied through the receiver. 'To what do I owe this pleasure . . . at nine A.M.? Need an extra shovel man at a dig?'

He chuckled. 'Not a social call this time, I'm afraid.' On the other end of the call, he heard a car door shut, an alarm chirp.

'Must be very important,' he said.

'It is.' He could hear Enoch's key chain jingle, then his hard soles clicking on cement. 'You're not in the tank yet, are you?' Amit had twice been called inside the Tel Aviv headquarters of Israeli intelligence to consult on hostage extractions in Gaza. And that's the impression the cement and steel Bauhaus bunker left: like being in the belly of a Merkava tank.

'Just making my way inside,' he said over the whistle of a breeze blowing through the parking garage.

'Maybe you can hold off on that.'

The footsteps stopped.

'Your mobile isn't monitored, is it?'

'No,' he said with some reservation. 'They still allow me a couple of liberties.'

'They' were the Mossad Merkazi Le-modiin U-letafkidim Meyuhadim, or the Central Institute for Intelligence and Special Operations – aka the Mossad. They'd assisted Amit's IDF unit on many operations. It was the two separate hostage extractions – both times, Israeli border soldiers had been abducted by al-Aqsa Martyr's Brigade and detained in Gaza City safe houses – that left the most indelible impression. The Mossad were a well-trained bunch.

Though the Mossad's director reported to the office of the Israeli prime minister, its estimated fifteen hundred employees were civilians, among them communications techs, weapons specialists, psychological profilers, field agents, international operatives, and hired guns. Its organizational chart was a pyramid of deniability – top to bottom. And when your business objectives included hostage extractions, terror-cell infiltration, sabotage operations, and assassinations, it worked much better that way, Amit thought.

Like Enoch, many in the Mossad's ranks had served in the Israel Defense Forces. Enoch had served his three-year conscription under Amit – back then, Enoch was a kid who had yet to shave and who was practically outweighed by his Galil (assault rifle).

'You all right?' Enoch asked with sincere concern.

'Eh. Been better. Have a few minutes for me?'

'Got a briefing in ten, but let's hear it.'

Amit made sure to squeeze everything he could into a two-minute recap of last night's assassination attempt. He mentioned the guy's tactics: his silencer-equipped Israeli pistol, his knowledge of explosives. Deciding to play it safe, he left Jules out of the story. 'Same kind of stuff we used to see in Gaza, if you know what I'm saying,' Amit told Enoch.

After a brief silence with more wind whistling through the receiver, Enoch finally came back with, 'Hell, I don't know what to say. Sounds to me like it has something to do with your excavations.'

'Definitely. The entire site was wiped out.'

An uneasy pause.

Enoch's reluctance was not subtle. Amit couldn't blame the guy – Enoch was a family man, and much better at it than himself. This was dangerous stuff that could have serious repercussions for him too. Then came the question Amit was hoping for.

'So how can I help?'

'I know it's a huge ask – puts you in a very difficult position. But if someone on the inside wants me dead, I need to know.'

'If they want you dead, it won't matter what you know.'

He had a point. Once you were caught in the agency's crosshairs, the Mossad wouldn't let up until a file could be rubber-stamped in red. *Should've killed him*, a tiny voice kept whispering to Amit. *Killed him and hid the body*. Then he'd at least stand a chance that the guy's employer would think the job was a success – that Amit and Jules were buried in the rubble. 'Just need a fighting chance. If there's a directive, maybe you can find out about it. See if I'm marked. And if so, why?'

More wind whistling through the receiver.

Enoch groaned. 'I'm in Collections now,' he finally replied. 'Nowadays, they've got me monitoring wire transfers and chatter. So I don't have clearance for that type of information anymore,' he said in a low, uneasy tone. 'But I still know some people in Metsada. You've got to give me some time.'

Amit grinned and gave Jules a thumbs-up. 'That's great, Enoch. Really great.'

Of the institute's eight branches, Metsada was the Mossad's special operations unit – the coordinators of assassinations and paramilitary and covert operations. Its huge database contained the agency's most guarded information.

'By the way,' Amit added, 'I have something that might help. I took a picture of the guy. I'm no photographer, and I used my phone to take it. Anyway, it should be enough that someone might recognize him. Do you mind if I send it to your phone?'

'Do that. It can't hurt. I need to get going. I'll call you as soon as I have something.'

Ending the call, Amit powered on his mobile only long enough to push the pix image over the airwaves to Enoch's phone. Then he powered it off just in case his hunter tried using it to triangulate his location.

'Think he'll help?' Jules asked as he got back into the Land Rover.

'Yeah, I do. Enoch's a good man.'

'What do we do in the meantime?'

He stroked his goatee. 'I think we should take a ride to the Rockefeller Museum. Have a talk with my friend Jozsef Dayan.'

25.

ROME

'You're sure this is going to work?' Charlotte asked as the taxi pulled to the curb along Borgo Pio.

'I don't see why not,' Donovan said. 'We've come this far . . .' He held up his hands and smiled. After paying the driver €40, he and Charlotte got out of the taxi toting their small travel bags. 'It will be fine.'

For some reason, she believed him. Just like she had when she let him talk her into driving to Phoenix Sky Harbor International immediately after they'd stopped at her home to get her passport and some essentials. Donovan had been wary of going to her house because he'd thought the men might have gone directly there after seeing the address on Charlotte's driver's license. But she'd informed him that after all that had happened at the Vatican, upon her return to the States she'd immediately switched her physical address to a local Mail Boxes Etc. store. That was the address that appeared on not only her license, but all mail and correspondence as well. Conte couldn't get all the credit for that, though; there were plenty of fanatics out there who put genetics on equal footing with abortion and murder. Some level of anonymity was prudent. However, since she'd left her purse at BMS, Donovan had put the pricey Continental airline tickets on his credit card.

Though the flight hadn't departed till six A.M., neither of them had slept during the four-and-a-half-hour trip to Newark or the hour-and-a-half layover there. Plenty of time for Charlotte to shed some more tears while Donovan tried his best to console her. It'd been the smooth eight hours crossing the Atlantic and Western Europe that had done the trick. They'd both woken up when the plane was in its final descent into Fiumicino around eleven A.M. Roman time.

She followed Donovan across the street.

'I'll need your passport,' he said, and waited for her to retrieve it from her bag. Taking it, he cast his eyes heavenward and said, 'Here's to the luck o' the Irish. Just give me a few minutes and wait here.'

She stood aside on the busy sidewalk. At the huge, ornate iron gateway crowned with a papal crest and flanked by Roman columns, she watched him approach a Swiss Guard wearing a blue jumpsuit, a sidearm, and a black beret. Over the busy commotion – cars and visitors queued in separate lines – she could barely hear the exchange. Though it didn't matter, since Donovan seemed to be conversing with the man in Italian. He presented their passports and the guard looked over at her. Next, Donovan produced a badge that was no doubt his outdated Vatican ID. Satisfied, the guard went behind the gate and waved for him to follow. Donovan confidently glanced over at her, smiled, and held up an index finger. Universal for *So far so good. I won't be long.*

When the first five minutes had gone by, crazy thoughts came to Charlotte – outlandish suppositions of why Donovan thought it best to come here, of all places. Could this be his elaborate plan to get her back into Vatican City – a trap? Maybe Conte was really alive, waiting behind the gate for Donovan's instructions to nab her.

But the laptop was more important than she – that's where the incriminating information really was. That's when it hit her: *My laptop. Christ, what if those men got hold of the files?* She took some comfort in knowing that the data was encrypted. Still . . .

Should it be surprising that she hadn't heard news reports concerning Conte's death? After all, Donovan had indicated that Conte wasn't even the mercenary's real name. And it was just another unsolved murder in Italy. Not prime pickings for CNN. But Santelli's death? Would that have made news in the U.S.? It's not like he'd been the Holy Father himself, but he was the Holy See's equivalent of vice president. Now she was wishing she'd had time to verify Donovan's story.

'I can't believe I'm doing this,' she mumbled.

A kind-looking priest was just exiting the gate and walked past Charlotte. Seeing her troubled expression and puffy eyelids, he smiled politely, glanced quickly at her bag, and greeted her with a warm 'Hello.' *Lucky guess*, she thought.

'Hello,' she said, smiling. Then she realized that her duffel bag, a complimentary joiner's gift from her local YMCA, had the facility's Phoenix address on it. The window of opportunity hadn't closed. 'Excuse me, Father?'

The man stopped and turned to her.

She took two steps to close the gap. 'I know this may sound like an odd question . . .' She rolled her eyes.

'I'm a priest. I get many odd questions, my dear.'

The kind, aged face reminded her of her dad. 'It's quite embarrassing that I don't know this,' she said, spreading her hands, 'but is Cardinal Antonio Santelli still with the Vatican secretariat's office?'

The man drew his lips tight and somberly shook his head. 'Sorry if you haven't heard. His Eminence passed away some months back.'

'Oh.' She feigned distress. 'That's terrible. What happened?'

'His heart gave out, I'm afraid. God rest his soul.'

She thanked the priest, and when she turned, Donovan was standing outside the gate waving her over. That's when she realized it was a beautiful day in Rome – clear skies and mild. And rising up all around her, the Renaissance architecture helped calm her spirit. A big improvement over her last visit. She strode over to him.

'What was that all about?' Donovan asked, curious.

'Oh, nothing,' she said. 'Just chatting.'

'You'll need this,' he said, handing her a laminated badge encoded with numbers, her name, and a high-resolution scan of her passport photo set beneath the flickering hologram of a papal crest. 'They'll hold our passports till we leave. Things have a gotten a bit more strict, I'm afraid.'

She shrugged and clipped the badge to the lapel of her rumpled blazer. 'As long as they still have showers in there, I won't complain.'

Passing through the gate, Donovan led her through the Vatican's tiny commercial district. As they passed Via dei Pellegrini she looked left, up at the rear face of the Apostolic Palace. When her eyes came down again, they were nearing the spot where she'd had a final showdown with Conte. The killer's final words echoed in her thoughts: *'Remember your confidentiality agreement, Dr. Hennesey. Or I'll have to come and find you.'*

And it was virtually on that very spot that Charlotte noticed a familiar-looking priest awaiting them.

'Patrick! So good to see you!' the priest said.

Donovan embraced the man. 'It's been a while.'

'Too long.'

Donovan turned to Charlotte. 'How rude of me. Charlotte, you remember Father James Martin? He was Cardinal Santelli's assistant?'

The poor man chained to a reception desk outside the cardinal's office. What she remembered most was the dark circles under his eyes and his pallid complexion, which seemed even worse in daylight. He looked like a creature of the night. 'Of course. Good to see you again, Father,' she said, offering a handshake.

He took her hand in his. 'Charlotte,' he said, cocking his head sideways as if trying to place her face. But really, hers was not a face to forget. He distinctly remembered – *May God forgive my impure thoughts,* he prayed – admiring her as she signed confidentiality agreements for Santelli's secret project; the project that now put his sister and her beautiful family in jeopardy. 'Yes, Dr. Charlotte ... Henry, was it?' He purposely botched the last name to alleviate suspicion. He'd remembered her name yesterday, when he'd immediately called the mobile number his abductors had provided. And only minutes ago, he'd placed a second call to Orlando on a new number, alerting him to the duo's unexpected arrival.

Her last name was printed in bold, twenty-point Times New Roman on her badge. Maybe he didn't want to be rude and look down since it was hanging over her left breast? Charlotte wondered. 'Close. Hennesey.'

'Sorry, I'm so terrible with names,' he said, some rosy color marbling his pale cheeks.

He finally let her hand free, leaving a damp, cold feeling behind.

'It's such a pleasure to have you staying with us again. Anything you need during your visit, you just give the word.'

'Thanks so much for your hospitality.'

'You're very welcome. Well then, let's get you both situated. You can freshen up, take some time to rest.' He led them up a walkway cutting alongside the Apostolic Palace. 'Are you available for lunch?' he asked Donovan. 'Take some time to catch up? You too, of course, Charlotte.'

'If it's all right with you, Charlotte,' Donovan replied.

'Sounds great.'

26.

TEL AVIV, ISRAEL

'So what do you make of all this?' Cohen asked.

Renowned professor of Israeli population genetics David Friedman leaned back in his chair. His protruding dull eyes were magnified through the lenses of thick bifocals. The gaunt thirty-something had no hair or eyebrows, the result of an extremely rare disease called alopecia universalis. The complete baldness of his body, coupled with his protruding steel-gray eyes, could make one wonder if he'd been beamed to earth by a flying saucer. His mind-boggling intellect was otherworldly too. But it didn't negate the fact that the man was socially awkward and irritable. And the fact that he staunchly denounced both God and Judaism was a huge tax on Cohen's patience.

'There's a lot of information here, Rabbi,' he said, looking exasperated. 'I'm going only by data and pictures, not a specimen. I'd be speculating,' he warned. 'And unless I was seeing this with my own eyes through a very powerful microscope . . .' He shrugged. The professor's gaze wandered to his office window, through which he could see students milling about Tel Aviv University's palm-treed quad.

'Please.' Cohen opened his hands and beseeched with uncharacteristic finesse. 'Speculate.'

Moaning, Friedman circled his gaze back to the monitor at the plot of forty-eight chromosome pairs. He shook his head and said, 'All right then. First off, I study the *human* genome. And this? This is too small to have come from a human.'

'How so?'

It had taken till midnight for Cohen to identify nine telling files that had been on Charlotte Hennesey's laptop. Ziv had copied them onto a flash drive now sticking out of a port on Friedman's juiced-up Macintosh. All nine files were running on multiple windows layered on the professor's oversize plasma.

Friedman clicked a tab on the bottom toolbar, and a data file maximized to fill the screen. 'See here,' Friedman explained, pointing to the different combinations and sequences of A, C, G, and T – each letter was assigned a different color. Running above them was a continuous series of vertical lines in varying thicknesses that resembled a bar code spread out to infinity. 'You know how many base pairs we'd expect to find in the human genome?' The question was rhetorical. Aaron Cohen was an excellent study and could easily find a second career in Friedman's lab.

'Three billion.'

'And what do you see here?'

On the monitor, next to a field labeled BASE PAIRS, was a number: 298,825,111.

'I understand it seems too small. But what if this *is* from a human specimen?'

'It's not, Rabbi. I assure you. Look at this . . .' His growing frustration made his bony shoulders twitch as he brought another active window into full-screen view. Feeling like a doctor whose patient wouldn't accept a cut-and-dried diagnosis, he said, 'Here, use those good eyes of yours, Rabbi – the scientific ones. Check your mysticism at the door.' Friedman pointed to the video showing fluoresced chromosomes being extracted with a needle from a cell nucleus. 'If this *was* real . . .' He shook his head again. 'This looks like science fiction to me. Watch what happens here.' He waited. 'Ah. There. See it? This pair of chromosomes here?'

The rabbi drew close. 'Yes.'

'These two chromosomes are instantly replacing extracted genetic material. Rebuilding the genome.'

'Is that not possible?'

'On earth? Impossible.'

'So how do you explain this?'

The professor threw his hands up. 'A computer-generated simulation. Hollywood. Who knows? I'm sorry to say that I think you've been duped.' Despite his harsh incredulity, the rabbi was not at all discouraged. In fact, he seemed quite pleased. Perhaps the professor himself was being duped? 'Does this have something to do with the Cohen Gene project? Is someone making you empty promises? Or are you just testing me?'

'I'd be speculating,' the rabbi noncommittally replied. This actually wrenched a chuckle out of the cantankerous brainiac. 'So there's no way to tell from this if it's real?' he persisted.

'Get a sample. Then I'll tell you if it's real – and which planet it comes from.'

Cohen smirked. 'Bring up the other image,' he insisted. 'The one with the two chromosome plots side by side.'

Luckily, Charlotte Hennesey's file-naming system was descriptive. This one was named 'karytope.subjectA-henneseyB.' And Ziv had easily discerned from the file's attributes that this had been the last file running on the geneticist's laptop prior to its recovery in Phoenix.

Friedman switched windows.

'If I were to bring a sample to you – from Hollywood,' the rabbi said, keeping it light to hold Friedman's tiny suspicions at bay, 'which sample would you need? The one on the left, or the one on the right?' Not that he'd dare share such a thing.

With little enthusiasm, the professor played along with the charade. 'This one labeled "subject" is hypothetically from a male,' he said. 'And this one here is obviously female, this one labeled "Hennesey," whatever that means. They seem identical, give or take the sex chromosomes, of course. In this fantasy world, it's this chromosome set here that really matters. For fun, let's call these two the "builders." Easy to spot because it doesn't even look like a human chromosome.' He tapped twice on the monitor – first on subject's unbanded chromosome pair, then on Hennesey's identical pair. 'So since the builders can single-handedly manufacture all the other chromosomes in the genome, I'd say that's where the magic is. Your Hollywood starlet,' he joked. 'And hypothetically speaking, since the builder chromosomes are present in both your male and female specimens, either sample would suffice.' He shrugged.

Either sample. Cohen's smile grew even wider.

Outside the Genetic Studies building, Cohen's driver had kept the Buick Lucerne sedan running. The rabbi ducked into the back seat.

'Has the jet returned from Rome?'

'Twenty minutes ago,' the driver replied. 'They're refueling now. I've already informed your pilot that we'll depart immediately for Inshas.'

'Excellent. Take me directly to the airport.'

'Yes, sir.'

Cohen sat back in his seat and let down the window to invite in the sweet Mediterranean air sweeping across Tel Aviv. It brought back memories of his first visit to Israel when he was fifteen – two years after he'd first been brought into his grandfather's secret circle, which set his life in motion. The teachings had been so detailed, so indelibly inked into his subconscious, that even then he'd felt a connection to this land – an innate familiarity. And by this afternoon, a different breeze blowing across ancient sands would meet him at the Nile Delta – the brother-land of his ancestors. The land that gave birth to Yahweh's gift – a family legacy.

27.

At the Rockefeller Museum, located directly outside the Old City's northern wall, Amit and Jules waited patiently in a blank corridor lined with administrative offices. Amit knocked a second time on Jozsef Dayan's office door – still no answer. He reached down and tried the door handle. Definitely locked.

'Strange. I've never seen this door closed. He practically lives here.' The guy had no kids and his wife had lost a tough battle with cancer only four years ago. The old man had been using this tiny room to fill the lonely void ever since.

'Where are the scrolls?' Jules asked.

'I left them with him, inside.'

'Don't you have a key?'

He shook his head.

'Maybe your friend took off with them.'

'Not a chance,' he said without hesitation. 'We need to get in there.'

The archaeologist squatted along the door frame to assess the lock, then withdrew his keys from his cargo pants.

'I thought you didn't have a key.'

'Not exactly.'

Amit pinched open the key ring and slid off two small matte-black tools that looked to Jules like they'd been lifted from a dentist's surgical tray.

'Just keep an eye out,' he instructed. Though security was tight at the museum entrances, and particularly in the galleries, Jozsef's lab, like his gentle personality, lacked any fancy protocols. When Amit was in the IDF, the main barriers to entry at a Gaza safe house would be masked kids with Uzis who'd drunk too much from fundamentalist Islam's spiked punch bowl. But once they'd been taken out, the door locks had been a lot less sophisticated than this one. Still, he'd give it a go. Inserting the flat tension wrench into the brushed aluminum lockset, Amit turned it clockwise.

Jules tried to play hall monitor, but she was more preoccupied with what Amit was doing. She snuck glances as he snaked the second tool into the keyhole alongside the first – a hooked-end thing that would have looked at home in her late grandmother's crochet basket.

Amit twisted the hook along the jagged innards of the housing, fishing for the tumbler's smooth pin pairs. He popped them up sequentially, *click, click, click* . . . Five seconds later, he palmed the handle and gently turned. *Clunk.* He signed to Jules, who answered with raised eyebrows.

'Where did you learn how to do that?' Jules asked.

'Standard IDF field training – at least when you're stationed in hostile places like Gaza, rooting out Islamic terrorists. Let's just say that ringing doorbells wasn't an option.'

Pocketing the tools, he stood and opened the door.

The pair slipped inside the unlit office and Amit closed the door quietly behind them.

'If you wanted to get me alone in a dark room,' Jules said, 'you could've just asked.'

'Save that thought,' he replied. He felt along the wall for the light switch.

A small click preceded a sterile wash of halogen light.

Immediately, Amit went for the light boxes. That's where yesterday morning, he'd watched Jozsef carefully cut away the jar's wax seal and remove the lid to reveal three loosely rolled papyri. Before Yosi pulled out the scrolls, he'd tried to temper Amit's excitement by explaining that most old vellums were too frail to open – something about collagen in the sheepskin being exposed to moisture, then drying. 'Now we may have to send them out for X-ray analysis,' Yosi had said. 'I've read about a new lab in Oxfordshire too . . . developed a light source ten billion times stronger than the sun that can decipher writings on scrolls too brittle to open. Can you believe this? Incredible!'

But when Yosi had pulled them out and laid them on the light box, ever so delicately testing their spring with a gloved index finger, he'd been pleased. Further prodding and a 'quick look-see' under intense magnification gave him the confidence to attempt to open one himself. The first unfurled with little effort, as did the second and the third. To Yosi's surprise, the condition of the *klaf* was nearly as good as the day it had been limed and frame-stretched. 'I've never seen such a thing,' he said. Then he'd sandwiched the vellums on the light box beneath a protective glass cover.

But all that meant nothing at this moment, because Amit was staring at the blank top of the light box. The one beside it was vacant too – no jar. Not even the wax Yosi had scooped into a glass dish had been left behind. Amit felt like he'd just been punched in the throat. 'Damn.'

'Still so sure he didn't skip town?'

This time, Amit was silent. He was already mourning the loss of his life's greatest discovery – and the blunt dagger had just been pushed deeper. Not to mention that he'd lost the best evidence implicating the guy whose face was a pix file on his cell phone. So it wasn't the opportune time to entertain any notion that his great friend was Judas in disguise.

Suddenly the door opened.

Startled, both Jules and Amit spun to it. It stayed empty for a moment. Then there was the sound of squeaking rubber on the tiles.

Jules tensely waited as a young man, maybe twenty, rolled through the door in a wheelchair – frail looking, pale as snow. Beneath his disk-shaped prayer cap, he had tightly cropped black hair with earlocks spinning down along his protruding ears.

'Oh, Professor Mizrachi,' the young man said in a timid voice. 'Sorry to disturb you.'

'Joshua,' Amit said, his neck muscles slackening. He was the docent from the main gallery, son of the museum's most exalted benefactor – the controversial Rabbi Aaron Cohen. Amit clearly recalled Joshua walking these same galleries only two years ago. But then he'd manifested some type of neurodegenerative disease that crippled him in mere months. A terrible thing for such a young man.

'It's just . . . the door was locked earlier' – he began nervously chewing at his fingertips – 'and I saw that the light was on.'

'No need to apologize,' he said. Since Amit was under the employ of the Israel Antiquities Authority, whose main offices were housed inside the museum, it was no surprise that his presence hadn't fazed the kid.

Amit took a moment to introduce Jules.

Joshua could barely maintain eye contact with the attractive Frenchwoman, his eyes fixating too much on the Egyptologist's slim, tan legs and the bandage covering her right knee.

'I was just looking for Yosi,' Amit explained. 'He'd given me a copy of his key . . .' Amit held up his hands. 'Figured we'd wait for him.'

Joshua's eyes went to the floor and his lips curled down. 'So you haven't . . . heard yet?' The finger-gnawing intensified.

That's not good, Amit thought. 'Heard what?'

'He died last night.'

'He *what*?'

'A neighbor found his door open. He was on the floor. I think they were saying something about his heart.'

Amit was thinking about an entirely different diagnosis as he looked back at the empty light boxes.

'That's awful,' Jules said with heartfelt sadness, even though she hadn't known the man.

'I know this may sound like an awkward question,' Amit said. 'But did you see him leave yesterday?'

Joshua nodded. 'Right after my father talked to him.'

'And was Yosi carrying anything with him? A box, a briefcase – anything like that?'

He shook his head. 'No. I think he had gone to some lecture at the Israel Museum. So he left everything here.'

Another punch to the throat. 'Poor man,' Amit said. It was tough to shake the feeling that he'd put Yosi in harm's way. Crushing.

'Well, it's probably best that we get going,' Jules said with some urgency, placing a consoling yet insistent hand on Amit's shoulder.

'Right,' Amit agreed. 'If you hear anything about services for him . . .,' Amit said to Joshua.

'Of course. An e-mail will be sent to everyone. You're on the list, right?'

'I am.'

They waited for him to reverse the wheelchair into the corridor. Amit turned out the lights, then he and Jules went outside and shut the door.

'Good to see you, Joshua,' Amit said.

Joshua bid them farewell. He worked the hand rims to swivel the chair, then proceeded down the corridor toward his post.

'Let's get out of here,' she said.

'Wait. There's one more thing before we go,' Amit said, his eyes not budging until Joshua had squeaked around the corner. 'This way,' he said, waving for her to follow.

28.

Amit led Jules through the octagonal Tower Hall with its Byzantine vaults, then swiftly through the South Octagon, where Jules caught a glimpse of a glyph-covered stele of Pharaoh Seti I. They headed straight for the South Gallery – one of the museum's two long, rectangular halls used in the 1950s and '60s as a scrollery for deciphering the Dead Sea Scrolls.

Amit greeted the pretty young docent named Rebecca, who was pacing the room with arms crossed behind her back; then he made for the room's center.

The refurbished gallery, with its elongated, high-set windows and Romanesque coffered ceiling, was filled with boxy, four-legged glass display cases that had been in use since the 1920s British Mandate era (all in keeping with tradition). Among the relics here, one could view the physical remains of Israel's ancient peoples: a two-hundred-thousand-year-old human skull excavated from Galilee; human remains from Mount Carmel, circa 100,000 B.C.E.; and human heads from Jericho dating to 6000 B.C.E.

Nothing, however, could compare to the gallery's most recent acquisition.

He stopped in front of a modern display case with ultrathick security glass. The podium that was its base was solid; it hid an elaborate security system. The relic housed in the case was gently lit from top and bottom.

'Take a look at this,' he said to Jules. 'You know about this ossuary, right?'

She studied the compact stone box covered in etched designs: rosettes and hatch patterns. Its arched lid was beautiful, though she noticed restoration work had corrected a jagged widthwise crack along its middle. Nothing came to mind. 'Should I?'

He gave her a surprised look. 'The theft at the Temple Mount? Back in June? It was all over the news. A firefight, explosions . . .'

To Jules, this was all vague at best. 'I was excavating outside Tanis in June,' she said defensively. 'It's not like I brought a TV with me into the desert. You know how digs can be . . . the isolation?'

'Yes. Of course,' replied Amit.

'So stop being a bully.'

He shook his head before proceeding to give her the *Reader's Digest* version of the crime that had taken place, explained how the situation had gotten so dire that a synagogue had been hit by a Muslim female suicide bomber (or as Amit preferred to call them, 'homicide bomber') and that in desperate response to the act, the Israeli police had almost wrongfully pegged a colleague of his named Graham Barton as an accomplice. Barton had been released only after Israeli authorities tracked the stolen ossuary to the home of a Muslim cleric who'd orchestrated the theft. The ossuary was then studied and brought here for safekeeping.

'This is what the thieves stole?' She regarded the relic more levelly now. 'An ossuary?' It didn't compute. 'Why?'

'Lots of conspiracy theories about that, but no one knows for sure. Probably had a lot to do with what had been inside it.'

'Which was . . . ?'

He shrugged. 'It came back empty,' he said, keeping his voice low in the echoing hall. 'So that's where the rumors get really interesting.' Thinking he heard the wheelchair's squeaky tires, he paused and glanced over his shoulder. Nothing. 'Take a look at this.' He pointed to the side of the box.

Jules sidestepped and bent to see what he was so interested in. That's when she noticed the carved relief that matched the strange pagan images they'd seen on the wall painting hidden beneath the hills of Qumran. 'That's weird.'

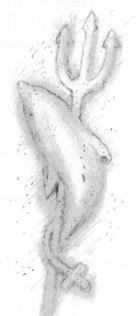

'Certainly is.' Her troubled expression showed him that she'd made the connection.

'So what do you think it means?'

'Tough to say, really. But some have interpreted it to be an early Christian symbol.'

'How so?'

'Well, when Jesus died in thirty-four C.E. or thereabouts, those who tried to continue his ministry were sought out by the Romans. So they concealed their identity by using pagan symbols.'

'A code?'

'A seal, to be more precise. It's meant to represent Jesus's crucifixion. Greeks and Romans revered dolphins as magical creatures that brought spirits to the afterlife.'

'Like angels,' Jules said.

'Like saviors,' he corrected her. 'And the trident is said to represent a lance that killed the dolphin.'

'The cross.'

'The cross,' Amit confirmed. 'Not to mention the trident's three tines—'

'The Trinity.'

'Good thing you weren't a Roman back then,' he said. 'Again, this is the type of stuff some are suggesting, and—'

'So they think this ossuary contained the body of an early Christian?'

He grinned. 'Oh, something like that. But not just any Christian.'

'Peter? Paul?'

'Think bigger.'

She looked at the ossuary and fished for the impossible. 'No way. Not Jesus.'

Amit nodded.

This made Jules snicker. 'Amit, you're talking to an Egyptologist,' she reminded him. 'You know how I feel about the whole Jesus thing.'

'And?' But he already knew where this was going.

'There's no evidence that Jesus was a living historical figure.'

He already knew her stance. 'So he's a literary creation?'

'Jesus reads like an Egyptian folk hero. Let me remind you – Osiris was brutally mutilated, his body parts collected by the female goddess Isis and put in a stone tomb, only to be resurrected three days later so that he ascended up into the sky. Crucifixion, burial, resurrection on day three, *and* ascension into heaven?' She spread her hands. 'Osiris, mind you, who judged souls in the hereafter, weighed the heart against Ma'at's feather and either granted the deceased eternal bliss or fed him to Ammit, the Devourer . . .'

'Heaven and hell,' he admitted. With Jules getting more impassioned, the female docent was now casting curious glances at them. Amit held an index finger to his lips so Jules would lower her volume.

'And in the Book of the Dead,' she continued more quietly, 'Osiris's son, Horus, fed five thousand with just a few loaves of bread.'

'Jesus feeds the multitudes,' he said, playing along.

'The five thousand, to be precise,' she said. 'There's the image of Horus suckling the breast of Isis, later spun as the Madonna and child,' she sarcastically added.

Amit knew there were dozens of parallels between Jesus and Horus – everything from virgin birth to consecration through ritual baptism, and both were even portrayed as a shepherd or a lamb. So he only hoped Jules would keep it short.

'And let's not forget this one: Isis, the healer and life giver' – she stuck out her right index finger; 'Osiris, the judge of souls' – the middle finger went up; 'and Horus, ruler of the heavens who happens to be the *son* of Osiris.' When the splayed ring finger went up, she tightly fused it with the other two. 'Sound familiar? Three separate gods recast as one?'

'The Trinity.' He nodded.

'And Jesus's assertions about the afterlife and the judgment of souls? That's philosophical thinking that's got Egypt written all over it. Just think about the *ba*,' she said.

The *ba*, Amit recalled, was the ancient Egyptian equivalent of a soul, which separated from the body at death to roam at will. And it was depicted as a bird, which Jules would no doubt consider the forerunner of the Holy Spirit.

'Forgive me if I'm not racing off to church every Sunday,' she said skeptically, crossing her arms tight in front of her chest and leaning back on her left leg.

He held up his hands in peaceful surrender. 'Got it, Jules. "All things Egypt." We could go through the same motions with the Old Testament too, and come up with the idea that the whole Jesus story was made up.' He began spouting off a few examples, tipping his head side to side to emphasize the parallels between stories: 'David was born in Bethlehem' – head to the left; 'Jesus was born in Bethlehem' – head to the right. 'Moses went up on Sinai for forty days' – left; 'Jesus went into the desert for forty days' – right.

Her eyes now seemed apologetic.

'You could also point out that Jesus's father was descended directly from David and Abraham and his mother descended directly from Moses's first high priest, Aaron, the Levite; a convenient fulfillment of Isaiah's prophecy – making the Messiah a priest *and* a king. And of course the whole thing with God offering his own son the same way Abraham tried to sacrifice Isaac—'

'Okay,' she said, rolling her eyes. 'Do I sound *that* crazy?'

He shrugged. 'You don't really think Jesus is just a created literary figure, do you?' He could only hope she wasn't aware that Jesus exhibited nineteen of the twenty motifs associated with the heroes of Greek mythology.

She sighed wearily – the way any sympathetic minimalist would. 'Then how do you explain that historians who lived during the time of Jesus – Philo and Josephus, to name a couple – never mention anyone even remotely close to Jesus *or* his disciples? Let's face it, a guy who walks on water, feeds multitudes with a sack lunch, and raises the dead isn't exactly B-list material.'

'Sure, no direct mention of Jesus himself. But Josephus's accounts vividly described the Essenes as one of three Jewish sects in first-century Judea. Philo wrote about them as well.'

'So what does that have to do with it?'

A knowing smile pulled at Amit's goatee. Doubters overlooked the historical record time and time again. "Essene' is actually a bad transliteration of the word Josephus and Philo ascribe to the Jews at Qumran. It was actually pronounced "Esaoin" – a word with roots in Greek, Aramaic, and Arabic. Since you live in Cairo, I'm sure you can figure this one out.' He could tell by the softened look on her face that she already had. Finally, something broke through her armor.

'"Follower of Jesus,"' she said with some reluctance in a low voice.

'Right. "Follower of Jesus,"' he repeated. 'And this Jesus happens to have an Egyptian spin to his name. So if you ask me, history does provide an account of a group many believe were the earliest Christians.'

'Now you're stretching it a bit.'

'Perhaps. But we both saw this same symbol in that chamber at Qumran,' he said, pointing to the ossuary's relief again. 'And like I said, some very intelligent archaeologists are whispering that this ossuary belonged to Jesus.'

Jules gave the ossuary another once-over, this time more seriously.

Seeing that she still looked skeptical, he decided to lay it on thicker. 'You remember John the Baptist?'

'Of course.'

'Many biblical scholars contend that his teachings echo teachings found in the Dead Sea Scrolls. He too was a minimalist who practiced ritual immersion, or baptism. And if you recall, he lived in the desert and baptized his followers in the Jordan River, which flows directly into the north end of the Dead Sea. Jesus was baptized by him, then remained in the desert for forty days. And where is Qumran located?'

She rolled her eyes. 'The northwest shore of the Dead Sea.'

'After Herod Antipas beheaded John, Jesus continued John's ministry. A changing of the guard, some might say.' He stared at the ossuary again. 'And what if I told you that the thief also returned a book that was determined to be the oldest Gospel ever recovered, dating to the early first century, and regarded as the original source for the books of Matthew, Mark, and Luke?'

'Makes for a compelling case,' she admitted.

'It certainly does. But the interesting part is that the last four pages of the text were purposely cut out so that the story ended with the crucifixion.'

'So I take it someone didn't like the ending?'

He nodded. 'The conspiracy builds. Another great example of how editing can rewrite history. And if you choose to believe the rumors, this same editor also didn't like what was inside this ossuary.' Jules still looked incredulous as she put it all together. *Stubborn as always*, he thought.

'So somewhere out there are four pages of the oldest Gospel and the physical remains of Jesus?' she clarified.

'That's the rumor.'

'Any way to get in touch with this Barton fellow you mentioned earlier?' she suggested. 'Maybe he can help us.'

Amit quickly dismissed the idea. Not only had the English archaeologist gone through his own tribulations, he explained, but there was a high probability that Barton was still being closely surveilled by Israeli intelligence, even though he'd long since returned to his home in London.

A boisterous American tour group suddenly poured into the gallery.

'Let's go,' Amit suggested.

They wove through the tourists, back toward Tower Hall. But halfway through the South Octagon, Amit spotted Joshua's wheelchair parked near the front entrance.

Amit grabbed Jules's arm and yanked her behind Seti's stele.

'What are you—'

'Quiet!' he demanded in a hushed tone. He peeked out to confirm that Cohen's son was talking to a man of medium height with an awfully familiar face. Amit panicked when he saw the fresh laceration just below the man's hairline, then the fresh white cast wound round his right forearm.

'My father told me to call you if anyone came asking about Yosi,' Joshua reported.

'You said someone was in his office?' the tall man said. The kid's voice message to him hadn't been very clear.

'Two people actually. Amit Mizrachi. And he was with a very pretty—'

'Are they still here?' the man broke in, looking like he'd just touched a live wire.

'I . . . I think so.' Joshua backed the chair up a bit, because the man looked like he was going to explode. Then his wild eyes began scanning the hall. 'They might still be in the South Gallery—'

But before he could finish, the man broke into a full sprint, practically bowling over the American tour group assembling in the hall.

29.
EGYPT

Exiting Inshas Airport, the driver turned the dusty Peugeot south onto highway 41.

Rabbi Aaron Cohen checked his watch: 12:32.

His private jet had covered the four hundred kilometers from Ben Gurion International in less than forty minutes. He'd instructed the pilot to expect to have the jet on the tarmac for a return trip later that afternoon. They'd need to work quickly before Egyptian authorities could start asking questions, he'd reminded everyone. But he took great comfort in knowing that the VIP charter flights coming in and out of Inshas enjoyed far more liberties than El-Al flights heading to Cairo International.

'You called ahead to let the others know we've arrived?'

'I did,' the driver replied.

Cohen settled into his seat.

The road paralleled the glistening Ismailiya Canal, where a magnificent sailboat was lazily motoring its way south, its mainsail down, an Egyptian flag flapping gently atop its mast. On the spacious aft deck, Cohen spotted a lithe woman with obviously surgically enhanced breasts and hair like raven's wings, sunning herself in a bikini. The shirtless, beer-drinking helmsman – also Egyptian – was much older than the woman and looked very, very proud. In a country full of Muslim fundamentalists who aspired to be the next great hope for an Islamic state, it flew in the face of Sharia, Islamic law, and exemplified how wealth came with great exception.

Vanity and pride have no place in the eyes of God.

He diverted his gaze out the right window to the flat swaths of sugarcane and rice fields.

They were heading to Heliopolis. Not the modern suburb on the outskirts of Cairo that locals referred to as Misr el-Gadida – or 'New Cairo' – but its ancient namesake about twenty kilometers north.

With Amit Mizrachi still alive, Cohen wasn't taking any chances; the archaeologist or the French Egyptologist who'd accompanied him to Qumran might have somehow deciphered the hidden meaning of the hieroglyph. Centuries of planning could potentially be undone. Besides, with the prophecy already set into motion, the timing for this visit couldn't have been better.

The driver turned west, following signs for Kafr Hamra.

Minutes later, they passed a tiny Coptic church with a mosaic on its belfry depicting Joseph guiding a donkey burdened with Mary. The Holy Mother was tightly cradling the baby Jesus. Laid out in colorful tiles, the narrative placed them along the palm-treed Nile, three distant pyramids rising up on the opposing riverbank. The imagery always made Cohen smile.

Churches like this could be found throughout the Nile Delta – Tel Basta, Farama, Wadi al-Natrun, Bilbeis, Mostorod, even Cairo. Each venerated its own ancient folklore built around the Holy Family's refuge in Egypt after escaping Herod's supposed infanticide in Judea: water springs brought forth by the baby Jesus; caves and sacred trees that had given the Holy Family shelter; wells from which the Holy Family drank; a granite trough used by the Virgin for kneading dough; the Holy Child's footprint and handprint set in separate stones; pagan idols that crumbled in the Holy Child's presence.

Despite these tales, Grandfather had taught him that many truths could also be found here in Egypt – and many facts had bled into ancient Christian scriptures deemed heretical by the Catholic Church.

Like the Essenes at Qumran who'd preserved the Dead Sea Scrolls from Roman destruction, the ancient Egyptian Christians, called Gnostics, had hidden their Coptic texts in buried jars. In 1945 thirteen leather-bound Gnostic codices had been accidentally unearthed by local peasants at Nag Hammadi. This caused much controversy for the Vatican since the texts spoke at great length about the resurrected Jesus as a spiritual being. *How the Vatican had twisted the truth*, he lamented. *And still they stop at nothing to protect their lies.*

Cohen particularly admired the stunning accuracy of the Gnostic codex entitled the Dialogue of the Savior, in which Jesus himself denounces the weakness of the flesh: 'Matthew said, "Lord, I want to see that place of life, [the place] where there is no wickedness, but rather, there is pure light!" The Lord said, "Brother Matthew, you will not be able to see it as long as you are carrying flesh around . . . Whatever is born of truth does not die. Whatever is born of woman dies."' And in the codex called the Apocryphon of James, Jesus's words resonated with Cohen even more so: 'For it is the spirit that raises the soul, but the body that kills it . . .'

The spiritual being – the eternal spark – was paramount to the

Gnostics, as well as to their brothers in Judea, the Essenes – all members of Cohen's legacy. Those who understood the weakness of the flesh were the enlightened – 'Sons of Light.' And they had been given secret knowledge that from the one true God did all light (spiritual essence) flow in perpetuity.

Heading north on Highway 400, they approached their destination – Tel el-Yahudiyeh, or 'Mound of the Jews.' Across the expansive delta plain, the tightly packed buildings of Shabin al Qanatir could easily be seen in the distance.

As they rounded a bend in the road, Cohen peered over at the ancient heap of marl and sand that rose up from the dust. It resembled a huge sand castle built too close to an ocean swell, washed over and stripped of detail. Some of the ancient fortifications could still be made out along the mound's expansive boomerang footprint.

This ruin had once been a grand temple-fortress built by Cohen's ancient ancestor.

The car drove past the mound and a wide-open field separating it from an industrial, corrugated steel warehouse. The driver slowed as he approached the warehouse and turned onto the short drive leading up to it. He waited as the bay door rolled back on creaking hardware.

Squeezing the Peugeot in beside a dilapidated tractor, the driver slid the gearshift into park. In the rearview mirror, he watched a man dressed in a white tunic press the button to close the door.

'Did you see anything suspicious?' Cohen inquired.

'Nothing,' he confirmed.

'Good.' He waited for the driver to open his door.

Cohen stepped out onto the cement floor. The warehouse's expansive, raw interior was lined with steel support columns and had a high ceiling with exposed rafters. Corralled into crude work bays were tool chests and various machines dismantled to their bare mechanical guts.

The moist air stank of motor oil and acetylene.

The building had been registered with the municipality as a machine repair shop. To legitimize that claim, the priests spent considerable time tending to local clients' broken-down tractors, tillers, and farm machinery. Lately, the decoy operation had expanded to include car repair too. A healthy profit fed the coffers of the Temple Society.

Cohen turned to the driver. 'Have them prepare the truck. I want to be out of here in an hour.'

Strutting with a slight limp – too much time sitting always aggravated his damaged hip – to the rear of the building, he opened the door to the office and stepped around a beat-up metal desk that hosted a greasy computer monitor and a stack of crisp yellow invoices.

He dragged a box of motor parts off a stain-covered Persian rug centered on the plank floor. Then he half squatted to grab a corner of the rug and peeled it back. What lay beneath was a rectangular hatch. He threaded his finger through its O-shaped hasp, heaved the door up, and let it fall open with a dull thud.

Patting dust from his black vest, he proceeded downward into complete darkness, the wooden treads groaning under his weight.

'. . . Eleven . . . twelve,' he muttered, counting the last steps.

He remembered that the priest who'd first brought him down here had performed the same counting ritual, which he'd always assumed was a tribute to either the twelve tribes or the twelve whom Jesus had recruited.

The final footfall connected with a spongy clay floor. Groping at the cool air just in front of his face, he found the pull-cord for the overhead light. A single bare bulb crackled to life just above Cohen's *zayen*.

The square basement was modest in size, just large enough to accommodate twelve shelving units along its mud brick walls, neatly stocked with chemical containers, tools, and welding supplies. Moving to the storage unit on the rear wall, he snaked his hand between some boxes until he felt a cold metal handle. He hooked it with his fingers and tugged. The shelving and the faux-brick laminate behind it noiselessly swung out on concealed hinges.

The solid metal door that lay behind it looked like the entry to a bank vault.

30.
JERUSALEM

In full stride, Jules was in the lead, Amit close at her heels. They'd doubled back through the South Gallery, slaloming through the dallying Americans. This had caused great alarm among the docents and tourists, but no one was moving to stop them.

Through the South Room they angled a hard right into a coin gallery.

'Go through that door!' Amit said.

Up ahead, Jules saw exactly the one he meant. It was a fire exit. She threw herself at the door and activated the shrill alarm. The door flew open hard enough to knock over an employee who'd been out back smoking. Facedown on the pavement, the poor man shouted his protest, but she wasn't stopping to make any apologies.

Now they were along the rear drive reserved for employees and deliveries. The Land Rover sat only twenty meters away. With key chain in hand, Amit had remotely opened it the moment he was outside.

Jules was already in the passenger seat and pulling her door closed as Amit was fumbling with the driver's-side door latch.

'Come on! Hurry!' he heard her yelling on the other side of the glass.

Yanking the door back, Amit hopped in.

Back at the exit door, the befuddled smoker was back on his feet, assessing the ragged tear in his pants, just over the right knee. Amit couldn't hear the swearing, but the guy looked awfully pissed off and was throwing his hands into the air. It would only be another second before his mood would surely worsen, Amit thought, jamming the key into the ignition.

By the time Amit looked back up, the smoker had been knocked facedown onto the ground again, his left leg blocking the door that was once more being forced open from the inside. There was a split second where Amit considered reaching for the pistol stashed in the center console. He'd left a round chambered, safety off. But as he made to get it, Jules screamed.

'Go!'

Cranking hard on the gearshift, Amit stepped down on the accelerator just as the arm-casted assassin muscled his way around the door and used the smoker's back like a doormat. In his good hand, he was clutching a replacement for the Jericho pistol taken from him last night. And now he was positioning himself for a clean shot.

Should've killed him when I had the chance, Amit thought again. 'Down, Jules!' He reached over and pushed her head below the dashboard.

The Land Rover's tires screeched as he ducked and pulled the wheel hard to the left. The gunshot was loud, the report of breaking glass just as harsh. The would-be assassin's left-handed aim wasn't so great. He'd only managed to take out the driver's-side rear passenger window. Amit peeked up over the dash just in time to cut a hard right that avoided a thick gatepost at the lot's exit. A successful maneuver, yet the Rover's rear tire caught the curb that stuck out beneath it, bouncing the truck into the air. Amit and Jules catapulted up from their seats, both smacking their heads on the roof.

But it was a fortunate thing, because the second shot that had cracked an instant earlier on a direct line for Amit's skull instead blew out the spare tire bolted to the truck's lift gate.

'Holy shit!' Jules yelled, cradling her pounding head in her hands.

Amit sped around the building. Then he confused Jules by bringing the truck to a sudden halt. He hit the switch that rolled down his window, then flipped open the console and pulled out the pistol.

'What the 'ell are you doing?' The French accent was really thick now.

'Trust me.' He gave it about ten seconds. 'Get down and stay down.'

'Amit, I don't think—'

'Do it!'

She did.

Then he eased down on the accelerator again and cornered stealthily onto the front circular drive.

His timing was good. The gunman was already outside working his car remote like a lobster with the two mobile fingers of his cast hand. Before the guy could figure out what was happening, Amit stomped on the accelerator and steered straight for him. Clutching the Jericho, Amit stuck his arm out the window, aimed, and squeezed off a shot that spat through the silencer. Unlike the assassin, Amit was a seasoned lefty.

The shot was close but missed. It did, however, force the guy to duck for cover behind his Fiat coupe.

That gave Amit just enough time to slow the Land Rover and maneuver for another shot. But this time, it wasn't the assassin he was going for. It was the front tire of the Fiat. He took aim and held the trigger down, forcing the pistol into semiautomatic mode. A slight circular sweep emptied three successive rounds into the Fiat's front wheel well and tire rim. A fourth tore apart the tire with a loud pop.

The assassin tried to come up over the hood for a shot, but Amit fired again to force him back down.

Satisfied, Amit ducked low and gunned the engine. One more shot came, but it merely shattered the driver's side mirror. Amit made a wild right onto Sultan Suleiman Street, which ran parallel to the Old City's northern wall. Not wanting to attract attention from the IDF guards stationed outside the Damascus Gate up ahead, he immediately slowed.

'You are one crazy bastard,' she said.

'Best defense is a good offense,' he reminded her.

31.

VATICAN CITY

It was nearing one o'clock when Charlotte heard a knock at the door.

'Just a sec,' she called out from the bathroom.

She checked her mascara and lipstick in the mirror one last time, hoping she hadn't overdone it. 'Sexed up' was not the look she was going for with a pair of priests. Just a little something to put some color back in her cheeks and jazz up her swollen eyes. With the amount of crying she'd done up until now, she might as well have poured acid over her eyelids.

But she had to remind herself that the last time she'd stared into a mirror inside a guest room at the Vatican's Domus Sanctae Marthae, her eyes showed a different kind of pain that no makeup could conceal. And she'd relied on chemo pills to suppress it, not Revlon.

Charlotte was glad she'd accepted Father Martin's offer to have her pantsuit dry-cleaned by housekeeping. As promised, it had been freshly pressed and discreetly hung on her door in a plastic garment bag by noon.

She snapped her black clutch shut, then decided there wasn't much need for it. After all, her passport was with the Swiss Guard, and everything else – money, keys, credit cards – was all left behind in Phoenix. And Donovan had said that Father Martin was hosting them inside the city.

'Keep it together,' she told herself. That's what her father would surely tell her in a situation like this. Being alone, even for this short time, hadn't settled her one bit. She just kept seeing Evan with a bullet in his head, over and over again. The thought of having company comforted her, got her mind moving in a different direction.

She went and opened the door. Déjà vu came over her when she laid eyes upon Donovan standing in the hall wearing a black suit and priest collar. It seemed he was feeling it too.

'Bringing back some memories?' he said with a smile, breaking the ice.

'You could say that.' She pocketed her key card and pulled the door shut. In the unflattering fluorescent-lit hall, Donovan looked especially fatigued. No doubt his harrowing experience in Belfast and the marathon transatlantic flights had taken a lot out of him. Yet still the man managed to keep smiling. And she could tell that it was more for her benefit than his.

'So let's see what the Vatican is serving up, shall we?' he said.

32.

Since the Holy Father was still enjoying a five-day retreat at Castel Gandolfo, Father Martin had managed to reserve the sumptuous dining room that typically hosted international dignitaries and diplomats. Being the personal assistant of the secretary of state did, after all, come with many privileges.

'*Salve!* Welcome,' Father Martin warmly greeted them at the wide entryway. He gave Donovan and Charlotte a double-clasped handshake.

'This is quite impressive, James,' Donovan said. He'd never actually been inside this room. The man was full of surprises.

Charlotte thought 'impressive' was an understatement. The Apostolic Palace's main entryway was over twenty-four feet high, flanked by Bernini's mammoth doors sheathed in bronze, which had been taken from ancient Roman temples. The Clementine Hall – the main reception foyer – was cavernous, covered in marble and trimmed with friezes. Three frescoes paid tribute to St. Clement's baptism, martyrdom, and apotheosis; a fourth honored the arts and sciences. Swiss Guards in full regalia were posted throughout.

'When I informed His Eminence that the legendary Father Patrick Donovan was making a return with a world-renowned guest . . .' He spread his hands. 'How could he refuse?'

'I'm not exactly the prodigal son,' Donovan reminded him in a whisper. He was trying to keep things lighthearted, but he couldn't help but look back at the two armed Swiss Guards standing at attention beside the door. 'So the honor is all yours, Charlotte,' he said to his companion.

'If you put it that way . . . I'm flattered,' she said.

'Come, let us sit,' Martin said, his right hand sweeping an arc to the far end of the room, where a cozy cluster of chairs faced the tall windows overlooking Piazza San Pietro and St. Peter's Basilica.

The dining hall pulled Charlotte's eyes in all different directions as she walked the ornate parquet floors around the grand Louis XIV dining table set beneath a magnificent chandelier.

There were more frescoes painted by the hands of masters – Cherubino Alberti and Baldassare Croce among them, Martin subtly boasted. Furthermore, he was quick to point out that the magnificent tapestry dominating the north wall was an original Raphael that had been among those used to cover the walls of the Sistine Chapel during the 2005 conclave.

Martin smiled when Charlotte picked a wingback chair, making her think she'd violated etiquette. 'Did I do something wrong?'

'No, no,' Martin said, holding up a hand. 'It's just that your country's president sat in that same chair during his visit with us last month.'

Charlotte instinctively raised her arms off the elegant fabric as if it were on fire. 'Seriously?'

'Oh yes. But if you don't mind me saying so, it suits *you* much better.'

She laughed genuinely, knowing that his preference referred to something other than appearances.

'I was thinking we could have a drink before we eat,' Martin said.

'Sounds great,' Charlotte replied.

Two glasses of Italian red wine and an Irish whiskey on the rocks were delivered by a nun wearing a white habit that covered all but her face and hands. Martin gave a toast, then settled into his chair. 'It's good to have you back, Patrick,' he said. 'You've been missed.'

'I'm sure the archives have functioned just fine without me.'

'I wouldn't be so sure. As luck would have it, the prefect's position is still vacant.' He gave Donovan a look of anticipation.

Donovan's noncommittal smile hinted that nothing was beyond the realm of possibility.

For the next fifteen minutes, they spoke of happenings inside the Vatican, both pleasant and distressing. Martin was good at pulling Charlotte into the conversation, but every so often, she was content to sip her Chianti and gaze out at Bernini's colonnades and Michelangelo's dome.

Soon thereafter, Martin sensed that Donovan was ready to segue into an explanation for his surprise return. So he allowed a gap of silence to encourage him.

Not knowing quite how to begin, Donovan explained, 'Lest I state the obvious . . . our visit doesn't concern my return to Vatican City.'

'I had a feeling that was the case,' Martin replied.

'And I'm sure you're wondering why Dr. Hennesey has accompanied me here.'

The priest's lips puckered. 'I would be lying if I said I wasn't curious about that too,' he confessed, watching Donovan's expression turn conflicted, contemplative. 'Tell me. What's troubling you?'

Some clarification of the events preceding his July departure was required. 'I'm sure you recall the secrecy of the project we'd arranged for Dr. Hennesey and Giovanni Bersei?'

'Certainly.' Then he looked to Charlotte and said, 'Let me express my deepest condolences for Dr. Bersei's passing.'

At a loss for words, Charlotte nodded.

'Though I'm not at liberty to discuss the details of that project . . .,' Donovan continued.

'I understand.'

Tentative, Donovan went on. 'It seems that someone outside the Vatican has information on the work that took place here – the analysis performed on certain relics acquired for the museum. Relics of extreme significance . . . and value.' Donovan paused to drain his whiskey – a superb pot-stilled Jameson – down to the halfway mark. *Keep it simple*, he reminded himself. 'Both Charlotte and I were separately approached by two men looking for these relics. There were threats. They had guns—'

Martin gasped. 'That's unbelievable.' His wide eyes rolled to Charlotte, and his mouth was agape. Recalling how the two men had thrown him into the back of the van made his response seem sincere.

'Bottom line is . . . I feel we're in serious danger. And I've come here to seek help – and protection.'

'There's no safer place for you to be than inside these walls,' Martin said with forced conviction. 'And you *are* officially a citizen of Vatican City.'

These words gave Donovan great comfort, because only roughly seven hundred clergy and one hundred Swiss Guards were granted official Vatican citizenship. The other three thousand lay workers, including Father Martin himself, lived outside the city – most in Rome. In accordance with Italy's Lateran Treaty, Vatican citizenship was granted *iure officii*, meaning that once employment was terminated, the cleric's citizenship would revert back to his original country of origin. Martin had assisted in arranging documentation with the secretariat's office to make Donovan a dual citizen – a privilege granted to only two hundred and fifty others. Therefore, his 'leave of absence' to attend to 'family matters' was still considered temporary.

'You are still provided full legal representation,' Martin confirmed, 'as well as complete access to the secretariat's resources, which, as you know, are quite extensive. If you are both in some kind of . . .' He paused. But he could tell they had already filled in the blank. 'Let's just say that there's no better place to be.'

'That's what I was hoping,' Donovan said, visibly relieved. 'Thank you.' Being a fellow Irishman, Donovan felt his bond with Martin went deeper than the cloth. And once again, Father Martin had come to his rescue. He emptied the glass, rattling the ice. 'And Dr. Hennesey?'

'I'll see to it that she's given the same protections.'

'Thank you very much, Father,' Charlotte said. She noticed his mood was confident and his complexion was looking much better this evening. Perhaps it was the ambient lighting. But she also registered a lingering suspicion about the man. After all, he'd reported directly to Cardinal Santelli – the lunatic who, according to Donovan, had ordered Conte to murder her.

'I know this may be uncomfortable for you,' Martin urged, 'but perhaps you could tell me more about these relics. Then maybe I can better determine how to direct my inquiries.'

The nun silently approached with a tray holding a fresh

tumbler of whiskey. Donovan invited the interruption, because he wasn't sure how to respond to Martin. Slowly, he swapped glasses, then took a deep breath.

'You can trust me, Patrick,' Martin stated. 'You know that.'

If it hadn't been for Martin, Cardinal Santelli's untimely demise might have been scrutinized far more closely – particularly since Donovan had left the cardinal's office just before Martin had found him dead. If an autopsy had been permitted, the poison Donovan had emptied through a syringe into the cardinal's shoulder could have been traced. But trust wasn't the issue. There was so much more at stake. Then again, it was the Vatican that had gotten Charlotte and him into this mess. And as it stood now, the Vatican provided the only hope of resolving matters.

Donovan looked over his shoulder and waited for the nun to disappear from the room. Then he looked to Charlotte for any sign of disagreement. She nodded for him to continue. 'Earlier this year, I was given a book,' he explained. 'A very, very old book . . .'

33.
EGYPT

Next to a keypad on the door frame, Rabbi Aaron Cohen pressed his thumb on a small glass pane. Within seconds, the biometric 'key' was accepted and the keypad illuminated. Next he punched in the twelve-digit password, each keystroke emitting a tiny digital chirp. The panel flashed three times, then a series of mechanized bolts slid out from around the door frame. The massive door disengaged, automatically opening inward on smooth hydraulic pistons. A motion sensor turned on the crisp LED lights in the space beyond.

On the right side of the door, Cohen placed his fingers over a slim golden mezuzah case angled toward the open door and inscribed with the Hebrew letter shin (שׁ), representing one of God's Old Testament names, Shaddai.

Stepping across the threshold, the rabbi paused at the beginning of what resembled a mine tunnel. He vividly recalled the claustrophobia he'd felt when he was first introduced to this place by the Levite priests.

The year was 1974 – a time of both great tragedy and personal transformation . . .

*

Aaron had just celebrated his twentieth birthday and had been in the second term of his junior year at New York's Yeshiva University. It was a snowy afternoon in late January when he received the portentous call from his oldest sister, Ilana. 'Father is dead' were the first words she'd said, in an eerily clinical fashion (at the time, she'd been an RN at Beth Israel). As shock had chilled over him, she'd gone on to explain in certain terms that earlier that fateful morning, the B41 bus slid on ice through a Flatbush Avenue intersection and plowed over three pedestrians caught in the crosswalk, injuring one critically, two mortally – including Mordecai Cohen.

'A father should never outlive his son,' Grandfather had said, weeping for the first time Aaron could recall. Not until his son had been put into the ground had the old man stopped rending his garments and chanting, '*Baruch dayan ha-emet*' – 'Blessed is the Judge of truth.'

Following the prompt burial and compulsory seven-day shiva, Grandfather had summoned Aaron to his office and, without a word, handed him a first-class ticket to Cairo. When Aaron had asked him what it was for, Grandfather cryptically replied, 'It is up to you now, my honorable grandson. Your future awaits. The fate of Zion rests with you.' Instructions had been provided, along with what would prove to be Grandfather's last pearls of wisdom. Aaron would later learn that Grandfather had died in his sleep as his plane departed for Egypt.

When his flight arrived at Cairo International's terminal, young Cohen was greeted outside customs by a white-robed Egyptian with crooked teeth and a horribly pockmarked complexion partially camouflaged by a patchy beard. The man discreetly presented a dolphin-and-trident talisman before asking Aaron to do the same. The Egyptian then escorted him to a beat-up pickup truck and insisted on blindfolding him for the ride to the warehouse – a scary episode for a young Jew in a hostile, foreign land less than a year after the Yom Kippur War.

The first thing he recalled about the warehouse was its grimy odor. When the blindfold finally came off and he found himself in the back office of a huge garage surrounded by a group of similarly dressed Egyptians, confusion and anxiety racked his thoughts. He remembered wondering how this place could possibly be the sacred ground Grandfather had spoken of.

'Sorry for this,' one of the men said, dangling the blindfold. 'I'm sure you understand that precautions are necessary.'

Though Grandfather had told Aaron that the Diaspora had scattered the bloodline all over the world, he'd been nonetheless taken aback when he first saw the Egyptian man's dark skin. Later in life he'd recall the episode when he learned that 99.9 percent of the human genome was identical, despite any outside appearances. The priest's amazing aquamarine eyes and the gleaming silver talisman hanging over his heart on the front of his white tunic, however, further confirmed a distant yet distinct familial bond.

'You look just like your father, Mr. Aaron. A bit taller, perhaps. He was a very, very good man. God's light will shine perpetually upon him.' The man's English was nearly perfect. 'My name is Khaleel.' He'd offered a warm handshake. 'It is an honor to have you here.'

Aaron was speechless, though Khaleel's kind words had eased his anxiety. He watched as one of the men worked on opening a door built into the floor.

'I trust your trip was comfortable?'

'Yes, sir.'

'Please, Aaron, call me Khaleel.'

His tone was remarkably calm. Aaron nodded.

Khaleel grinned. 'Well then, come. Let us begin,' he said, pointing to the dark opening. 'We have so much to discuss.'

In the cramped, dank basement, Khaleel had unlocked a crude, dented metal door with a skeleton key. Its hinges groaned grittily when he opened it. On the other side, he groped for a light switch that brought to life a string of work lights dangling along the center of a tunnel. 'Not great,' he admitted, looking up at the dull bulbs, 'but it's a huge improvement over the torches we'd been using up until the twentieth century.'

That managed to bring forth Aaron's first smile. Khaleel, he'd quickly determined, was a gentle, wise man.

Aaron watched the Egyptian swing the creaking door back into place, his long fingers turning the dead bolt. Realizing he'd been locked in an obscure pit in the Egyptian no-man's-land, he felt his hands begin trembling. He stuffed them into his pockets. Grandfather wouldn't have liked it, but even God would have trouble seeing his hands (or his head) down here.

Khaleel placed his right hand on Aaron's shoulder and extended his left invitingly down the tunnel. 'It may not look like much, but what it leads to is very special. Come.'

They walked abreast, the tunnel just wide enough to accommodate them.

Aaron flinched when he saw a scorpion darting along the earthen floor. Khaleel, however, paid it no mind as it skittered over his sandal.

'Your grandfather has told me you've learned quite a lot. "An excellent student," he says.'

'I know it is very important to study our history,' Aaron replied.

'Our history is the doorway to our future,' Khaleel agreed. 'You have read about Onias and the tell?'

'Yes, sir . . . I mean, Khaleel.'

To calm his anxiety, Aaron told him what he'd learned from reading Josephus's detailed accounts in *The Jewish War*. In the second century B.C.E., Onias had been the high priest at the Jerusalem temple. He'd vehemently opposed the pagan sacrifices being allowed on Yahweh's sacred altar. The temple had been poisoned by Hellenic culture – defiled. When the Syrian king Antiochus threatened war against the Jews, Onias fled to Alexandria to seek refuge under Ptolemy (who detested Antiochus). Onias was granted this land in what had then been the nome of Heliopolis. And here Onias had constructed a fortress city atop a man-made mound. Upon its highest point, he'd built a new sanctuary – a new temple to God, modeled after the one in Jerusalem, but on a smaller scale, and free from any pagan influences.

'It happened just as Isaiah prophesied,' Khaleel added. 'The prophet told us that in a place called the City of the Sun, the language of Canaan would be spoken in the land of Egypt, and an altar to the Lord would rise up. And just as Isaiah had said, here is where the Savior came to begin His mission to rescue the Israelites.'

They walked further down the passage in silence. Halfway down the tunnel, they turned along a slight bend. The lighting remained dim, so Aaron could barely make out what lay at the tunnel's terminus – a rectangular outline of some kind.

'You know what happened to Onias's temple, yes?' Khaleel asked, testing him.

'The Romans burned it down. Not long after they destroyed the Jerusalem temple in seventy C.E.' Josephus, Aaron recalled, had been very explicit about that too. 'The Romans were looking to destroy any hope of another Jewish rebellion. Not only was Onias a priest, but he had his own army here in Heliopolis. The Romans considered this the last Jewish stronghold – a rallying point for further sedition.'

'Excellent, young Aaron,' Khaleel said. 'And since the days of Onias, time and nature have colluded without hindrance to reclaim what little remains of his grand temple city. Up there' – he pointed through the five meters of earth that hovered overhead – 'we're left with only ravaged foundations. But down here, Onias's real legacy has been preserved. Are you ready to learn about it so that you may truly become a Son of Light?'

'Yes.'

'Are you ready to *see* it? To see what Onias's army was protecting?'

See it? 'I . . . I think so.' When he looked into Khaleel's eyes, he experienced the same rush he'd felt when his father was about to bring him into Grandfather's secret room – two men embarking on a journey. 'You cannot be a Kohen without first going to Egypt,' Grandfather had told him. 'There, everything you have learned will become clear.'

Khaleel's voice suddenly dropped low. 'Did your grandfather also tell you that Yeshua walked down this very same tunnel?'

This shocked Aaron. 'Jesus?'

'That is right. As Isaiah foretold, the Savior came here, just as you have. To learn. To understand. To believe.'

They stopped at the intimidating steel door that materialized from the shadows.

As Khaleel worked a second key into its lock, he said, 'And inside this room, Jesus was given God's most wondrous gift.'

I am a Son of Light, Cohen thought.

The earthen walls looked the same now as they had in 1974,

with the exception of some steel reinforcement beams recently retrofitted along some of the crumbling ancient stone arches, and the electrical conduit that snaked between the modern overhead light fixtures.

Five meters below the surface, the subterranean passage ran a perfect line stretching two hundred meters to a secret chamber beneath Tel el-Yahudiyeh's foundation. The dusty parcel situated directly above it attracted little attention, but it hosted the faint remains of a massive elliptical fortification built by the Hyksos in the seventeenth century B.C.E.; like the mound, the site was protected by the Egyptian Supreme Council of Antiquities. Therefore, excavations required SCA authorization – virtually impossible to attain. The last meaningful excavation performed here had been in 1906 by Flinders Petrie (the incriminating findings were published in *Hyksos and Israelite Cities*) – and luckily, even though the renowned father of modern archaeology had pinpointed this as the city of Onias, he had not been granted permission to dig below the tell's foundation.

At the tunnel's terminus, the rabbi stopped in front of the second security door, which looked nothing like the one Khaleel had trusted to a simple lock and key. Unlike the tunnel and its improved entrance door, here Cohen had insisted upon major modifications. Regularly, new safeguards and enhancements were added to keep pace with ever-improving technology.

Cohen pressed his thumb on the lock's scanner, then keyed in a second password. The panel flashed blue three times. The steel door's mechanical guts came to life, multiple jamb bolts smoothly disengaging. The pressure seal released a small *pop* just before the door began opening along a smooth arc. Beyond, a dense matrix of iridescent green lasers snapped off.

Cohen entered the cube-shaped vault.

Stainless steel panels sheathed steel-reinforced zero-slump concrete slabs (with special additives that made their crush value ten times greater). Behind that, the two-meter-thick ancient block walls constructed by Onias's builders had been maintained.

Cohen stared in wonderment at the supervault's extraordinary centerpiece.

Less than a minute later seven priests in white tunics funneled through the entry and awaited instructions.

34.

JERUSALEM

Amit and Jules entered the Old City's southern wall through the Zion Gate. They kept close to the stone sidewalls to avoid the cars negotiating the tight L-shaped bend in the tunnel.

'So exactly where are we going?' Jules asked in a loud voice. Amit had been tight-lipped as he parked the Land Rover in the tourist lot outside the gate. Contemplating a plan, she intuited.

Amit didn't want to compete with the sounds of tire rubber squealing along the glass-smooth ancient paving stones. So he provided the answer only once they'd emerged into the Armenian Quarter along busy Shaar Tsiyon, lined with cafés and souvenir shops.

'We are going to the Jewish Quarter,' he told her.

Passing through a security checkpoint and metal detectors at the entrance to the Jewish Quarter, Amit only hoped that their sly pursuer wouldn't be able to circumvent the metal detectors. A Mossad agent like Enoch could easily bypass security barriers. The agency's outside contractors, however, didn't have that luxury.

He brought Jules through the Roman Cardo, down through

Hurva Square (where the only people she spotted were Hasidim), and through the narrow maze of streets that put them on Misgav Ladach. Finally, he stopped in front of a nondescript three-story building neatly edged in Jerusalem stone. A bronze placard engraved in Hebrew and English with THE TEMPLE SOCIETY hung above the unassuming entry, which seemed little more than a storefront.

'Here?' she asked, looking up at the sign. 'What are we doing *here*?'

'Rabbi Cohen's office,' he flatly replied, thumbing at the door. 'I figured we might ask him if the scrolls were still in Yosi's office when he met with him yesterday. If the scrolls had been moved, he might know it.'

'That's your plan?'

Exactly the reaction he'd expected. 'Got anything better?'

She put her hands on her hips and huffed. 'Yikes. We are screwed.'

'To be determined,' he optimistically replied. He reached out and pulled the door open. 'After you, mademoiselle.'

'Rrrr,' she growled as she walked past him.

They entered the reception foyer, whose walls were covered in Torah-themed scenes that would have impressed Michelangelo himself: Moses raising his staff to part the seas; Moses atop Sinai; Moses presenting God's sacred commandments to the Israelites. A massive gold-plated menorah rose tall behind a reception desk. Seated directly beneath it was a middle-aged woman wearing an ultraconservative navy blouse buttoned to the collar. Like that of many Hasidic women, her thick, wavy hair was a wig.

'*Shalom aleichem*,' Amit greeted her.

She responded in kind, then asked, 'May I help you?'

'Yes, I've come to speak with Rabbi Cohen,' Amit replied.

This seemed to confuse her. 'Sorry, but my husband is out of the country on business. Did you have an appointment with him?'

'Not exactly,' Amit said, his optimism immediately deflated.

'Perhaps I might be of assistance then?' she pried. 'What is it you'd like to speak with him about?'

'Well . . .,' he sighed. 'When do you expect him back from . . .?' Amit let the words linger, hoping she'd fill in the blank. Surprisingly, she did.

'I expect him to return from Egypt this evening.'

'Cairo, was it?' Amit pressed.

That's when Cohen's wife realized that she'd already said too much. 'If you'd like to leave your name, telephone number . . . I'll certainly see that it gets to him.'

'That's okay. I'm sure I'll see him at the Rockefeller Museum. It's nothing urgent.'

'Your name?'

Amit wasn't about to give his own. 'If you could tell him Yosi stopped by?'

'Certainly.'

'We came to see the museum as well,' Jules tactfully cut in, as if reminding Amit. She pointed to a sign above a door to Mt. Sinai's left side – an arrow next to the word MUSEUM.

'That's right,' Amit quickly agreed. 'I heard you've recently remodeled the galleries?' He could tell this lightened Mrs. Cohen's mood.

'We just reopened two weeks ago.'

'Then two tickets, please,' he cheerily replied, reaching for his wallet.

35.

The spacious gallery was bustling with tourists, many of whom, Amit could tell, were American Jews eager to decipher their heritage.

'Do we really have time for this?' he protested.

'Do you really want to draw more suspicion to yourself?' Jules quickly rebutted. 'Why didn't you just go ahead and wrestle the woman? Besides, we might learn something here. And it's certainly safer than walking the streets.'

In the main exhibit hall, the walls were covered in wonderfully detailed oil paintings – a virtual storyboard going back to 1300 B.C.E. to trace Moses and the Israelites along their grueling trek out of Egypt, through the forty-year desert pilgrimage and the centuries-long Canaan wars, to King David's conquest of Jebus in 1000 B.C.E. – the capital city he'd renamed 'Jerusalem' – and Solomon's construction of the first temple shortly thereafter.

In a separate room, the Babylonian invasion and subsequent exile of the Jews was recounted on twelve framed canvases, and over three dozen more bridged the Jewish dynasties and occupying empires leading up to Rome and its destruction of Herod's temple in 70 C.E. A large display table in the room's center sat beneath a sign reading, in English and Hebrew, THE THIRD TEMPLE. Encased in a Plexiglas cube was an elaborate architectural model showing the Temple Society's vision for a new Temple Mount, absent all Islamic buildings currently on the site, including the Dome of the Rock and al-Aqsa Mosque.

'What do we have here?' Jules asked, stepping up to it.

'That,' Amit said, 'is what these guys think should be sitting on top of the Temple Mount – in place of the Dome of the Rock.'

'That's one ambitious building project,' Jules whispered.

'Mmm.' Amit studied the model more levelly now, something clicking in his thoughts. This wasn't the re-creation of Herod's temple that many of Cohen's conservative predecessors had imagined, but a modern complex of glass and stone set in three concentric courtyards, each with twelve gates. The design seemed vaguely familiar. But he couldn't place it.

They moved on to the next exhibit room, where rectangular glass kiosks housed authentic replicas of the sacred vessels to furnish the Third Temple. Amit explained some of them to Jules: the gold-plated ceremonial shofar ram's horn, the handled gold cup called the *mizrak* used to collect sacrificial blood, the ornate silver shovel used to collect ash from burnt offerings, the Table of Showbread to display the twelve loaves representing the Israelite tribes, the crimson lottery box used during Yom Kippur to draw lots for sin offerings, and the gold oil pitcher used to replenish menorah lamps. There were even beautifully crafted harps and lyres for Levitical priests to play orchestral music in the temple courtyards.

'Seems like they're ready to move in,' Jules said in a hushed tone.

'Indeed.'

'And what do we have over here?' she asked, eyeing a life-sized mannequin wearing a cobalt robe interlaced with gold thread, a gold breastplate encrusted with twelve gems, and an elegant turban with a gold tiara. 'Who's the genie?'

Amit chuckled. 'Those are the vestments for the temple's high priest.'

'Snazzy,' she said, shaking her head.

Amit read the placard aloud: 'And to Moses God said' – he took the liberty of saying 'God' where the placard read 'G-d' in compliance with the Jewish law forbidding the writing out of God's name – 'Have your brother Aaron, with his sons . . . come to you from the Israelites to serve Me as priests . . . You are to instruct all the skilled craftsmen, whom I have filled with the spirit of wisdom, to make Aaron's garments for consecrating him to serve Me . . .' The excerpt was noted as Exodus 28.

But Jules was already moving on to the next display.

'And this?' She crouched to get a better look at a massive limestone block etched with ornamental rosettes and hatch patterns.

He walked over to her and read the Hebrew placard. 'Apparently, that's going to be the Third Temple's cornerstone.'

'These designs . . .,' she said, pressing her face closer to the etchings. 'Look familiar?'

Drawing nearer, he saw what she meant. 'Same as the ossuary I showed you today. Amazing.' More gears clicked in Amit's mind. Jules's suggestion of a tour was actually paying off.

Passing beneath a sign reading THE HOLY OF HOLIES in Hebrew and English, they entered a final exhibit room and stood before the display that was its focal point. Dramatic orchestral music played low through hidden speakers. Here, a raised platform sat in the room's center – empty.

'Not much to see *here*,' Jules said with a smirk.

Amit put his hands on his hips, assessing the space. 'Well, before Herod's temple was destroyed by the Romans,' he offered, 'its most sacred room, the Holy of Holies, actually *had* been empty.'

'Why would the Jews build a temple around an empty shrine? That's a bit ridiculous, isn't it?'

'Not really,' he said. 'What it had once contained wasn't something that could ever be replaced.'

'And what was that?' But she noticed his attention had wandered, strangely enough, to the room's faux stone block walls. 'Hello?'

'My God,' he gasped. The short hairs on his neck bristled. 'That's it.'

She followed his eyes and wasn't seeing a damn thing. 'What do you mean, *it*?'

Now her failure to piece these things together was starting to disappoint him. But he needed to remind himself that he was dealing with an Egyptologist, not a biblical archaeologist. 'The walls, Jules,' he calmly replied. 'The ceiling, the floor?' He pointed to them in turn. 'Look at the shape they form. Don't you see it?'

Her frustration was setting in too as she scanned the space again. 'What? You mean the squares?'

'The cube,' he sternly whispered. 'This room is a cube. The ideal of perfection used in the design of the Tabernacle's innermost sanctuary. *And* those vaults I showed you in Qumran.'

She shrugged. 'Okay, I get it. They were cube shaped.'

'Exactly!' He anxiously eyed the empty platform at the room's center one last time, then stared up at the surveillance camera mounted close to the ceiling. 'We need to leave. Right now.'

36.
EGYPT

It was at Inshas Airport's security gate where the problem began. Rabbi Cohen's returning Peugeot hadn't aroused suspicion, but the blue pickup truck following closely behind it had.

As instructed, Cohen and his driver waited in the car, idling in front of the lowered security barrier. A mustached guard stood by them while two others circled around the truck to question the driver and inspect the sizable wooden crate stowed in its bed.

Cohen had already explained to the Egyptians that his diplomatic privileges should not be questioned. He'd shown them his passport and the diplomatic papers that he maintained as a former member of the Knesset. But the stubborn guard wasn't hearing any of it, and the rabbi knew why. Though Egypt showed no outward hostility toward Israel, the two still remained ideologically, politically, and theologically split – bitter enemies. And Cohen was no ordinary Israeli; he was a Hasid . . . a Hasid bringing a very suspicious package onto the airstrip.

Gazing out across the runways, he could see his blue-striped jet oriented directly toward Israel, exhaust haze streaming out from its running engines. Calculations ran through his head.

How long would it take to break through the barrier, load the crate, and take off before the Egyptians could do anything to stop them? The place was heavily secured. But he was willing to gamble they wouldn't risk shooting down an Israeli jet, no matter what they suspected was inside the crate.

Cohen turned in his seat, craning his neck to see what was happening behind them.

One guard stayed with the truck's driver, machine gun at the ready.

The second guard was circling the truck's cargo bed, scrutinizing the crate's Arabic markings, which suggested that its contents were auto parts. The inspector pulled out a black security wand that blinked wildly as he ran it over the crate's lid.

This caused more commotion as the guards began screaming back and forth to one another.

Cohen gritted his teeth. No matter what the cost, he'd be returning to Tel Aviv with the cargo. He spoke quietly to the driver in Hebrew. 'You know what to do if this gets messy.'

The driver nodded. He let his hand drop slowly along the seat, ready to take up the Uzi concealed there.

The inspector paced back inside the security post and came out with a second device that Cohen couldn't identify.

'If they even attempt to open the crate . . .,' Cohen whispered to the driver.

With another subtle nod, the driver's hand went down further along the seat.

Back at the truck's rear, the guard fidgeted with the device, which looked like some kind of handheld vacuum. Once it powered on, he used the thing to scan the top and sides of the crate.

Cohen's hands curled into fists.

After a few more sweeps, the inspector finally yelled out his findings in Arabic to the mustached guard who'd taken a post at the car. Though the man's accent was thick, Cohen could make out that he was saying everything seemed all right – then something about there being no radioactive material.

The mustached guard slung his machine gun over his shoulder and bent down along the Peugeot's window. 'We cannot be too careful these days,' he said by way of a mediocre apology. 'You are free to go.'

The security gate opened and the car moved forward, followed by the blue pickup.

Unclenching his fists, Cohen breathed a sigh of relief and checked his watch – almost three P.M. The unanticipated complications in packaging the relic had substantially delayed their departure. Difficult to fault the priests (the relic's custodians), since the meticulous protocols hadn't been carried out in almost two millennia.

Regardless, within an hour they'd arrive in Tel Aviv, with the crate. He'd then instruct the pilot to continue on directly to Rome, where another urgent delivery would be awaiting pickup.

37.

VATICAN CITY

Following the leisurely two-and-a-half-hour lunch, Father Martin brought Donovan to the Swiss Guard security office. There he made good on his promise to help restore Donovan's clearances to the Secret Archives, the clerical offices of the Apostolic Palace and the Palace of the Governorate, the museums, and the various administrative buildings throughout Vatican City.

Though Donovan acted outwardly enthusiastic about Martin's offer to arrange meetings for the following morning with the archbishop in charge of the Pontifical Commission, as well as the inspector general of the Corpo della Gendarmeria (Vatican City's police force in charge of general security and criminal investigations), he was most interested in performing an investigation of his own – an investigation that would commence at the heart of Vatican City: St. Peter's Basilica.

Donovan knew little about the cunning enemies he was dealing with. Nevertheless, of one thing he was certain. The critical information they'd been given could only have come from someone inside Vatican City. And earlier that afternoon, he'd very discreetly sprung a trap to test his hypothesis.

Donovan didn't use his new key card to enter St. Peter's Basilica, since his last after-hours visit there back in June had left a digital trail in the security center's activity log. And what needed to be done here required utmost furtiveness.

At six thirty, he came in the grand front entrance, just like every other tourist. And for the next half hour, he slowly paced the voluminous nave and transepts, reacquainting himself with the shrines and statues, which spoke to him like old friends.

Soon the docents announced the basilica's seven P.M. closing and began shepherding everyone outside. That's when Donovan nonchalantly slipped through the balustrade leading to the deep grotto set at the foot of the main altar, beneath Bernini's towering baldachino.

He moved quickly down the semicircular marble steps, past St. Peter's shrine and the Confessio set before it, back beneath the mammoth white plaster-covered arches supporting the basilica's main floor. Deeper he went into the underground graveyard where late popes and dignitaries had been laid to rest in massive sarcophagi and elaborate crypts, until he came to the tomb of Benedict XV.

Looking back over his tracks, he made sure he still had a straight sight line to the Confessio and St. Peter's shrine. Then he crouched beside the mammoth *cippolino* marble sarcophagus topped by an incredibly lifelike bronze effigy of the late pope laid in state.

It took another fifteen minutes before he heard a docent descend the steps for a final run-through. Staying low, Donovan quietly shifted around the tomb's base to stay out of view as the docent roved past, whistling.

Five minutes later, the sconces throughout the grottoes dimmed to blackness, and security lights glowed gently in the necropolis's main corridors.

Now he would wait.

38.

If the four-course meal served up at the Apostolic Palace – antipasti, braciole, *zuppa di faro*, and *linguine al pescatore* – hadn't made Charlotte's eyelids heavy, the two glasses of Montepulciano d'Abruzzo certainly had. She'd endured the most stressful day of her life, short of the hellish Monday back in March when her oncologist first told her she had bone cancer.

So while Father Donovan sorted out the administrative details of his return to Vatican City, she'd returned to the dormitory, emotionally drained and physically spent. Though it violated her cardinal rule for skipping multiple time zones – *immediately acclimate to the local time and let your body adjust* – she surrendered to a late afternoon nap.

When the alarm clock went off around six P.M., she hit the snooze button three times, then shut it off altogether.

Her sleep was deep, yet far from peaceful.

Images of Evan's murder kept cycling through her subconscious – oddly, in black and white, as if it were a movie from the forties: the strange gunman disguised as a lab tech . . . the gun arcing up at Evan . . . the silent shot . . . Evan's head snapping forward in slow motion . . . a gush of black liquid . . . falling . . . falling . . .

She could see herself, there in the office, screaming through the deafening silence. Helpless.

Wake up . . . WAKE UP!

. . . The gunman turns to her, two words growling from his twisted lips: *'The bones!'* . . .

Then Donovan sitting in the Volvo, calmly saying, 'The bones? Why would they want the bones?'

. . . Cut to chromosomes furiously replicating and dividing in microscope view to the roar of unearthly shrieking and howling . . . souls tormented by hellfire . . .

Silence.

Next: blackness giving way to blinding light.

A skeleton on a stainless steel table.

Gouged ribs.

Ground-up bones around the wrists and feet.

Broken knee bones.

. . . A leather whip streaming through the air – *WHOOOOSH* – its barbed thongs tearing across bare flesh . . . blood spilling out from long, ragged gashes . . . *again* . . . slashing . . . *again* . . . ripping . . . *again* . . . shredding . . .

A sturdy wooden beam laid upon rocks . . . a bloodied, semi-naked figure splayed across it . . . indiscernible shapes shifting through the surrounding thick haze . . . limbs pulled and stretched over the wood . . . sinewy fingers clamping down . . . more hands clutching jagged spikes . . . silent screams . . . pressure on the wrists . . . a hammer cutting the air . . .

WAKE UP!

Charlotte awoke with a start.

Though the images in her nightmare had instantly

disappeared, the pressure on her wrists had not – a sharp pain bolted up to her shoulders.

There was an instant where she thought she was still dreaming. But the pain – the terror – was all too real.

When she tried to scream, an enormous hand came down over her mouth and nose. She detected some kind of fabric against her lips and nostrils, the pungent smell of chemicals.

The broad-shouldered man came into her sights as he jumped onto the bed, straddling her stomach. The one who'd broken through her office door! The gunman who'd murdered Evan! Recoiling, she tried to kick, to flail, to bite. But any resistance was ineffectual.

Through blurring vision, she spotted the second intruder only an instant later, turning the door lock, racing over.

. . . Can't breathe . . .

Her starving lungs struggled for air, only to pull in more chemicals, their smell much sharper this time.

Within seconds, a numb pressure settled over her limbs and torso, as if concrete was being poured over her body. Her head felt impossibly heavy – woozy.

The hand fell away from her face.

As they lifted her from the bed, her head fell limply back. The last thing she saw was the crucifix nailed above the headboard.

Then her field of vision telescoped backward. Total blackness.

39.

THE TEMPLE MOUNT

Ghalib's searing caramel irises glared out the window at the Dome of the Rock, his wiry fingers steepled beneath his chin. The lights circling the shrine's cupola made King Hussein's gold leaf blaze against the darkening sky – a magnificent juxtaposition. It pleased him immensely to know that Israelis from all over Jerusalem and its surrounding hills could see this most potent symbol of Islam's occupation of the world's most sacred ground – this fiery torch lighting the darkness.

Oh, the fury the Jews must endure as they weep in the valley below.

But never could this victory be taken for granted. And that was exactly what the Waqf had done: shirked their duties. Oversight of the Temple Mount was not limited to mere religious functions. This place was a fortress that needed to be closely guarded. The preeminent post within the Waqf was that of Keeper. Just as the name implied, by accepting this assignment, Ghalib had sworn to preserve Islam's foothold not only in Jerusalem, but throughout God's world.

He was a sentinel for Allah.

'Glory to Allah for taking His most righteous servant from the sacred mosque to the most distant mosque,' he muttered, his unblinking eyes still trained on the gold dome.

Oh, how the *kalifah* had taken the divine words of the Great Prophet to weave the grand tale that made this place the third-most-sacred shrine in Islam. The cryptic Qur'anic reference at the onset of the sura entitled Bani Isra'il gave very little detail about what place had truly been designated the Distant Mosque. But the oral traditions in the hadith told a great story that it was this very place – the site where the grand Jewish Temple presumably once stood. How clever the caliphs had been when they'd conquered Jerusalem in the seventh century and re-created Jerusalem's identity – al-Quds. Just as the Jewish king David had once laid claim to this site, so too had the *kalifah*. And the Jews' most sacred place was hence transformed into the Islamic Haram esh-Sharif – the Noble Sanctuary.

'*As-salaam alaikum*,' a soft voice said from over his shoulder.

Swiveling round in his chair, Ghalib studied the young man who stood in the doorway – average height, slight of stature, Palestinian by blood. But his pale complexion, green eyes, and soft features had often been confused for Israeli – one might even guess that he was a Sephardic Jew. Precisely the reason Ghalib had summoned him here. He knew him by first name alone: Ali – Arabic for 'protected by God.' And as requested, Ali had shaved away his beard. The added effect was quite dramatic.

'*Wa alaikum al salaam*,' Ghalib said, waving him forward. 'Come, let us talk.'

Ali sat tall in the guest chair, eyes cast down at his hands in a show of respect.

'You can look at me, Ali,' Ghalib insisted. The green eyes shifted up, blazing with a familiar fire. He got right to the point:

'I've been told that you have offered to give your life for Allah . . . for your people. You wish to be a martyr?'

'Yes,' he replied simply, without emotion.

'Tell me. Why do you believe that you are worthy to make such a sacrifice?'

Ghalib already knew the answer. He'd heard it many times before from countless young Muslims – mostly male but occasionally female – who flooded the rightist Islamic madrassas throughout the Middle East and Europe to be consumed by the radical interpretations of Islam's oral tradition. A common thread bound them all: their lives had been stripped of hope, opportunity, and dignity.

Like many others, Ali and his family had lost their home and land to Israeli settlements funded by American Christian evangelists and zealous Jews. His older brother had been gunned down for throwing stones during the second intifada. Ali had grown up witnessing frequent Israeli raids and the destructive aftermath of rocket attacks. His family was locked behind concrete and barbed wire eight meters high – Israel's ever-growing security barrier. They lived in a camp and relied on handouts, or *zakah*, from Hamas for their survival. And the Israelis forbade them to enter Jerusalem to pray at the great mosques.

No home. No freedom. No land. No future. The perfect martyr.

The worst thing any man could take from another man is his dignity, Ghalib thought.

'I give myself to Allah – body, soul,' Ali replied with utmost certainty. 'I am His now. And to honor Him, I must fight against what is happening to our people. I fight for Palestine. For what is rightfully ours.'

Ghalib smiled. It wasn't the promise of countless virgins in a garden paradise that fueled this one. Just as the Merciful One had created Adam from clay, so too Ali's spirit had been molded by the teachings. But as much as Ghalib would have loved to strap shrapnel bombs to the *shaheed*'s torso and send him into a nightclub on Ben Yehuda Street, there was a more pressing matter at hand.

'You will be greatly rewarded when the final day comes, Ali,' Ghalib said in praise of him. 'In the meantime, there is something very important I would like for you to do.'

'Anything you ask.'

Reaching under the table, Ghalib brought out a neatly folded blue jumpsuit and set it in front of Ali. The embroidered white insignia on the front pocket – depicting a menorah inside a circle – brought much confusion to Ali's fair-skinned face, as did the identification badge and security access card Ghalib placed atop it.

40.
VATICAN CITY

The figure appeared much sooner than anticipated – a dark shadow descending from above, sweeping down the gentle curve of the staircase, faint footsteps echoing off the marble-clad grotto. From the shadows deep within the necropolis, Donovan leaned out from behind the tomb in wait.

The face was difficult to make out beneath the dim glow from the oil lamps circling St. Peter's shrine. But Donovan had little doubt about the intruder's identity. And he was relieved to see that the traitor had come alone. There was a sizable bag in the figure's left hand – far too big for what he'd come to steal.

Father Martin knelt before the arched niche where the golden casket shimmered behind a glass door. He glanced up into the eyes of Christ's mosaic set behind it and crossed himself.

With a trembling hand, he raised a key to the door frame and turned the lock. Slowly he pulled open the glass door.

'And what ever happened to the bones that you found in the ossuary?' he'd asked Donovan over lunch. Though at first Donovan had been reluctant to respond, he'd come back with 'Just after I left Santelli's office, I put them in a very safe place.'

That was when Martin recalled the night of Santelli's death, when he'd found Donovan here in the basilica, after hours, creeping up from this very shrine. Donovan said he'd been praying. But Martin remembered that he'd been carrying an empty satchel. There would have been no way for him to have hidden the bones in one of the papal sarcophagi or tombs, since all were permanently sealed. He'd have needed tools, and no doubt someone to help him. But that night, there'd been neither.

That left only one possibility.

With gleaming eyes, Martin studied the golden ossuary.

The photograph of his sister's family came into his mind's eye, along with the haunting words: 'The most efficient path to truth comes from the blood of loved ones.' Now, by the grace of God, he could spare them by giving Orlando what he wanted. He hadn't asked to be dragged into this mess. This wasn't his war. Donovan and the American geneticist would take responsibility for what had happened.

'You get the bones and have them ready for us,' Orlando had told him on the phone earlier that afternoon. 'You'll also need to find a way to get us into the city.'

There came a moment of doubt when Martin considered the size of the box. Could such a small vessel hold an entire human skeleton? Reaching out with both hands, Martin wrapped his fingers around the relic's ornate lid, his movement more urgent now. He pulled the lid away and set it down on the marble tiles at his knees. The shadows made it difficult to see inside the box and he scrambled for the bag to retrieve the flashlight he'd brought along.

He leaned over the box and shined the light down into it. Reflections shone crisply off some glass vessels stored inside. *Cruets filled with ceremonial oils?*

'What?' Despair immediately gripped him, knocking the wind out of his chest.

'The bones aren't there, lad,' a voice suddenly called out in a heavy brogue.

Taken aback, Martin spun wildly. In the process, he slipped on the relic's lid and it scraped along the tile, making him fall backward against the wall and hit his head. The flashlight fell out of his hand, hit the tile, and rolled away until it partially spotlighted Donovan – his face visible but blended into the darkness. The glow from the overhead lamps silhouetted his hairless skull.

'Where are the bones?' Martin demanded, scrambling to his feet.

Donovan's muscles tightened. Martin stopped at arm's length, the light shining up under his chin making his wild eyes more pronounced – demonic looking. 'Not here; not in Vatican City,' Donovan bitterly replied. 'You will never know. I promise you that.' When he'd left Vatican City, the bones had left with him. And now they were in a much safer place.

'I must, Patrick! I must know!' he ranted, stepping closer to Donovan, limbs quaking. 'You don't understand!'

'Get hold of yourself,' he replied in disgust. 'There's plenty I understand. Especially deceit. I've seen too much of it inside these walls. But I never expected it from you.'

Then Martin broke down. 'They've threatened to kill my sister . . . the children. If I don't give them what they want . . .' He dropped to his knees, sobbing.

'You have no idea what you've done. People have *already* died because of what you've said.'

Martin buried his face in his hands, shaking his head in denial, not wanting to hear the words.

'Tell me who they are. I'll help you. We'll find a way to protect your sister and her family. We can bring them here until we find these men.'

'Just give them the bones,' he weakly pleaded.

'I can't. I won't.' It took everything in his being not to lash out at him. Donovan dropped to one knee and yanked Martin's face up into the light. 'Who *are* they?' he growled in frustration.

Martin shook his head, his lips quivering. 'Do you think I know?' he sobbed. 'Do you think they actually told me? I have no idea who they are!' He pulled away and dropped to the floor like a wounded animal. 'It doesn't matter now anyway,' Martin murmured.

Donovan didn't like the way this sounded.

'They're already here, in the city. When I don't give them the bones tonight . . .'

Adrenaline surged through Donovan and he lunged at Martin, seizing the lapels of his jacket, shaking hard. 'You let them in here? Are you insane!'

'It wasn't only the bones they wanted,' Martin whispered, his body flaccid. 'They wanted her too . . . Charlotte.'

Stunned, Donovan shoved Martin back against the wall. Wasting no time, he sprang to his feet and raced up the steps into the basilica.

'It's too late!' Martin screamed after him. 'You can't save her now!' His next words went unheard by Donovan. 'God forgive me.'

41.

JERUSALEM

'Why are we going here?' Jules asked as Amit turned the Land Rover off Jaffa Road and its headlights swept across Jerusalem's Central Bus Station – a modern eight-story pile of Jerusalem stone and glass. 'Are we skipping town?'

'I need to check my e-mail,' he told her, 'and I'm not about to go to my apartment to do it. Suicide bombers like to target buses. So security here is super tight. Lots of cameras, police, metal detectors.'

'Good idea.'

'Thanks.'

'And you're still not going to tell me what you're thinking?' The stubborn Israeli had raced her out of the Old City saying barely a word. And he'd given her no clue as to why the Temple Society's tribute to the hypothetical Third Temple shrine had spooked him.

'If I tell you what I'm thinking right now, trust me, you'll think I'm completely nuts,' he told her.

'Too late for that,' she grumbled.

Winding through the underground garage, Amit parked the

Land Rover close to the elevator. He waited a good minute with the Jericho grasped firmly in his hand, making sure no one was following them inside. Once he was satisfied that the area was secure, he locked the pistol in the glove box.

'Let's go,' he said, jumping out. 'There's an Internet café upstairs that one of my students told me about.'

Along the shopping concourse, Amit strode quickly to Café Net, with Jules double-timing her steps to keep up with him. At the counter, he paid seven shekels for fifteen minutes of Web surfing. While he settled in at a terminal close to the front, Jules perused the pastry and sandwich selections at the display case running along the opposite wall.

By the time Amit had fussed with the access code and gotten the browser up and running, Jules had returned with a tray holding a café au lait and omelet ciabatta for each of them.

'Might as well get something to eat while we're here,' she said. She set a mug and a plated sandwich in front of him.

'Good thinking.' Famished, he immediately went for the sandwich.

'So what exactly are you looking for?' Her tone was more conciliatory now. It was obvious that Amit was putting together the pieces of a very intricate puzzle.

It took him a moment to finish chewing before he said, 'Yosi always sends me an advance copy of his transcriptions,' Amit explained. 'To keep us both out of trouble, he sends them to my Yahoo account.'

'Sneaky,' Jules said.

'Smart,' Amit corrected. 'Yahoo affords some pretty sophisticated firewalls and encryption. Not to mention my name is not attached to my account. So it's all fairly anonymous.' He clicked on his in-box and the screen filled with unread messages. 'And this transcription would have been very easy for Yosi – quick. So if we're lucky . . .' He cast his eyes heavenward.

She swallowed her first bite of the ciabatta. 'Any stuff in there I'm not supposed to see?'

He shook his head.

'How about this one?' she inquired, pointing to a new message with the subject line enlarge your penis – 1 inch in 3 days. 'Are you sure your account is anonymous?'

Amit chuckled. 'I guess the secret's out,' he said. 'Junk mail.' But the smile dissolved quickly when he scrolled down and spotted the message from Yosi, the subject line stating one ominous word in caps: 'URGENT.' 'Ah. Here we go.'

Jules leaned closer.

'Listen to this.' Amit quietly read aloud Yosi's message: 'In all my years, I've never seen anything like this. So many have tried to extrapolate meanings from the Qumran texts, seeking connections to the Gospels – contradictions, perhaps.' His voice began to waver slightly. '"But as you know, only ambiguous interpretations exist. If these scrolls truly date to the first century, and I have no doubt they do, what you have discovered will' – he had to pause to clear his throat – 'challenge everything we know.' But the last sentence stumped him, because it stopped abruptly.

Jules picked it up for him: 'I fear that such a controversial message might—' And she let her voice break off just as the words had. 'What happened there?'

'He obviously sent this in a rush. Didn't get a chance to finish.' Amit checked the time and date of the transmission. 'See here . . . this came yesterday, right before Joshua said Yosi left the museum.'

'You mean when he was talking with that rabbi?'

Amit's face went pale. 'Exactly.' He tried to imagine the timing of it all. 'Rabbi Cohen must have interrupted him.' The thought of this troubled him deeply. Cohen was a powerful man.

'Yet he still felt the urge to get the e-mail off to you?'

'Yeah.' Amit could only guess that what the transcription revealed had profoundly unnerved Yosi. Now, with great trepidation, he stared at the tiny paper clip icon next to the subject line. Could Yosi have felt that he was in danger?

'Come on. Open it,' Jules urged.

He quickly moved the mouse pointer over the paper clip icon to open the document Yosi had attached. The moment it came up, he knew it was the transcription. But there was no time to read it. Amit clicked the print button. 'We've got to get out of here right now,' he told Jules, jumping up from the chair.

'What are you—'

But he was already at the printer snatching up the pages. Verifying that he'd gotten the whole document, he paid the cashier for the printout. Then he raced back, logged off his e-mail account, and grabbed his sandwich. Jules was already standing, emptying her mug.

Amit threw back his coffee too.

'Ready,' she said, and followed him out. 'What's with the sudden rush?'

'This guy is most likely monitoring everything. My credit cards, my passport . . . I'm sure he's already traced all of Yosi's e-mail. Which means he already knows that Yosi sent this e-mail to me. So I have no doubt that my Yahoo account is being monitored too.' He explained how stationary computers were open books and that techs with even basic knowledge of Internet protocol addressing could easily pinpoint where activity was originating.

As they moved through the throngs of commuters, Amit's

radar was working overtime – his eyes scanning faces, store-fronts, escalators . . .

'So now what?'

'We get ourselves safely away from here and read this tran-scription. But first, I need to use a pay phone.' His eyes motioned to a cluster of phones next to the entrance doors.

Once again, Enoch picked up in two rings.

'Hey, it's me,' Amit said loudly over the bustling commuters moving about the terminal. 'Find out anything yet?'

'Plenty. Got some very interesting info for you,' the Mossad agent said without formality. 'Good news and bad news.'

Amit's fingers tightened around the receiver. 'I could use some good news.'

'Good news is, the tank hasn't marked you.'

That definitely came as a relief. 'Bad news?'

'That picture you sent me? Outside contractor. And I don't think I need to tell you his specialty.'

His fingers clamped tighter. 'Assassinations?' Jules was stand-ing close beside him, and her eyes went wide.

'Among other things.'

His worried eyes swept over the sea of faces moving all around him, looking for anyone suspicious – particularly a man with a fresh head wound. 'Were you able to get a name?'

'Come on, Amit. You know how those guys work.'

'Right. Aliases and anonymous bank account numbers.' *Deniability.*

'You got it,' Enoch said. 'And I picked up lots of activity with the credit bureaus, immigration, the works. Not in-house. Someone on the outside, trying to track you down.'

'Can you trace it?'

'Tried. No good. The connections bounce through phantom routers, stay live for less than a minute at a time. But he's got all your information.'

'So this guy has help?'

'Very good help.'

'Great,' Amit grumbled. 'You know Rabbi Aaron Cohen, right?'

'Who doesn't?'

'I have a feeling he might be involved in all this. Call it a hunch. I found out today that he took a last-minute trip to Egypt. Can you find out where he went, what he's up to?'

A tired sigh on the other end of the line preceded Enoch's reply.

'I'll see what I can find out.'

'You're the best. I'll be in touch shortly.' Amit hung up the phone and turned to Jules. 'Come on.'

He led her down the escalator to the main level, in the direction opposite where they'd come into the station.

This was all happening way too fast for Jules and she was getting frustrated. 'Slow down,' she said, tugging his thick arm. 'We parked back there,' she said, pointing behind her.

'Forget my truck. I'm sure that's being watched too. We'll take a taxi from here.'

42.

VATICAN CITY

Donovan was in full sprint as he flew out the rear exit of St. Peter's Basilica onto Via del Fondamento. He had no cell phone to call ahead to Charlotte's room – to warn her that Martin had snared them in his trap. And there was no time to double back to the Swiss Guard barracks to arrange a rescue team.

Worst of all, Donovan was unarmed.

He only hoped that the dormitory's deskman had stopped the men from entering the building, or at least called ahead to security if anything seemed suspect.

As he rounded Piazza di Santa Marta, a group of nuns scattered from the sidewalk to make way for him, gasping as he tore past. A searing burn was radiating up his leg muscles as he pushed harder.

Breathless, he slid to a stop at the dormitory entrance, yanked open the door, and darted into the vestibule. 'Call secur—!' he began to yell to the curved front desk. But no one was there. He quickly hurled himself halfway onto the counter to try to see if the deskman was in the rear office through the open doors on the left and right. '*Ao!*' Donovan yelled, not seeing any trace of the guy. '*Ao!*'

But then his eyes caught reflections glinting off the pool of red spreading over the tiled floor beneath the desk. The deskman was sprawled out on his back, lifeless eyes frozen in terror, a clean hole pierced through his forehead.

Donovan recoiled, his chest heaving up and down.

The bank of security monitors was still live, and on the closed circuit for the second floor, he spotted a large man pushing a bulging laundry bin toward the elevator. This time the man wasn't wearing a lab coat. Father Piotr Kwiatkowski, or whatever his name was, had donned the gray uniform of a maintenance worker.

Donovan feared he might already be too late. The Petrine Gate was very close by, as was the Arch of Bells. If Martin had gotten them into the city legally, they would easily make their exit past the Swiss Guards posted there. Then a couple of quick turns onto Via Gregorio VII and they'd surely disappear.

If, however, Donovan could immediately warn the Swiss Guard, they might respond in time to stop the intruders prior to their leaving the city. He reached across to the desk phone and snatched up its receiver. The line had been cut.

On the monitor, the elevator doors had just closed. He could hear the machinery come to life behind him.

Did deskmen carry guns? His frenzied eyes went back to the body, the navy blazer that had flapped open when it hit the floor. No gun belt or underarm holster.

His eyes scanned furiously for anything resembling a weapon. The far wall – a red fire extinguisher, and a formidable ax encased in safety glass beside it.

43.

The instant the elevator doors parted, Donovan sprang out with the extinguisher's hose aimed straight. With Kwiatkowski in clear view, Donovan pulled on the cylinder's unpinned lever and sprayed a blast of ammonium phosphate directly at his face.

The stunned assassin's reaction was a split second off – his hands came up only after the searing chemicals jetted into his eyes. He went down screaming and simultaneously thrust the linen bin out at Donovan, knocking him back onto the floor.

Donovan relinquished the extinguisher and scrambled for the fire ax. Jumping back to his feet, he jigged around the bin, hooked his free arm inside the elevator, and jabbed blindly at buttons on its control panel. Kwiatkowski was already getting to his feet, struggling to see.

When he lunged for the closing doors, Donovan swung down at his outstretched arm; the ax blade split open his thick forearm with a wet *thwack* and blood sprayed wildly. The assassin howled in pain, giving Donovan a final opportunity to plant a firm kick that made him stumble and collapse against the rear wall of the elevator car. Another quick poke at the panel inside the car brought the doors together and sent the shocked assassin on his way to the fifth floor.

Trembling all over, Donovan pulled back the sheet covering what was inside the laundry bin. Charlotte was there, curled into a ball, unconscious . . . but still breathing.

'Thank God!' Donovan cried.

Next he went for the fire alarm near the stairwell. But as he made to pull down on the handle, he heard a commotion on the stairs. He only glimpsed the man storming down at him and knew immediately that it was Kwiatkowski's partner.

Donovan yanked on the handle and ran past the bin. There wasn't time to get Charlotte to safety, but at least security would respond. The fire alarm immediately began squelching in fast intervals – the sound was so ear-splitting that Donovan didn't even hear the shot.

But he certainly felt the force of its impact as the round punched through his left shoulder and tore out of his chest. His body pitched violently forward and spun, then smashed down against the marble floor.

Seconds later, Father Donovan went still. An ice-cold sensation crawled over his skin as the piercing alarm faded to silence.

44.

JERUSALEM

The taxi turned off Ruppin Boulevard and climbed the steep tree-lined drive leading up to Jerusalem's most famous complex of art and history galleries – the Israel Museum. *My third museum today*, Amit mused.

As the roadway crested, he stared out the window at the Knesset building dominating the nearby hillside in Givat Ram – a bland, 1960s rectangular eyesore with a flat, over-hanging roof supported on all sides by flared rectangular columns. It was lit up against the night sky, making it even harder for him to imagine that its unnatural symmetry and harsh lines had been inspired by the temples of Egypt. But what did impress him was the huge power base Rabbi Aaron Cohen had built inside its unicameral hall during his tenure with the Israeli parliament.

Cohen was a powerful man whom many considered a vision-ary. But he was also a Zionist at heart – as pure as they came. Amit somehow knew that he was responsible for what happened at Qumran, not to mention Yosi's coincidental death, followed by the disappearance of the scrolls. Now in his pocket he had the

221

printed translation that might answer many questions concerning the rabbi's motive.

Outside the museum's entrance, Amit settled up with the driver and he and Jules proceeded through the glass entry doors.

Jules was busy watching some guests arriving by limousine, who were dressed elegantly in gowns and tuxedos. Some impolite stares came back at her. 'I'm feeling a bit grungy,' she muttered. 'What's going on here?'

'Probably a private showing for VIPs. And don't worry, you look fabulous,' Amit added.

She smiled.

He was actually feeling naked without the Jericho, so the metal detectors and security guards inside provided great relief. 'We'll be safe here for the time being,' he told Jules, recognizing one of the security guards on detail – an older, gaunt man with pure white hair.

When the guard stood and reached out for a handshake, Jules noticed his sleeve hike up, revealing some numbers tattooed just above his wrist.

'Amit, how are you, my friend?' he said with a heavy Polish accent.

'Good, David. Yourself?'

'Another day aboveground,' the old fellow cheerily replied, as if he'd just won the lottery. When his eyes turned to Jules, he couldn't help but whistle. 'With this lovely lady at your side, you should have *no* complaints.'

Amit formally introduced his companion.

'You know we closed at nine tonight?' David said, verifying on his watch that it was already past the hour. 'I don't mean to be rude . . .,' he said, giving both their outfits an obligatory once-over as more sweet-smelling guests in sleek black filtered through the lobby. 'It's a private function, I'm afraid.'

'We're not looking to crash the party. Just wanted to show Jules a few things.'

Looking both ways, David leaned closer and stage-whispered to her, 'He may not be on the list, but he's certainly a VIP in my book.' He winked and motioned with his head to the inside. 'Get going.'

'I appreciate that,' Amit said.

'Just don't cause any trouble in there, eh?'

'By the way, David,' Amit said before heading in. 'Tell me, were you here for the symposium yesterday?'

'Of course.'

'Yosi came, didn't he?'

This immediately saddened David. 'Sure. He was here. The poor fellow. What a shame. I guess God was ready for him.'

Amit was sure that God was surprised to see him, but he said, 'Came as a shock to me too.' He let the moment pass before asking, 'This may sound like an odd question, but was he carrying anything when he came in? A briefcase? Anything like that?'

David scrunched his eyes, pondering for a second, then shook his head. 'Everything was going through the scanner,' he said, pointing to the conveyor-belted machine behind him. 'He did have a fancy pen in his pocket that made him ring. Besides that . . .' He shook his head.

'You're sure he wasn't carrying anything else?'

Now David took mock offense. 'I may not be a kid anymore, but my wheels keep turning.' He pointed to his brain.

Amit knew there was no chance Yosi would've left the scrolls in his car. He would have fretted about the humidity, the heat – not to mention the possibility that they might get stolen. And

David's story did agree with Joshua Cohen's recollection of Yosi leaving the museum empty-handed. 'Thanks, David. You take care of yourself and tell your wife I send my love.'

'Make an honest man out of him, will you?' David said to Jules, and waved them through the metal detectors.

45.

The delivery van that had awaited Rabbi Aaron Cohen's arrival on the tarmac at Ben Gurion International was parked behind the modern wing next to the Rockefeller Museum exhibit halls.

Adjacent to the Israel Antiquities Authority's director's office, Cohen's entourage entered a handsomely appointed octagonal meeting room set below a domed ceiling. Along each wall, eight niches were furnished with seats for the Archaeological Advisory Council's auditors. And onto the room's central table, Cohen's men carefully set down the heavy consignment safely returned from Egypt.

Unlike the ossuary on display in the Rockefeller Museum's South Gallery, what was inside this crate was certainly not intended for exhibition. This was not something to be admired. It was to be respected and feared. And soon, for the first time in over three millennia, fear would return to the enemies of Zion.

'Lock the doors,' Cohen instructed his men. He pointed to the windows. 'And shut the blinds.'

Luckily, the return to Tel Aviv hadn't been nearly as eventful as the departure from Inshas. The perilous journey was nearly complete.

'Open it,' he ordered them. He stood back and watched them unpack their tools.

Like Moses preparing to claim the lands of Canaan, Cohen stood upon the threshold of a New Jerusalem – a new world. The bitter conflicts in the Middle East and Israel; the fall of the modern Babylon, Iraq; the godlessness and lasciviousness of Western culture poisoning the world; even the scourge of new pandemics like AIDS and the volatile climatic shifts that churned up more frequent tsunamis and hurricanes – all telling signs that the prophecies were finally being realized.

Since 1948, the promised land had virtually been reclaimed, and the tribes had gathered from around the world. Cohen knew that the return of God's law patiently awaited the final signs, just as He'd promised to Ezekiel: 'Although I sent them far away among the nations and scattered them among the countries . . . I will gather you from the nations and bring you back from the countries where you have been scattered, and I will give you back the land of Israel again . . . And I will also purge you of those who rebel and transgress against me.'

Only one spark remained, one single event culminating a final conflict that would usher in the Day of Judgment – a bloody clash between the Sons of Light and the Sons of Darkness.

As the men lifted the lid off the crate, Rabbi Aaron Cohen grinned widely.

As Grandfather had only dreamed, soon Zion would rise up like a phoenix.

The muted chiming of his cell phone inside his briefcase interrupted the moment. On the opposite side of the conference table, he set the briefcase down and opened it. He fished for the phone, which had slipped between the three plastic-sealed papyri safely recovered from Yosi's office and an aerial schematic of the Temple Mount showing a bright blue line drawn through its midsection from west to east.

Agitated, he hit the receive button. 'What is it?'

What the caller told him was gravely unsettling.

'You hold him there. I'm on my way. Do nothing until I arrive.'

46.

Amit turned right off the main walkway, splitting away from the herd of well-attired invitees en route to the Samuel Bronfman wing. Jules kept pace beside him up a paving-stone path cut through the lush campus surrounding the Israel Museum's Shrine of the Book exhibit hall. A warm breeze sharpened the bouquet of the garden's fragrant flowers and cypress trees.

'Let's sit over here for a few minutes,' he suggested, pointing to the stone wall angling around a colossal basalt monolith.

While Amit unfolded the printout, Jules gazed across the plaza at the shimmering reflection pools and fountains around the illuminated shallow white dome of the exhibit hall.

'Ready?' he asked her.

'Ready,' she said, turning to him.

He paused a moment to look into her eyes. 'I know this isn't the best date you've been on,' he said, 'but I'm really glad you're here with me.'

She leaned over and kissed his cheek. 'You really know how to show a girl a good time. There's no place I'd rather be.' Funny enough, she actually meant it – danger and all. 'So let me hear it.'

Amit let out a long breath and began reading . . .

For forty days Moses convened in the light of God at Sinai.
There, God bestowed unto Moses the Testimony so that the
Israelites would walk the righteous path. When the people abided
by the Testimony, good fortune followed them and He protected
them. When His children were blinded by pride, great punishment was delivered unto them. Through great sacrifice and
bloodshed, the lands promised to the tribes of Abraham were
thus delivered unto them so that a new nation might rise in honor
of God.

The covenant was fulfilled, as told in the books of our ancestors.

King David built a city upon Abraham's rock, and there his son
Solomon erected a temple to honor Yahweh. In the Sanctuary,
the Testimony was placed, for it was the heart of a new empire.
There was peace and rejoicing throughout Zion.

The great empires to the south and to the east and to the north
did look upon Israel with lust, for God's blessing came with great
fortune and prosperity.

Many kings did come after Solomon, though none as wise.
The Israelites had forgotten their promise to Yahweh and Israel
became weak. From over the mountains came armies that surrounded the walls of Jerusalem and threatened to lay siege.
Thinking God had forgotten his children, the kings of Israel
bowed down not before the Testimony, but before their enemies.

And so the righteous sons of Aaron who guarded the
Testimony prepared for the day when Israel's most sacred shrine
would be plundered. The great prophet Isaiah counseled King
Hezekiah, telling him, 'The time will surely come when everything in your palace and all that your fathers have stored up until

this day will be carried off to Babylon.' He then told the king that God had ordered a safe place to be built for the Testimony. For if it was lost, so too the Israelites would perish. So Hezekiah followed God's will.

The kingdom of Babylon did rise up like a lion to devour Israel. They laid waste to the city and took away the many treasures from the temple. But when they entered the Innermost Sanctuary they found it empty.

As this is written, many more kings and empires have come and gone and a new temple is rising high above Abraham's rock. But the Idumean king Herod the Great builds it not in humility to God, but to honor vanity and pride. So too the priests blaspheme God by straying from His laws. Therefore its grand Sanctuary will remain empty. For to restore the Testimony, Israel must once again turn to God, disavow false idols, and see that it is not Rome that oppresses them, but faithlessness.

As Moses spoke the Testimony to the Israelites who knelt before the false idol, I too bring a message of hope for all children of God, for a new covenant will be made. Those who seek the light will be enlightened. And as Abraham prepared to sacrifice his son to God, so too a new sacrifice in blood will be offered upon Mount Moriah.

For this, the unbelievers will make a great mockery of me. They will gather against me. They will pierce my flesh and hang me from a tree. Fear not, for the flesh will be sacrificed so that the eternal spark may live on. Only then will I be given back to God to prepare the way for His eternal Kingdom.

Hear now that Israel will then perish, its idolatrous temple laid to ruin, and those who do not fall to the sword will be scattered. Many will lay claim to Abraham's altar before the glorious temple rises up again, many lifetimes from now. You will know when that day comes, for my broken body will be reclaimed from beneath the sacred rock as a sign that a new covenant will be made.

Look not for the Testimony here, for Onias and the Sons of Aaron have brought it to a more righteous place in the land where the Israelites had once been captives. Forty days after God shakes the land of Zion shall it be brought and set upon Abraham's rock.

Then the spirit of the Son of Man will descend upon the Chosen One to restore the Testimony.

The disbelievers will heed not the signs put forth before them. Thus a great battle will follow between the Sons of Light and the Sons of Darkness. But fear not, O Israel, for out of the ashes, the sheep will lie with the wolf and all peoples in all lands will look in wonder upon Zion and praise God.

Letting out a prolonged breath, Amit was speechless.

'If that's what those scrolls said' – Jules had to get up and pace in a circle – 'sounds to me like they were written by—'

'Jesus,' Amit said.

'Do you know what this means?' she rhetorically asked. 'The implications? My God, this is the find of the century!'

'*Was* the find of the century, Jules,' he reminded her.

Her enthusiasm immediately shrank.

'Obviously someone doesn't want this to be made public.' And more and more Rabbi Aaron Cohen fit the bill.

'But why? It's tremendous.'

'If you don't mind me saying, I'm not sure that you're quite getting it right,' he said. 'This is a prophecy, Jules. A prophecy triggered by the discovery of Jesus's bones beneath the Temple Mount. And all this talk of the Testimony . . .' He shook his head.

She wasn't hearing him. 'So what do you think the rabbi wants out of this?'

A much clearer picture was forming in Amit's mind now. And it was a terrifying proposition. When he looked over at the Shrine of the Book's white dome, a final puzzle piece snapped into place in his mind. 'Let me show you,' he said, getting to his feet and waving for her to follow.

47.

Charlotte's consciousness was a patchy haze, her senses tuning in and out in wild disarray.

Smells came first – spicy, pleasant. Cumin? Cloves? Maybe an exotic Middle Eastern dish. Strange.

Sounds came next – muffled, distant. Then sharper. Voices – maybe two, maybe five. It all seemed to blend together so that only their pitch created any distinction between them. But certainly men. A blaring whine came and went through her head, loud enough to make her wince. Then the voices became clearer. They were speaking in a foreign tongue. Definitely no romance language. Yiddish, maybe?

No sight. This scared her at first, until she could feel her eyelashes sweeping against the blindfold wrapped over her eyes. There was no hope of removing it, because her wrists were pulled tight behind her back with some kind of strap. And when she tried to move her left ankle, she felt resistance there too. Her leg had been tied to something.

She felt like she could vomit.

Then the numbness in her arms and legs began to give way to sharp pins and needles. Twisting cramps came next – neck, shoulders, back, hands . . . It took all of her power not to scream out. As she squirmed to ease the pain, the reclined leather seat she'd been propped in groaned.

She froze.

The voices went on.

There was definitely a sense of motion – smooth coasting. The way the sounds resonated around her, it certainly was too big to be a car. A bus was a possibility. Then a brief interval of turbulence dispelled any guesswork. The seat belt indicator chimed briefly overhead. More bumps, rougher this time.

The voices were laughing now. One of the men was taking a ribbing, probably because he was overreacting to the bumpy flight.

Then the pain ripped up her spine and circled up the back of her head, making her moan loud enough for them to hear.

The voices stopped. There came a brief exchange that she knew was something along the lines of:

'*You do it.*'

'*I already checked on her. It's your turn.*'

One of them let out a tired groan and she could hear his heavy feet thumping along the cabin floor.

She tried her best to pretend she was still out. But she could feel him close, leaning over her, his warm breath reeking of scotch. The smell of metal came up into her nostrils too. She felt a large hand cup her breast and squeeze.

'Get off me!' she screamed, recoiling from his touch – more pain exploded along her shoulders.

The laughing intensified.

'Sounds like she needs more drugs,' another voice called over.

Then the blindfold was stripped away.

Charlotte's eyes squinted against the cabin's bright lights. When everything came into focus, she saw the tall man from Phoenix, his complexion clammy (except for the blotchy, blistered burns below his chin where Evan's coffee had left its mark), his tearing eyes glazed red. And his left arm was wrapped in a blood-soaked towel, the hand immobile and blue. It was a grotesque sight.

'See what your friend did to me?' he slurred.

Donovan! What had they done to him? Then Charlotte's stomach revolted and she retched violently.

'Bitch!' the man cursed furiously, just before jabbing a syringe into her thigh.

'Good night,' was the last thing she heard.

48.

JERUSALEM

Once past security, the rabbi stormed in hobbled strides across the Western Wall Plaza toward the blazing white work lights that lit up the entry to the Western Wall Tunnel. He tried his best to be cordial to the teenage IDF soldiers guarding the entrance, but because of their incompetence he now had another mess to clean up.

Past the pallets of stone and portable cement mixers, he trounced down the stairs and cut through the massive subterranean visitors' hall without giving it a cursory glance. His eyes were locked on the security door up ahead.

At the door, he grumbled as he swept his key card through the reader to free the lock. What good was such a useless protocol now?

Through the narrow channel running along the Temple Mount's foundation he came to the group of men huddled outside Warren's Gate.

'What happened?' Cohen yelled before he'd even reached them.

The men separated and fell back, revealing the subject they'd surrounded – a young man, hands tied behind his back, on his knees. One of the men maintained his hold on a handgun pressed firmly behind the man's ear.

'How did he get through?'

'He had a key,' one of the men replied. 'An ID badge too.' He handed both to the rabbi.

'Eleazar Golan,' he read from the authentic ID. Cohen squared off in front of the intruder, arms folded across his chest, glaring down at the top of his head. 'Look at me,' he said.

No response.

The man holding the gun grabbed a fistful of Ali's hair and jerked his head back so that the green eyes had no choice but to see the rabbi. Deep red blotches on the Palestinian's cheekbones were already darkening to blue, and his nose was bloodied and bent sharply to the right. His left eyebrow was split in half by a ragged gash oozing blood as thick as oil.

'You look Israeli, I'll give you that,' Cohen said. 'Very deceptive indeed.'

'He went inside,' the gunman informed him, pointing to the breach in the Temple Mount foundation. 'Saw everything. It wasn't until I spotted him making a phone call that we figured it out.'

Rage flushed over Cohen. 'Give me his phone.'

The man passed it to him.

Immediately the rabbi huffed. He could tell by its cheap design that it was of the prepaid variety, most likely bought on a street corner for cash. His slim fingers adroitly navigated its simple menu to find any stored numbers. As expected, it was empty. Then he hunted for the last outward call – no doubt a second drone – and hit a green button to patch the number through. Someone picked up within two rings, but no reply came. On the other end, a muezzin's chant swirled in the background. Cohen summoned his best Arabic and offered '*As-salaam alaikum.*'

The call immediately disconnected.

Cohen smashed the phone against the wall. Then he bent at the waist and pressed his face close to the Muslim's. 'Whatever your real name is,' he hissed with teeth bared, 'it will die with you today. No honor will come to your family because of what you've done here, I assure you. And for you, there will be no garden paradise on the other side, no rivers of honey, no virgins to pleasure you.'

The Palestinian's green eyes boiled with hatred – a pulverizing stare. '*Allahu Akbar,*' he proclaimed. Then he spat on Cohen's shoes.

'God is indeed great. However, though your words may honor him, your deeds mock Him. Blasphemy!'

And in Leviticus, the prescription for blasphemy was clearly written.

Cohen straightened, went over to a nearby wheelbarrow heaped with debris, and palmed a jagged rock. He stepped aside, told the gunman to remain where he was, and signaled to the others to come forth. Eleven more men came in turn, each taking up a formidable stone.

Crouching before Ali, Cohen held the rock tauntingly, turning it over in his palm. The Arab trembled, and it pleased him. '"And he that blasphemes the name of the Lord, he shall surely be put to death; and all the congregation shall certainly stone him."'

The eleven men fanned out around the Palestinian.

The gunman backed away, still aiming the gun at Ali.

The Muslim bowed his head and began to loudly pray in Arabic.

Tilting his chin up, Cohen held out the stone in his right hand, paused . . . then brought his left hand down upon it as a sign to commence the execution.

The first stone flew through the air and struck bluntly, tearing open the scalp. Ali teetered severely but remained on his knees, his chant pressing on in an unrecognizable garble.

Four more stones pummeled the Palestinian, peeling the flesh and hair clean back from the skull, dropping him to the ground. The prayer abruptly ceased; the green eyes rolled back into their sockets, so that only twitching white orbs were visible. Froth bubbled from his lips.

Another six stones pulverized his face – the nose flattened, the cheekbones mashed, the jaw snapped inward. Teeth clattered out across the ground.

Cohen handed the twelfth stone to the gunman, who now stood with the pistol lowered.

The final bludgeoning strike brought forth brain matter in globules.

'Throw the body into the cistern,' Cohen instructed the men. 'Then prepare with haste,' he said, pointing to the breach. 'For the time is upon us.'

49.
JERUSALEM

Since the Shrine of the Book housed the majority of the Dead Sea Scrolls recovered from Qumran, it was Amit's home away from home. Thus the IAA had granted him his own key, thanks in part to the clout of his late friend, Jozsef Dayan.

Unlocking the glass entry door, he urged Jules into the dim space beyond – a corridor designed to invoke the feeling of spelunking through a cave. Coming in behind her, he led the way to the main gallery, which had been constructed in 1965. American architects Frederick Kiesler and Armand Bartos had designed the Shrine of the Book's domelike roof to resemble the lid of one of the clay jars in which the ancient scrolls had been stored. Inside, the ceiling rose in concentric coils to a central oculus, lit by a gentle amber light.

Directly below the dome, an elevated platform commanded the center of the circular exhibition hall. There, a meticulous reproduction of the great Isaiah Scroll was displayed in an illuminated glass case that wrapped around a huge podium resembling a scroll handle. Other display cases spread along the room's circumference featured additional scroll reproductions.

Amit had studied many of the originals, which were stored in an airtight safe beneath the gallery.

'It's just over here,' Amit said, moving quickly along the looping ambulatory.

He stopped in front of a curved glass display case where faux vellums were laid against a black backdrop, top-lit by dim lights.

'This scroll came from Qumran, Cave Eleven,' he told Jules. 'It's called the Temple Scroll. Nineteen parchments totaling just over eight meters in length. The longest of the Dead Sea Scrolls. See the characters there? That's Assyrian square script.' He pointed to the scribe's writings, inked just below horizontal guidelines cut superficially into the parchment with a stylus.

She nodded.

'This was written by an Essene.'

'A follower of Jesus,' Jules proudly replied in a show of solidarity.

He smiled. 'The Temple Scroll speaks about a revelation made by God through Moses. God basically explains what the true temple should look like – explicit dimensions, precise layout, how it is to be decorated, you name it. And its design is much grander than what Solomon or Herod built.'

'So what should it have looked like?'

He pointed up to a placard hanging in shadow above the case. 'See there?'

She moved closer, squinting to make out the details.

'The gray area is the Temple Mount that exists today,' he said. 'The outermost square would be the footprint of the new and improved Temple Mount – a fivefold expansion to about eighty hectares that would virtually swallow Jerusalem's Old City and connect the Kidron Valley to the Mount of Olives.'

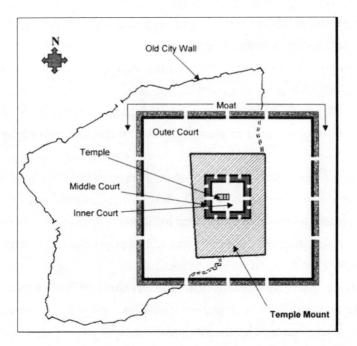

This was tough for Jules to envision, since at fourteen hectares of surface area, the Temple Mount was already a massive construct, even by modern standards. 'That's a mighty ambitious building project.'

'According to the Temple Scroll, that's what God specifically commanded. And of course you'll notice where the temple sanctuary must reside.'

Focusing on the rectangular bull's-eye inside the squares, she answered, 'Directly over the foundation of the Dome of the Rock.'

'And does the design of the temple look familiar?'

It did. 'Nested courtyards . . . twelve gates . . .,' she muttered. She blanched. 'Same as the model we saw at the Temple Society.'

'*Parfait*,' Amit said, praising her. 'The courtyards mimic the original Israelite desert encampments where Moses and the twelve tribes would have set up camp around the tent that acted as the first mobile Tabernacle.'

Amit further explained that from the middle courtyard, there would be three gates in each of the four walls, each named for one of the twelve tribes of Israel. The expansive outer court extended eight hundred meters in each direction, enclosed by a perfectly square wall. From there, another twelve gates led out to bridges spanning a fifty-meter moat to the residential precincts surrounding the Temple City.

'The scholars who've studied the Temple Scroll, me included, have theorized that the Gospels are encoded with this stuff.'

'How so?'

'Three inner courtyards and three rooms in the temple – the Trinity. Twelve gates – twelve disciples gathered from twelve tribes. It's built into the temple's physical design,' he said, spreading his hands. 'And Jesus himself references the temple's design in Matthew nineteen, verse twenty-eight. Jesus says to his disciples, "I assure you: in the Messianic Age when the Son of Man sits on his glorious throne, you who have followed Me will also sit on twelve thrones judging the twelve tribes of Israel."'

She pursed her lips. 'Amit, you know any theologian will say those passages are a metaphor for the afterlife and heaven.'

'Not so,' he said, correcting her. 'Religious authorities in Judaism, Christianity, and Islam all agree that the Messianic Age is a time of great peace and prosperity, which the Messiah will bring to the living earth prior to the Final Judgment – the End of Days, or whatever you choose to call it. This reference clearly describes a new kingdom in the here and now. And Jesus refers to himself as "the Son of Man," not only in this passage, but throughout the Gospels.'

Amit explained that the phrase 'Son of Man' had actually been ascribed to many great prophets – human prophets – by God Himself. He used Ezekiel as an example.

'In the first sentences of Ezekiel two, when the prophet is standing in God's presence, God says to him: "Son of Man, stand up on your feet and I will speak with you." Then Ezekiel states: "As He spoke to me the Spirit entered me and set me on my feet." "Son of Man" is then used numerous times throughout the text. It's a reference to an earthly prophet transformed by the essence of God. Same with Isaiah, Jeremiah, and the others.'

'But still in human form?'

'Of course.'

The implications shook her to the core.

'The Temple Scroll also goes on to spell out how this new kingdom should be governed and protected with a praetorian guard. There's another scroll in the Dead Sea collection that is dedicated to a New Jerusalem – it details how this Temple City would flourish during two millennia of peace under messianic rule. That's a lot of time to grow, so they'd certainly have envisioned a mighty big palace. I'm sure you'll also remember that in the Gospels, Jesus points to the buildings on the Temple Mount and tells his disciples, "Don't you see all these things? I assure you: Not one stone will be left here on another that will not be thrown down!"'

'Jesus's prediction about the Roman destruction of the temple in seventy C.E.?'

He shook his head.

She rolled her eyes. 'So what does the learned Amit Mizrachi have to say about it?'

'It could just as easily mean that Jesus was announcing the Essenes' plan for the Temple Mount's refurbishment – knock it down and rebuild according to God's original plan given to

Moses.' He paused to study the diagram again. 'Which leads one to ask: was Jesus one of the architects of the Third Temple?'

'All right, smart guy. So do you have any idea what he was planning to put in the empty room?' she added.

He shot her a confused glance.

'The Sanctuary? The Holy of Holies?' She was thinking back to the Temple Society's last exhibit. 'I doubt Jesus would have planned on leaving it empty, right?'

Amit's face went ghost white. 'That's right.' He checked his watch. 'There's a phone in the back office. Let me make a quick call to Enoch, see what else he's got for us.'

50.

Charlotte's numbed senses responded sluggishly as consciousness returned once more. Slowly her eyes opened, eyelids fluttering spasmodically against the intrusive overhead lighting.

Something was covering her mouth, straining her breathing. When she tried to touch her face, she found that her hands were still immobilized. Looking down, she saw a thick silver strap – *duct tape?* – digging so tightly against her wrists that her fingers felt nothing but pins and needles. Her forearms were pinned to the armrests of a metal chair. The tight pressure around her chest and shoulders was another thick wrapping of silver tape that kept her snug against the chair back. Testing her feet confirmed that each of her ankles had been bound to a leg of the chair. Her cracked lips barely moved against the tape wrapped tight over her mouth.

What the hell . . . ?

Her eyes darted back and forth. Definitely not a plane. This time she was in a cramped, windowless room. She was facing a metal door and it was shut tight.

No sign of Donovan.

The room's storage shelves, stacked with cleaning utensils, brought to mind Salvatore Conte's makeshift surveillance room in the basement of the Vatican Museums. Could these bastards have hurt Donovan . . . or done something worse? God, the idea of it was torturous. They'd already killed Evan.

What wack-job is behind all this? she wondered.

Wriggling her fingers, she tried to get some blood back to her milk-white hands.

Panic began to set in, making it even harder to breathe. Nothing good could come from being terrified. She had to keep her wits. *Calm down*, she repeated in a loop. *Breathe . . . use that yoga.*

She meditated deeply to ease the cramping that was quickly setting into her tight muscles. This would be the point in the movie, she mused, where the crafty heroine would produce a hidden blade, a nail clipper, or a rough-edged fingernail to cut the bindings. Nothing doing here. Wrong script, wrong heroine. Even her nails were nonexistent – snipped as short as short could be. Prissy nails had no place in the clinical confines of a laboratory. Now she wished she had the whole package – half-inch talons with perfect cuticles and a French manicure.

Helpless. Utterly helpless.

Just to spice things up a bit, the place was like a sauna too. Charlotte was drenched in sweat. Not that that was having any effect on the integrity of the damn duct tape. *What a great product testimonial this would make*, she thought. She could picture the thirty-second spot featuring her taped to this stupid chair. Rolls of the stuff would be flying off stores' shelves.

Now she turned her attention to the room, her eyes poring over its contents. That's when she realized something peculiar. On a shelf just over her right shoulder, there were dried food containers, stacked canned goods, and juice bottles. The awkward sight angle made the labels tough to read, but the ones she could make out had both English and Hebrew writing. And there was a common symbol on the packages that she could swear certified the goods as being Kosher. *First the Yiddish, now this?*

That's when a tiny red light blinking high up near the ceiling caught her eye. Craning her neck to the limit, she was able to glimpse the circular lens glaring down at her.

Not for the first time, someone was watching.

The nausea was threatening an encore. She needed food. Water.

Then came sounds from outside the door. Cocking her head sideways, Charlotte watched the lit crack beneath the door as a heavy shadow swept into view.

She heard the tinging sounds of a key ring.

Then there was the scratchy metal-on-metal sound of a key being pushed into the lock.

The doorknob slowly turned until the bolt disengaged with a *clunk*.

Last, the door swung open in three clumsy stages, revealing the person on the other side.

Charlotte was completely taken aback. It was a young Jewish man, plain looking, wearing a crisp white shirt, black trousers, black shoes. And he was confined to a wheelchair.

51.

Tempted to lash out at her invalid captor – not that she could have if she wanted to, thanks to the tenacity of her bindings – Charlotte merely watched in puzzlement as the frail young man rolled into the room. Clearly someone in such a condition couldn't possess the physical stamina to perpetrate an abduction. So how could *he* be involved in all of this?

The man's sallow complexion looked ghostly beneath the fluorescent bulbs. At first he appeared to be much older than she was. *Much* older. But upon closer examination, Charlotte thought that he actually appeared more boy than man.

'Are you all right?' he asked in a hushed tone. 'Nod if you are.'

All right? Is he kidding? Eyes tightening with frustration, Charlotte shook her head.

'I'm not supposed to talk to you,' he confessed in a whisper. His paranoid gaze went back to the door. 'I'll take the tape off your mouth if you promise not to scream.' Another glance at the door. 'They will hear you,' he confided.

Unsure what to make of the situation, Charlotte nodded. 'Okay.'

Working the hand rims, the boy maneuvered the wheelchair closer. Reaching out, he worked his spidery fingertips under the edges of the tape strip covering Charlotte's mouth.

Charlotte noticed the kid's front teeth gnawed incessantly at a callus on his lower lip. There were raw calluses on the fingers too – some almost bleeding. *Obviously some type of compulsion disorder.* The kid was a wreck.

'This might hurt,' he said apologetically. Digging his fingertips in deeper, he squeezed the tape and tugged it free.

Charlotte immediately drew some fresh air into her lungs and exhaled. Though her breath was one notch below toxic, she wasn't making any apologies. Her throat felt like a sandbox. With an unblinking stare steeped in resentment, she remained silent, waiting to see what the boy would say.

Slouching in the wheelchair, the boy dropped his eyes to his lap, where he wiped Charlotte's sweat onto his pants. He began neatly folding the tape. 'You're very pretty,' he muttered, glancing up.

Unlike most people, who were usually fascinated by Charlotte's emerald eyes, this guy was fixating on her long, shiny chestnut curls. *Give the kid a chance*, she told herself, fighting like hell to curb her tongue. 'Why am I here?'

The boy's timid eyes retreated to the tape folding. 'I'm not allowed to tell you that.'

'The man who was with me . . . Is he okay?' Adrenaline rushed into her. He'd *better* be okay.

Without looking up, he mulled the question for a five-count before responding. 'I don't know,' he replied.

'Is there someone else here with me?' she clarified. 'A man . . . a bald man?'

Looking confused, he shook his head.

Charlotte fought against despair. It was too early to assume the worst. Time to get down to business. 'You – those men. Are you terrorists?' she asked matter-of-factly.

The boy flashed her a surprised glance, then giggled.

'It's not funny,' Charlotte chastised him. 'Taking people hostage is *not* funny.'

Curling into himself, he raised a trembling finger to massage a twitch that flicked his eyelid. 'Sorry,' he said.

'Who did this? Who *are* you? Who are those men?'

Unwilling to respond, he shook his head.

'I have a right to know.'

More shaking.

'God, this is ridiculous,' Charlotte grumbled.

The kid's head snapped up, eyes wide. 'You can't say that,' he said in a hushed tone, eyelid pulsating. 'Do not take the Lord's name in vain.'

You've got *to be kidding me.* 'I don't recall the Lord endorsing kidnapping,' Charlotte curtly retorted. 'Why am I here?' she repeated succinctly.

He cowered and dropped his eyes back down to his hands. The tape was now wrapped into a tight square, his chewed fingernails picking at its frayed ends. Two reluctant words emanated from the boy's lips: 'The bones.'

A jolt shot through Charlotte. This was definitely the time to play stupid. 'What bones?'

His expression hardened as he confidently looked up. 'The Messiah's bones. You touched them. You know where they are. They need to be returned. You shouldn't have touched the bones,' he coldly added.

No answer.

The kid's head was shaking again. That damn head just kept

shaking. Her frustration was building fast. 'Listen, I don't know who you are, but you need to help me. This is all one big mistake. I don't know where the bones are.'

'Joshua!' a voice blasted from the doorway.

Startled, both Charlotte and the boy jumped at the same time.

An older woman of medium height and build with a stern face, wearing a wig and a black ankle-length dress, stormed into the room like a raging bull.

'What do you think you're doing?' the woman roared, grabbing the boy's wrist and squeezing so hard that her fingertips turned white.

'Owww . . . you're hurting me, Mother,' the boy whined.

'If your father ever heard what you just said . . .,' she gravely warned him.

Mother? Father? Charlotte couldn't believe what was happening. So this was some kind of family affair? *Really* creepy.

The woman's bitter stare swung to Charlotte. 'It's best for you not to say anything more.'

Sensing that the mother wasn't on board with whatever was happening – judging from her wavering tone, rapid breathing, and guilty eyes – Charlotte nodded and kept her mouth shut.

Relinquishing her crushing grip, the mother clasped the wheelchair's handles while the boy rubbed at the red marks she'd left behind. Pulling her son out of the room, she parked the wheelchair in the corridor. Then she came back in clenching and unclenching her hands, pacing around Charlotte's chair.

'I'll free your hands and feet,' she offered. 'Only if you realize that should you try to escape, they will kill you.' Her eyes motioned to the corridor.

'I understand,' Charlotte softly replied, now realizing the woman was equally terrified.

From a shelf situated behind Charlotte, the mother retrieved a pair of scissors and began cutting into the bindings. 'Listen to what I say. This is very serious, what is happening to you – to everyone. I'll bring you food, water. He is coming back shortly to speak with you.'

'Who?'

'My husband.'

52.

Thank heavens the woman cut away the bindings, Charlotte thought. Not that any great debt was owed to a woman who took part in an abduction. Luckily she'd kept her promise to bring food and water, though the food was predominantly matzo and some mushy, bland cheese that would no doubt bring her bowels to a screeching halt. That wasn't a bad thing, she thought, considering the 'bathroom' was a metal bucket in a corner, well within the surveillance camera's range.

The sound of a key turning in the knob broke the room's dead silence. Charlotte sat up as the door eased open.

A morose Orthodox Jewish man came into the room, looking like he'd walked straight out of Manhattan's Diamond District, where she and Evan had ventured after a pharmaceutical convention and dared to window-shop for an engagement ring only two months ago.

'Dr. Charlotte Hennesey,' the rabbi said accusatorily, claiming a second folding chair beside hers.

The way he sat immediately annoyed Charlotte: his shoulders were pulled back and his chin was tipped up as if he'd just reclaimed his throne.

Her lack of response brought a smirk to his face. 'Let me make this very easy. Your coercion with the Vatican has caused me great difficulty. What they stole belongs to me and to this nation—'

'What nation?'

'Israel, of course.'

'Israel?' This rendered her mute for a three-count. 'I don't know what—'

But he held up a hand to silence her, shaking his head. 'We recovered your laptop. I've seen everything. So let's not waste time playing games. You've witnessed many things, Dr. Hennesey. Many marvelous things. Your PowerPoint presentation was most impressive. But how little you know, child. Those were no ordinary bones you so unceremoniously unpacked from that ossuary. Then again, you know that better than anyone, don't you? I must admit that even *I* was surprised to learn about the physical secrets Yeshua possessed. You, a *geneticist*, must have been astounded.'

To this she didn't respond. The answer would be obvious.

Charlotte pulled her arms tight across her chest. Could this lunatic be after the DNA codes, the formula for the viral serum? No doubt, its commercial potential was incalculable. And in the hands of an unscrupulous opportunist . . .

If she could just figure out what was charging this guy's batteries.

Then the Hasid's expression registered something very odd: admiration? His guarded posture – arms drawn protectively over the chest, shoulders rounded, hands overlapping in a tight clasp – showed vulnerability.

'You've acquired the gift. That's a critical omission on your part.'

'Gift?'

'Come now, Dr. Hennesey. I *am* smarter than that. So I ask you this: how is it a woman who was in contact with the bones of the Messiah just so happens to have acquired His most precious gift?'

'I'm still not following.'

'"Hennesey" is an Irish name. Safe to assume you're a Catholic, yes?'

'I was raised Catholic, although I haven't been to church in quite some time.' Over a decade ago, cancer had stolen her mother away. It was tough to find solace in scripture after seeing someone die so mercilessly.

'But you believe in Jesus, don't you? The stories . . . the miracles?' She stared at him for a good five seconds. 'The sacred writings tell us that by simply laying his hands on the sick, he could make their ailments disappear. The sacred writings tell us that, like you, he sought truth. He too *wanted* to believe. That was how he was given the gift. The question is, how did it find its way to you?'

Could he possibly know about the serum, how it cured her? Even if he'd seen the genetic data, how would he have known what he was looking at? 'Why don't you tell me what the "gift" is, then perhaps I can tell you if I've got it.'

Grinning, the rabbi combed his beard with his fingers. 'You strike me as a very complicated woman. Intelligent. Brave. Strong. I would venture to guess that you're wondering if science could ever explain miracles. Am I right?'

'You don't need to be a scientist to be a cynic.'

He smiled tightly. 'I'd like for you to explain something to me. See if your science may provide some insight.'

'I'll see what I can do.'

'Devora!' he called loudly. He waited for a response.

Seconds later, quick footsteps sounded in the corridor and the rabbi's wife popped her head into the room.

'Yes,' she quietly replied, eyes cast to the floor.

'Bring Joshua to me.'

'I'm not so sure he's ready—'

'Don't question me!' he snapped.

'As you wish.' She immediately acquiesced.

'Most women are not like you, Charlotte.'

She felt her stomach turn.

It didn't take long before Devora reappeared in the doorway. Charlotte was confused when she didn't see her guiding the son's wheelchair into the room. In fact, she hadn't even heard the wheelchair's squeaky rubber tires.

The mystery behind the son's noiseless approach was quickly revealed when the terrified boy walked into the room.

53.

THE TEMPLE MOUNT

The Dome of the Rock was empty as Ghalib – the Waqf's Keeper – silently crept barefoot along the ornate blood-red carpeting lining the octagonal inner ambulatory. Beneath the *qubba*, or dome, the Sakhrah – the rock – glowed in ocher light, looking like the stark terrain of a distant moon.

Throughout the shrine, ladders had been erected in and around the cupola, and at key positions along the outer ambulatory. Half a dozen men busily went up and down them, running wire, installing small brackets and hardware.

Ghalib greeted each of them as he strolled by to inspect their progress.

Minutes later, after completing his circle, he paused along the railing and stared at the unique impression on the rock's surface said to be the hoof mark left behind by the blessed steed, Buraq, as it leapt from the earth to deliver the great Prophet to the heavens.

Ghalib grinned, knowing that soon the angel Israfel – 'the Caller' – would be sent to this very spot to sound the trumpet that would commence the Last Judgment – al-Qiyamah. Then the Merciful One would gather all humanity in congregation and place before every man, woman, and child the book of judgment, detailing a lifetime of deeds that would determine each soul's fate. Upon the Scales of Justice those deeds would then be weighed to foretell the outcome of each soul's perilous walk along the razor-thin bridge, as-Siraat, across the blazing bowels of hell to the glorious gates of Paradise.

For those whose sins burdened the Scales of Justice, their path across as-Siraat would lead to a fateful end. Into the writhing, fiery pit – Jahannam – they would surely plunge. There the black hearts of sinners who shunned Allah would be met by eternal fire and agony beyond comprehension: searing heat that broils flesh, heavy chains whose weight never subsides, putrid drink that never quenches thirst, and rancid, thorny plants that would never sate hunger.

Their torment will be perpetual.

For the righteous, however, the Last Judgment would be a glorious moment when the walk along as-Siraat would deliver them to a place of eternal spiritual redemption: the garden paradise, Jannah. There loved ones would reunite in perpetual peace and delight among the angels. Rivers would flow with milk and honey; there'd be goblets of gold, countless pleasures of the flesh, and above all, the countenance of Allah Himself. And those receiving the greatest reward in Paradise would ascend to its highest level – the Gardens of Bliss – to be nearest to Allah.

The soul of the martyr is the most loved by Him.

'*Taqwa*,' he reverently whispered. 'Fear God.'

Making his way to the shrine's south side, the Keeper passed beneath a freestanding marble archway and descended the wide marble steps that accessed the natural subterranean hollow beneath the rock called the Well of Souls.

He stepped down onto the ornate Persian carpet covering its flat excavated floor, and the damp air in the spacious cave nipped his bones. A bright floodlight bit the shadows off the chamber's rocky outcroppings, which curved gently upward from floor to ceiling.

On the far side of the cave, two Arab men worked diligently with hammer and chisel, chipping away stone to install mounting brackets and wiring.

'So what do you think?' he asked the foreman in Arabic. 'Will it work?'

The bearded man nodded. 'Yes. I'll make sure of it.'

'Excellent.' He turned his attention to the others. 'Brothers, please stop for a moment. Be still.'

The workers ceased activity. Five seconds later, the cave plunged into a perfect silence.

Ghalib closed his eyes, paused his breathing, and listened intently. Beneath the cave, the muffled sounds of digging were unmistakable – chipping, scratching – more prevalent now than yesterday. Ghalib could even sense something new: subtle vibrations tickling his bare feet.

Opening his eyes, he smiled. 'Continue,' he told the men. 'And may His peace be upon you all.'

The Keeper made his way back to the steps and disappeared up the passage.

54.

At the Israel Museum, Jules struggled to keep stride with Amit as he climbed the steps leading up from the Shrine of the Book gallery. When they angled back across the open courtyard, Amit glanced at the shrine's white dome, then over to the black monolith rising high opposite it. Each symbolized a combatant in the final battle between good and evil detailed in the Dead Sea Scrolls – the spark that would trigger the Messianic Age. The Sons of Light versus the Sons of Darkness.

'So what did Enoch find out?' Jules asked. This time around, when Amit had placed a call to Enoch in the exhibit hall's administrative office, he'd mostly listened. So she had no clue what new information Enoch had conveyed. But the alarmed look that had come over Amit was deeply unsettling.

'Early this morning, the rabbi's jet took him to a private airport north of Cairo – Inshas. He was back in Tel Aviv by the afternoon.'

'Inshas?' Jules suddenly slapped Amit's arm. 'That's right near old Heliopolis!'

'Exactly. The secret of the hieroglyph revealed.'

261

'What was he doing there?'

'Enoch didn't know for sure, only that when he arrived at Tel Aviv, he unloaded a rather large shipping container.'

'Really? What was in it?' She was practically jogging alongside him. 'God, slow down, will you?' She tugged at his arm.

'Sorry,' he said, bringing his pace down a notch. 'Enoch wasn't able to find out. Problem is, these diplomats can pretty much come and go as they please,' Amit told her. 'Even the Mossad can't poke around too much with the big guys.' He recalled Enoch's warning: *Be careful with this guy, He's a heavy hitter.* 'If you ask me, however, I'd say it's something that would make a nice addition to the Third Temple. Remember in the transcription . . . all of Jesus's references to the "Testimony"?'

'Yes.'

On the main walkway, they doubled back to the museum's main entrance.

'The Testimony refers to the entirety of the laws God gave to Moses at Sinai.'

'The Ten Commandments?'

'That's the condensed version, the "Testimony for Dummies." In Leviticus, God speaks to Moses in the first person and actually provides *six hundred and thirteen* directives, or mitzvoth, that were the road map for the Israelites' daily living – diet, dress, death, health, marriage, divorce, sexuality, criminal justice, and so forth. It was all part of the covenant that needed to be abided by so that the Israelites could be delivered to the Promised Land.'

'And what does that have to do with the temple?'

'Everything, since two hundred and two of the directives spoke to temple worship. But it gets much deeper than that. You see, the Testimony was transcribed onto stone tablets – including the text paraphrased into the Ten Commandments. And God told Moses to build a vessel to hold them.'

'The Ark of the Covenant?' she said, half smiling.

'Right. And that was what the entire temple model was built upon. So to answer your question, at the very center of the Temple City would reside the Ark.'

Amit opened the door of the visitors' center and ushered Jules through.

'Oh, come on now,' she scoffed. 'You're not really suggesting that Cohen just went to Egypt to reclaim the lost ark?' During her last excavation in Egypt, she'd heard plenty of wild legends from the locals in Tanis about Menelik – the love child of King Solomon and Sheba – secretly bringing the relic to their hometown. They'd even joked with her that she might uncover it beneath the sands outlying the city. She'd quickly reminded them that Indiana Jones had already beaten her to it.

Raising his eyebrows, Amit clammed up as they ducked inside.

They stopped to bid David farewell.

'By the way,' David began to explain, 'some fellow called here looking for you—'

Then, without warning, one of the clear doors facing the parking lot let out a resounding *crack* that made Amit spin round. A tiny hole had punched through it and fractured the glass. Instantly, he dropped, yelling, 'Get down!' as a second round zipped past him and struck David in the chest with a *thwump*.

The old man gasped and spun back off his chair, crashing onto the tiles behind the bag scanner.

At the same time, Amit tried to grab Jules, but his hands got nothing but air. She was already falling backward, tumbling onto the floor, hands clutching her side. Blood was seeping through her fingers.

'Jules!' Staying low, Amit immediately went and pulled her behind the bag scanner just as another round pinged off the tile, then ricocheted off the bulky machine's thick metal housing. Peeking out, he could see the white arm cast swinging through the darkness, closing in fast.

David was splayed beside him, blood seeping along the tile grout lines beneath his right armpit. It was spilling out of his chest and over the handle of his holstered Beretta.

Outside, taxi drivers scrambled for cover as the gunman sprinted toward the front entrance.

Peering inside the foyer, the assassin could make out the guard's outstretched arm sticking out from behind the clunky bag scanner. There was a thick swath of blood smeared along the tiles where the woman had fallen. The Israeli archaeologist wasn't in sight but was certainly pinned down behind the hulking machine.

He deliberated for a moment.

Wait for the target to make a move? Not an option; too much time for the police to respond. The archaeologist had been moving quickly, cleverly shifting from place to place and covering his tracks very effectively. This guy was no amateur.

The assassin had already been sidetracked for a good hour by the Land Rover abandoned in the bus station's parking garage. Then he was finally provided with tracking coordinates for the archaeologist's mobile phone. Though the phone had remained powered off, the latest satellite tracing had been able to detect a chip in its battery. But that had required some administrative runarounds. So at this point, prolonging the chase wasn't an option. He quickly determined that this might be his last opportunity to finish the job.

Keeping his eyes peeled on the foyer, he pushed on the door, but it didn't budge. He quickly glimpsed the sticker above the thick handle that said PULL. He reached for the handle with his broken arm, but the stubs of his fingers poking out beyond the plaster cast weren't able to grip it.

Cursing, he pinched the gun with three fingers of his left hand and hooked the pinky and ring finger around the handle.

Much to his regret, that's when the archaeologist sprang up over the scanner, wielding a pistol gripped firmly with both hands.

The shot was loud, the glass exploding out into his face even louder.

Shards ripped into his eyes, but something else had pierced much deeper into the side of his neck. He felt metal nick bone as the round exploded beneath his right ear. And he knew in an instant that it had cut through his spinal cord in the process, because the entire right side of his body shut off immediately – paralyzed. His right leg went out from under him, and he toppled sideways.

Dropping his gun, he clamped his left hand over the spray of blood spurting onto the cement. The archaeologist was standing over him seconds later, pointing the gun in his face, yelling questions that his ears could not register.

The blood gurgled into his throat, choking him. Then his mission came to a most unsuccessful end.

55.

'You all right?' one of the livery guys yelled over, still shielding himself behind his limo door.

'I'm okay,' Amit said. 'But I need an ambulance inside.'

'I'm on it,' the guy said, and pulled his phone from his belt with the speed of a gunslinger.

Then something strange happened.

Another phone came to life, but the ringtone certainly wasn't Amit's. It was coming from the assassin's pocket. Amit crouched over the body. As he pulled out the phone, the guy's key ring came out along with it.

Without thinking, Amit hit the receive button. He answered abruptly in Hebrew, as he guessed the assassin would. 'Yes?'

'We need you back at the Rockefeller immediately.'

Then the connection clicked off.

The Rockefeller? Amit stuffed the security guard's Beretta into his belt and pocketed the phone and keys.

Racing back inside, he knelt by Jules.

'Crap,' she grumbled. 'This was my favorite T-shirt. I look great in this T-shirt.' She laughed nervously, half in shock, half in amazement. Strangely, there wasn't much pain. 'Did you get him?'

'He's dead,' Amit said with little emotion.

'Good shooting, cowboy.'

Amit pulled away her hand and began to lift her shirt.

'Easy . . .,' she said in a shaky voice, hands trembling fiercely.

'Now I'm definitely going to get a look at what you're hiding under here,' he said to comfort her. He raised the sodden shirt up below her left breast. Luckily, the bullet had only grazed her abdomen, just below the ribs. The blood was already thickening. 'You're going to be okay. I've got an ambulance coming for you.' Torn, he looked over his shoulder. 'I hate to do this, but I've gotta—'

'I'm fine,' she told him. 'Just . . . kiss me before you go.'

He looked at her quizzically. Despite her fear, there was desire in her lucid eyes. He gently cradled her chin and brought his lips to hers. Not his best work, he knew, but as passionate as the situation permitted.

The moment he pulled away, he knew things had irreversibly changed between them. And her genuine smile made something melt inside him.

'Now go get them,' she said.

56.

Though Joshua quickly reached out for his mother's arm to steady his wobbling legs – the musculature had no doubt atrophied during the months he'd been confined to the wheelchair – the result was nonetheless overwhelming. Charlotte gasped.

'A miracle, would you not agree?' the rabbi quickly cut in.

Such a quick turnaround was hard to attribute to anything else, she thought. 'Is this some kind of trick?' Charlotte was so caught up in the transformation that she'd just now noticed that the boy's right hand was wrapped all around in bandages. The nail biting wasn't *that* bad. So what had happened to the kid's hand?

'You're familiar with ALS, Dr. Hennesey?'

'Of course,' she said.

Amyotrophic lateral sclerosis, or Lou Gehrig's disease, was an aggressive neurological disorder that attacked the motor neurons in the brain and spinal cord, which regulated voluntary muscle movement. The incurable wasting disease gradually affected mobility, speech, chewing and swallowing, and breathing. Its later stages brought on severe pain. Though ALS more often struck the middle-aged, it wasn't uncommon for a young person to fall victim to it.

'Then you're aware that curing ALS is no *trick*,' he said. 'Joshua's symptoms began only two years ago,' he explained without emotion. 'He would fall often. At first, we thought he was just clumsy. Then he began dropping things. Simple things, like cups, forks, pencils. Within no time, his legs weren't functioning at all. The neurologist spotted the symptoms immediately and the tests began. So many tests.'

Charlotte's sad eyes went over to the boy. *Poor kid.* But given the circumstances, she needed for him to be more specific before she'd buy into this story. 'Did his doctors try drugs?'

'Baclofen, diazepam, gabapentin, to name a few,' he swiftly replied. 'Not to mention a regular cycle of antidepressants.'

So far, he was getting it right. She had seen it firsthand when she'd been treated for cancer. Parents of chronically ill children, particularly those with a terminal prognosis, gained clinical proficiency along their taxing journey – a defense mechanism against the utter helplessness that was the alternative. The drugs he'd named were prescribed for muscle spasms and cramping. The antidepressants were no surprise. Like bone cancer, ALS was a diagnosis that amounted to little more than a death sentence. For a young man, it must have been psychologically overwhelming, hence the compulsive nail biting. And like bone cancer, ALS had no cure – just therapeutic damage control.

Genetic chaos. Bad coding. Corrupted chromosomes. Evan had *injected* the serum into her bloodstream. She had no contact with the kid, except for . . .

'When I touched you, I felt something in my fingers,' Joshua said. 'Tingling. Not the bad kind I normally feel, though. When I left you, it began to spread . . . down to my legs and feet.'

Touched me? She shook her head in disbelief. Then Charlotte remembered the cracked skin on Joshua's fingertips peeling the tape away from her mouth. His *wet* fingers. The sweat from Charlotte's cheeks. An exchange of fluids? 'It can't be that simple,' she said. 'You can't just touch . . .' Her words trailed off.

But what the kid just explained had jolted a memory Charlotte would never forget . . .

'Are you ready?' Evan asked, holding her hand in his left hand. In his right hand, a plastic syringe was pinched between his fingers, thumb resting over the plunger. He'd already tapped the air bubbles out of the clear serum that filled it.

Charlotte peered out the suite's open window and glimpsed a Lufthansa 747 lifting off the Fiumicino airport's runway, jetting directly heavenward to the clouds on broad wings. Tears trickled down her cheeks. 'I think so,' she said in a choked voice.

Releasing her hand, Evan used his index finger to massage a throbbing vein running down her left forearm.

'I thought you loathed venipuncture,' she said. He'd said it was one reason he didn't want to become a surgeon: blood bothered him.

'I make exceptions,' he said with a comforting smile.

'I can't believe I'm doing this.'

'It's not too late to say no,' he reminded her. 'Just say the word.'

'We've already talked this thing to death,' she calmly replied. 'What choice do I have? Just get on with it,' she said with a small grin.

'Okay.'

He was trying his best to keep his hands from trembling.

'Just a quick sting.'

Charlotte directed her attention back out to the planes. The doubts came fast and hard as she sat there wondering if Evan's concoction could possibly have any effect on her myeloma. People once thought flying was impossible, she reminded herself. Yet just outside that window, a huge metal machine had been climbing up into the sky. *Nothing's impossible*, she told herself.

After drawing a deep breath, Evan steadied his hand and plunged the needle's tip into the vein. She glanced down as he pulled back the plunger a fraction and some blood swirled up into the serum. Surprisingly, he'd gotten it in on the first try. Gently, he depressed the plunger until the entire 4-cc dose was emptied from the syringe. Withdrawing the needle, he held a thumb over the injection point, set the syringe down on the bed, and loosened the rubber tourniquet strapped tightly below her elbow.

The sensation was instantaneous. 'Ooh,' she said, grabbing at her arm.

'What? What is it?'

'Nothing,' she said, letting out a breath. The poor guy was already on edge and she could tell that she'd scared him. 'It just feels . . . strange.'

'What feels strange?' he asked, struggling to hide his concern.

'My arm. It's . . .' She had to pause to place it. 'It's tingling.'

The rabbi jumped back in, saying, 'Would you not agree that ALS is a terminal disease where the chance of spontaneous recovery is *zero*?'

Snapping back into the moment, Charlotte tried to understand how even a spontaneous recovery could explain how Joshua was walking only hours later. ALS irreversibly destroyed nerve cells, and plenty of diagnostic tests could prove it.

This viral DNA is wildly contagious.

'I think what's happened here is scientifically *inexplicable*,' the rabbi added. 'So perhaps you might just admit that a miracle has taken place. A miracle for which *you* are responsible.'

Mute, Charlotte didn't know how to respond. She stared blankly at the perfectly smooth skin on her own wrists where the raw marks from the duct tape his wife cut away had disappeared in a matter of seconds. *Almost spontaneously.*

'*That*, Dr. Hennesey, is the gift,' the rabbi proudly stated.

As Grandfather had taught, since Moses, only Jesus had acquired the *most* sacred genes. Perhaps the Messiah's skeleton was indeed with the Vatican. But Cohen knew that what made the physical remains so special wasn't the bones themselves; it was the incredible gift stored inside them. And now it had been transferred to the geneticist – the Chosen One. How the prophecies did surprise!

'I want you to come with me. There is something you must see.'

57.

Amit killed the headlights on the assassin's Fiat, with its bullet-riddled right-front wheel well above the recently installed spare tire, and rolled to a gentle stop outside the Rockefeller Museum. The exhibit hall's interior was completely dark, as were all the windows in the adjoining wings. But in the circular tower of the administrative building that was home to the Israel Antiquities Authority, a thin outline of light shone around each of the blinds closed tight in the top-floor room.

Easing the car door shut, Amit crept around the building, the Beretta at the ready.

He spotted a flatbed truck loaded with two full pallets of pre-cision-quarried limestone parked near the service entrance. The stone looked similar enough to the Rockefeller building's exterior. Perhaps a renovation was under way?

His eyes kept scouting the area as he moved out from the cover of the wall.

No watchmen.

This isn't Gaza, he kept reminding himself; there wouldn't be a highly visible security detail protecting a hot zone. Cohen had included Mossad contract killers in his entourage. Just because one now lay dead on the doormat of the Israel Museum, he wasn't about to let his guard down or get haughty about his marksmanship. There was a reason these killers were very good at what they did – lots of practice. And they didn't do it by show-ing themselves. They were masters of stealth.

Parked in front of the flatbed was what Amit had expected: a white delivery van.

Most likely, the museum door closest to it was open.

But that didn't stop Amit from trying a couple other doors first. Locked, of course.

It was going to be tough making a subtle entrance.

58.

The two burly guards who'd manhandled Charlotte out of the basement had taken up posts at the wide doors leading out of the octagonal conference room. The rabbi had had them position her directly in front of something plunked down on the glossy tabletop commanding the room's center. The object was covered by a silky blue veil with gold embroidery depicting two winged creatures. *Angels, maybe?* she guessed. Though the form beneath it was largely rectangular, the veil was draped clumsily over two peaks on its top.

Pinched between Rabbi Aaron Cohen's fingers was a vial of blood, and he rocked it back and forth, watching how the thick crimson swished side to side. 'You're quite familiar with the sophisticated tests used to study blood?'

Another rhetorical question, so Charlotte chose silence. No use encouraging him.

'While you were sleeping, I took the liberty of taking this from you,' he said, holding up the vial.

Was nothing sacred with this guy? 'You've taken a lot more than that from me,' she said, seething.

He knew precisely what she meant. 'Sacrifice, Dr. Hennesey. It must be made. Shortly, you'll have a much better understanding of that. You'll realize that no death would be too great a price for what you are to witness.

'Since the beginning of human history, blood has been the symbol of life and sacrifice. It is the tie that binds us to our ancestors.' His expression hardened. 'Blood also separates us.'

Charlotte felt like she'd been picked from an audience to assist in performing a bizarre magic trick. She couldn't help but think the rabbi would jam her into the box and saw her in half. Maybe then he'd get what he was really after.

'Let me show you what I mean,' he said. He summoned one of the men to the table. Then he pulled up a corner of the blue shroud so that the top corner of the box was revealed.

Charlotte was amazed to see that the surface of what lay beneath glinted wildly in the light. Gold? And its decorative edging looked an awful lot like the ossuary she'd studied at the Vatican. What most perplexed her was the fact that the small section of the box's exposed face was covered in neat columns of ideograms. The top corner had a unique edging to it that suggested a lid or removable panel.

'Give me your hand,' the rabbi told his drone.

The man gave it no thought, offering his left hand palm up.

The rabbi took a small blade off the table and deeply incised the flesh along the base of the man's pinky.

From there, the man didn't need instruction. Curling the hand into a tight fist, he held it over the box and squeezed hard. The blood swelled from the slit, then rained down onto the box.

The instant the blood hit the gold sheathing, bright sparks crackled it into tiny droplets, then completely burned it away to nothing – all in under a second.

Charlotte didn't know what to make of it. The effect was like that of water dripped onto a hot frying pan, but more potent. Though this could have come across like a rudimentary science project in electrical conductivity, it didn't. She was engrossed.

The rabbi had watched her reaction, her incredulity, very closely. 'Now watch, please,' he demanded as he uncapped the vial.

Holding the vial over the same spot where the man's blood had completely disintegrated, he slowly tipped it so that Charlotte's blood spun out in a thin string. When it connected with the gold lid, nothing happened. No sparks came.

The rabbi smiled victoriously. 'Blood binds us, blood separates us. Purity and impurity.'

'What's the point?'

'You see, Dr. Hennesey,' the rabbi said, his tone suddenly more reverential, 'the most pure blood holds God's covenant given to Moses at Sinai. The blood of the Messiahs is the most pure . . . the most *sacred*. This box hasn't been opened in two thousand years. Jesus was the last to touch it – to be given the Spirit. But the prophecies have foretold that a Chosen One would come after Him. He sacrificed Himself on Golgotha so that his bones – His sacred blood – would be passed on to the next Messiah at the appointed time.'

Now Charlotte had to fight the urge to smirk. This was crazy talk.

'If you don't believe me,' he said, 'put your hand on the box.'

'Put *your* hand on the box,' she retorted.

He shook his head. 'You still don't understand.' Cohen signaled to the men and they grabbed her to bring her closer.

'Hey!' she protested, shaking her arms free. 'No need to get rough. I'll touch it.'

The rabbi motioned for them to back away.

'Fine,' Charlotte said. 'I'll play your game.' Stepping up to the table, she couldn't help but admire the relic's craftsmanship. The scientist in her found herself peeking around its sides for hidden wires that might have activated the light show she'd witnessed. Yet something else stirred in her when she found nothing.

Stretching out her hand, she could see the men backing away on the periphery of her vision. The rabbi himself seemed to be holding his breath.

Time for the big show, she thought. Very slowly Charlotte lowered her left hand over the golden lid.

59.

When Amit finally reached the rear service door, he'd waited a full two minutes behind the van, deliberating on how to proceed. In his head, various scenarios were playing out, and every one of them featured lethal Mossad contractors exiting the building and engaging him in a blazing gun battle. That had him thinking of what it would feel like to be shot a few times without the luxury of a bulletproof vest. Couldn't be pleasant, and he wasn't curious enough to want to give it a try.

Nevertheless, what Rabbi Cohen had gone to such great lengths to protect was most likely sitting in the IAA's conference room. No doubt it was Amit's discovery at Qumran that was the cause for Cohen's hasty trip to Egypt. And Amit was willing to wager his genitalia that the very same relic that had once resided within the heart of Solomon's temple was now inside this building.

But it was the thought of the bullet that killed poor David, and the second one that almost erased the first genuine connection he'd had with a woman since God knew when, that finally got him moving closer.

Yet after all that consideration, when the last ever-so-carefully-placed steps brought him right up to the door in perfect silence – the gun hand ready to respond, the right hand grasping the doorknob and preparing for a three-stage disengagement of the door latch – the door was locked.

Locked?

'Shit,' he spat with little regard for silence.

He did his best to listen for any activity coming from inside, but the thick door wasn't exactly the off-the-shelf variety. There could be someone standing right behind it yapping away and he might not hear it.

Setting the gun in the waistband of his pants at the small of his back, he dipped his fingers into his inside vest pocket to retrieve his Gaza lock-buster set. The flat tension wrench slid into the keyhole with barely a whisper, and he turned it clockwise. The hook-ended fisher slid in beside it. Ten seconds of hunting and twisting popped the lock.

Still got it.

Smoothly withdrawing the tools and returning them to his pocket, he took up the gun and reached for the knob. His eyes had a momentary standoff with the circular casing of a second lockset – the dead bolt above the knob. If he had to open that one too, things could get a lot noisier.

Biting his lip, he started the steady three-step turn. 'Come on' – a little resistance – 'give it up' – a little more – 'you nasty—'

Tickunk.

Exhale.

Pause. Regroup.

The next motion was all or nothing.

Another breath and he went for the pull.

Staying low, Amit cranked the door open and trained the gun

straight out, fully prepared to take a bullet. But the corridor beyond was dark and empty. And thankfully, no after-hours alarm seemed to have tripped. Cohen had most likely turned it off when he'd entered the building. The guy seemed to have the password to all of Israel – and apparently some obscure precincts of Egypt too.

Amit stepped inside. He slipped off his obnoxiously squeaky rubber-soled shoes and carried them in his right hand as he penetrated deeper into the building.

60.

The box's golden lid felt warm and tingly under Charlotte's fingers – similar to the sensation she recalled from Evan's injection, which had shot the sacred DNA into her bloodstream. There certainly was an energy stored up inside this vessel, she thought – though probably not one that could be measured in volts.

She actually heard a couple of the men gasp. They'd certainly been harboring some doubts that she was the Chosen One, because they seemed fully prepared to be dragging a flame-broiled carcass out of the room.

'Ah!' Cohen joyously blurted, bringing his hands together with a clap. 'See! Do you all see this? You are witnessing the fulfillment of a prophecy!' he said to the assemblage.

He kept on with it, but Charlotte had tuned him out, because there was something very strange happening over the veil's sheer surface that the others weren't picking up on. Something seemed to billow – a distortion that was invisible yet dynamic in its shifting. It could easily have been dismissed as a quick bout of blurred vision. But the interference was contained in only one spot – and when she tested it by shifting her eyes slightly sideways, it remained stationary. Frightened, she immediately withdrew her hand.

It went away.

What the hell was that?

'Don't be afraid, Ms. Hennesey,' the rabbi said soothingly, stepping up to her and placing a hand on her shoulder.

She knew he wasn't referring to what she'd seen – or thought she'd seen. It was her recoiling hand that had drawn his attention.

'What you feel is the Holy Spirit,' he explained. 'Just as Jesus did when he laid his hand upon that very spot and it entered into Him – just as it entered into Moses atop Mount Sinai. The sacred blood is a gift,' he repeated. 'A gateway into the one light that rules over all creation.'

'Then take the blood from your son,' she fumed. 'If you say I healed him by using this power, then it must have transferred to him, right? Or just let me heal whatever ails you, then you can go and do whatever you want with the box, the blood . . .'

Shaking his head, he flatly stated, 'It doesn't work like that, Dr. Hennesey. If it were that easy, I wouldn't need you.'

She noticed the rabbi's eyes shift away as he said this.

'I'm not following you,' she said.

'You were chosen. Why, I don't know. But question not the Lord's plan.'

More eye shifting suggested that the rabbi was holding back. 'You tried it already, didn't you?'

The rabbi's jaw clenched tight and his eyes burned with fury.

That's when the truth hit her. 'Your son's hand,' she said accusatorily. 'When you saw that he was walking, you brought him directly here, didn't you? You had him touch the—'

Without warning, the rabbi's hand flew through the air to connect firmly with Charlotte's cheek.

'Silence!' he yelled.

What had happened to Joshua was a horrible thing. The smell of burning flesh still lingered in Cohen's nostrils. He'd pulled the terrified boy away from the Ark almost instantly, yet the damage had already been done. A scream like no other had come from Joshua's lips and he'd covered the boy's mouth with his hand to suppress it. Joshua's fingers had been broiled, curled into a tight claw. Yet while the rabbi sat there cradling him, he could actually see the flesh regenerating ever so slowly. By the time he'd composed himself and brought Joshua downstairs for presentation to the geneticist, the boy's pain had already subsided; the hand was still on the mend. Gazing into his son's eyes, he'd known immediately that another wound – a much deeper, irreparable wound – had been inflicted. The rabbi himself suffered as well as the extreme disappointment of a broken son – a broken legacy – returned. He'd asked Devora to cover the hand so that it wouldn't detract from the message he needed to relay to Charlotte.

'After patiently waiting for centuries,' he replied, 'nothing falls to chance. Unnecessary risk is unacceptable.'

Charlotte held a hand against the hot fire rushing into her cheek. She noticed that during this whole exchange, the rabbi's wife had been standing in the shadowed corridor, listening. The rabbi himself, however, had not picked up on this. 'And injuring your own flesh and blood is a necessary and acceptable risk?' she added. 'You couldn't have used yourself as the guinea pig?'

He stepped up so close that his nose practically touched hers, ready to strike again. His eyes were wild.

'You're no savior,' she raged on. 'You're a coward – a coward who sends assassins to kill the innocent. A coward who is willing to sacrifice his son to save his own skin. How do you think God feels about that?'

'Abraham was ready to sacrifice his son. Even God sacrificed His own.' He drew a cleansing breath and withdrew. 'Enough of this,' he said, his voice eerily calm. 'The time has come.'

'*What* time?' She knew ancient Jews were hugely amenable to making sacrificial offerings. Plenty of animals carved up on an altar came to mind, but she was sifting her memories for more prolific examples. Another quick glance at the doorway showed that the rabbi's wife had already staged her retreat.

Cohen ignored her question and directed his attention to his entourage. Pointing to the relic, he said, 'Place it back in the crate and load the truck. You know what to do with her. We'll leave immediately.'

The men came at her quickly, overpowering her, binding her hands behind her back, then gagging her mouth.

61.

In the fire stairwell Amit set down his shoes and peeked out through the fire door's small glass window. The red glow of the exit sign hanging above the door's other side gave him about two meters of muddled visibility through the corridor extending left and right. But he heard the commotion before he saw what caused it.

First came a crate set on a dolly that a man was wheeling toward the elevator adjacent to the fire door. Another five armed men trailed closely behind, and between them was a very pretty woman bound and gagged. For Amit, the sight of her raised a whole new set of questions.

Finally came the morose master of ceremonies wearing all black and bringing up the rear.

Definitely not a favorable scenario for playing hero. But the rabbi *was* at the back of the line, and if Amit could somehow take him by surprise . . .

The compulsion to use the element of surprise was short-lived as he tried to imagine what Jules would say. Probably something along the lines of 'Settle down, cowboy.'

The elevator doors opened and the bright light from its interior spilled into the dark hallway. Amit shrank back against the wall and listened as they all crammed into the elevator alongside the dolly. Once he heard the doors clatter shut and the gears engage high up in the shaft, he waited a few more seconds near the tiny window. Then he swung open the door, staying low and thrusting the gun forward. He was greeted once more by silence.

At the end of the dark corridor, however, he could see light coming from the conference room – the last door on the left. Instinct told him to check the room and see if anything had been left behind.

Easing the fire door closed, he slipped quietly down the hall in his socked feet. His two outstretched hands were wrapped around the Beretta, his left index finger hooked firmly around its cold trigger.

As he neared the folded-back doors, he slowed to a shuffle and took cover behind the closest one. He peeked through the thin gap separating the doorjamb. That's when he spotted two people moving about inside, tidying up the room's center. He noticed both of them immediately. The woman was Cohen's wife, the Temple Society's not-so-pleasant receptionist. Amit second-guessed his recognition of the boy's face when he saw that he was actually up and about, not stuck in a wheelchair. *Joshua? What the hell?*

Now a new opportunity presented itself. If he tried to simply follow the rabbi and his posse, there was a very good chance he'd get only so far. Amit could risk losing them altogether and not be able to pick up the trail until it was too late. But if he could somehow get advance information on what Cohen's plan entailed . . .

Maneuvering around the door, Amit inspected the room more

thoroughly to make sure it was only the two of them. Next, he stormed in with the gun trained on the rabbi's son.

'Don't scream or I'll put a bullet in your head,' he said in a calm voice.

62.

'Hello, Mrs. Cohen,' Amit said wryly. 'A pleasure to see you again.' He held the gun straight out, trained on Joshua's head. The wife's arms dropped limply to her sides, the right hand still clutching the cloth she'd been using to buff the crate's grimy streaks off the tabletop. 'I see that your husband returned safely from Egypt.'

The woman remained silent, well composed. Her eyes, however, looked weary, lifeless.

'Seems he didn't come back empty handed,' Amit said. 'Care to tell me what he has in that crate?'

After studying the archaeologist for five seconds, she responded: 'Why should you care?'

'Because whatever it is, he tried to kill me for it. Sent an assassin for me. And your husband had two of my friends murdered.' He turned his gaze to Joshua. 'Including Yosi.' The boy had been fond of the old man too. Who hadn't been?

'Yosi died of a heart attack,' Joshua insisted.

Devora had already figured out Amit's real name shortly after she'd advised her husband of the man's sudden appearance at his office, when he'd introduced himself as Yosi. When she'd explained what the visitor and his female companion looked like, her husband had immediately become alarmed. Playback of the Temple Society's security recordings confirmed what he'd already suspected.

'No, Joshua. It wasn't a heart attack that killed Yosi. And as we speak, another of my friends is in the hospital having a bullet hole in her side plugged up. All because of your husband,' he said to Devora. 'So I care *very* deeply about what is in that box.' There were also selfish reasons for his interest, traceable to a culmination of years of research and the slim possibility that the Bible's most cherished relic still existed.

'He's killed many others too,' Devora weakly replied, staring blankly at a Greek inscription glazed onto a ring of ceramic tiles just below the domed ceiling. She remembered her husband telling her it was a quote from Plato that was the oldest known reference to the study now dubbed 'archaeology.' But perhaps Aaron had lied about that too. After all, she couldn't read Greek – and she certainly couldn't read him. 'He's done many things you may not like. But it is God's will that—'

'No,' Amit cut her off. 'Murder is *not* God's will. Now I'm running out of time. So tell me, what is in that box?'

'You wouldn't believe me.' Devora shook her head.

'Try me.'

But Devora stood her ground.

It was the son who offered up the answer. 'The Ark of the Covenant.'

'Joshua!' the mother said in a warning tone, shaking her head.

'Thank you,' Amit said with an air of vindication. But the confirmation brought even more anxiety.

'It doesn't matter now, Mother,' Joshua reminded her.

Devora paused as she looked over at Joshua's bandaged hand.

What her husband had done to his own flesh and blood was unspeakable. Yet it was no surprise, since he'd never shown Joshua true love or respect. Being a son in the Cohen family was no small responsibility. Only the able-bodied could perform the duties of a priest. To Aaron, Joshua had become first and foremost a break in his genealogical chain. Crippled, the boy stood no chance of serving God as a *kohen*.

And given the gloomy prognosis for Joshua's condition, a grandson had been considered an impossibility. Nor could Joshua's corrupted genetics have supported artificial means of conception, even if it were to come down to that. The bottom line was that Joshua could never carry on the Cohen family name and the ever-so-precious pedigree that came with it – his *yichus*. Not to mention that Devora was able to bear only one child before a series of benign cysts strangled her ovaries so badly that they required excision. Since Joshua's illness began, Aaron had not been able to reconcile how the imperfections of the next generation could run so deep. His obsession with genetics had grown even stronger. If there was any way to retain the bloodline, he was determined to find it.

Though she hadn't acknowledged it for many years, Devora had become aware that there was something wrong with her husband – something bordering on mania. It wasn't hard to imagine what he was capable of doing to others. And now that he'd achieved so many things and brought the Ark back to Zion, there was no telling what he'd do next.

Amit's gaze bounced from mother to son and back to mother. They were serious. 'Is it real – the Ark?'

Devora's eyes were still locked on Joshua's hand as she answered Amit: 'The Ark is real.' There was defeat in her voice – decades of it. 'The Ark is *very* real.'

'My God,' Amit mumbled. Seeing that neither mother nor son posed a threat, he lowered the gun. Though his first inclination was to question her sincerity, there was something else playing out in the woman's hurt gaze. With his guard down, he noticed a sleek safe case sitting on one of the chairs. He sidestepped closer to examine it – a fancy model with a digital combination lock. The rabbi's attaché? Could the missing scrolls from Qumran be inside it? 'What is this?'

When Mrs. Cohen told him, his alarm heightened. He asked who'd be coming to pick it up. The answer wasn't pleasing either. 'When?'

'Any minute now,' she replied. 'They are in the building.'

Amit moved the case further across the room and gave her specific instructions on how to handle the transaction. Keeping his attention, and the gun, on the door, he lowered his voice.

'You need to save the Messiah,' Joshua blurted out.

Puzzled, Amit asked, '*Who?*'

'The woman . . . Charlotte. The pretty one they are taking with them. She's the Messiah.'

Messiah? Amit looked back at the mother, hoping to see recognition that her son had a few screws loose. But much to his surprise, Devora nodded in agreement.

'It's true,' Devora conceded. 'She is the Chosen One. Do you not see how my son walks now?'

This was all a lot to take in. First the Ark, now the Messiah? Things were moving too fast. 'She's the Messiah,' he whispered to no one in particular. 'So tell me about her. I also want to know what she has to do with the Ark – and I want to know what your husband is planning to do,' Amit insisted.

63.

'Look at this fucking mess,' Kwiatkowski grumbled, unwrapping the blood-caked towel from his mangled forearm. Blinking sporadically, his bloodshot eyes were still tearing from the chemical burns. Leaning over the bathroom sink, he turned on the squeaky chrome spigots.

Watching his ashen-faced partner peel away the final layer, Orlando cringed as the towel's crusty twill pulled away some of the crescent-shaped scab. The raw, deep wound split like smiling lips, the skin surrounding it a gruesome shade of purple. Blood zigzagged down Kwiatkowski's forearm muscles into the basin, turning the shallow water pink. 'That priest really got you good.'

As Kwiatkowski stuffed the bloodstained towel into the garbage can, his inflamed red eyes knifed into Orlando. 'He just got lucky. That's all.' An attempt at wiggling the bluish-purple digits produced good results for the pinky and ring finger, limited motion in the middle finger, and nothing in the other two. 'Damn nerves are severed. Shit.'

All told, it had been six hours since they'd slipped out of the

Vatican dormitory and loaded the geneticist into the rented van. They'd easily rolled out the Petrine Gate as the Swiss Guard focused its attention on the fire alarm that had gone off in the dormitory. The priest had unwittingly made their escape easier. At Fiumicino, the woman had been transferred to the rabbi's private jet. As Cohen had promised, diplomatic privileges allowed them to bypass all security. The man seemed to have more pull than the pope. The bumpy flight from Rome to Tel Aviv took less than two and a half hours. Once they'd landed, a transfer to a second van completed the last leg of the delivery to the Rockefeller Museum.

Now it was time to collect final payment.

Repulsion giving way to curiosity, Orlando stared at the wound more clinically. 'Did he break the bone?'

'I don't think so.'

'Could have been worse.'

'Are you fucking kidding? This isn't exactly like cutting myself shaving.' He bent over and held the grotesque arm under the running water. Chunks of the scab and oozing gore slid off into the drain. 'As soon as we get the money you can drop me over at Hadassah. I'm going to need surgery.'

'No problem,' he said, patting him on the shoulder. Big problem, actually. It was Kwiatkowski's shooting hand. Clearly the best surgeon in Israel would have a difficult time restoring the reflex in his trigger finger. Which rendered the man useless. 'You did good. There'll be plenty of time to rest up after this job.' *Plenty of time.* He handed over a fresh towel.

Kwiatkowski sighed. 'The rabbi's wife has the cash?' He glared at Orlando in the mirror.

'That's right.'

'Euros, not shekels?'

'Right.' With a lightning-fast draw, Orlando pulled out his gun and fired once into Kwiatkowski's left ear.

The giant rocked sideways and struck the wall where the round had cracked through the tiles. Blood and brain matter smeared as he crumpled to the floor.

Holstering his gun, Orlando made his way outside.

64.

Orlando moved quickly down the corridor toward the light coming out of the conference room, the gun swinging like a pendulum in his right hand. 'Mrs. Cohen?' he called out.

As he drew nearer the conference room, shadows moved across the light. Then the matronly Hasidic woman in her ankle-length dress seemed to glide out of the room, hands folded.

'Yes, in here, please,' she said in a lukewarm manner.

The assassin's muscles eased up as he passed by her and cautiously entered the room with the gun drawn.

'Where is your partner?' she asked, coming in behind him.

'He went ahead to the hospital.'

'His arm?'

'An awful thing,' the contractor confirmed. 'I'll be handling matters on his behalf,' he firmly replied, his deadpan face clearly communicating that he shouldn't be questioned any further.

A haunted expression came over his face when he saw the rabbi's son across the room, standing next to the silver safe case. When he'd first arrived, the emaciated, ghost-white kid had been curled up in a wheelchair. Less than an hour after he came out of the room where the geneticist had been detained, he'd started rambling excitedly about his legs, how he could feel strange sensations. Then the kid had clumsily pulled himself up from the chair. It hadn't been pretty, but the kid managed to stand, using the wall and the chair for support. But he was definitely up and about, crying like a baby, his cheeks flushed with rosy color. The circumstances seemed highly suspicious, so Orlando had immediately fetched the rabbi. The rabbi's genuine astonishment had not been what he'd expected.

The boy's condemnatory stare sent a freakish coldness over Orlando. He paced over to the case and ran his fingers over its small keypad.

'Don't worry. Your blood money is all there,' Mrs. Cohen said.

The woman certainly wasn't looking to win any popularity contests. 'The code?' He tucked the gun into his underarm holster since he'd need both hands to open the case.

She gave him the sequence.

Orlando keyed in the numbers and the locks snapped open inside the case. Grinning, he unhinged the cover. The smile immediately faded when he looked down at the neat stacks of bills. 'Shekels?' he grunted.

'It's perfectly good money,' the wife confirmed.

'I specifically requested Euros, not this Jew money. Now where am I supposed to go to trade this at this hour?'

'So open a bank account in the morning,' she coldly replied.

'You think you're funny?' he hissed. Pulling his gun, he swept it up at the son's pale face. 'I can be funny too.'

Without warning, the wooden panel covering the front of the table splintered open around a clean hole. At the same time, Orlando felt a wretched pain tear up through his abdomen and into his chest – an invisible spear impaling his body. 'Wh –

what . . . ?' Blood pulsed out in quick bursts from above his navel and sprayed onto the shekels. Absorbed in the absurdity of it, he hadn't noticed the boy scamper off behind him. He backed up from the table, dazed. Delirious, he swung the gun side to side, squeezing off haphazard shots – at the table, at the ceiling, over his shoulder. 'Fucking scumbags!' he slurred.

The gun's ammo clip emptied quickly.

That's when a broad man with a goatee sprang up from underneath the table and fired three more rounds into his chest.

Orlando crashed onto the conference table, blood spreading out smoothly over the freshly polished finish. He tried to curse them once more, but the words drowned in the bile and blood that gurgled into his throat. The rabbi's wife came and stood beside the table, arms crossed tight in front of her chest. It was the first time he'd seen her smile.

He felt her spit strike his eye just as the darkness took hold.

65.

By the time Amit got his shoes on, made it back downstairs, and bounded out the rear service door with gun drawn, the delivery van was gone. No surprise. Oddly, however, the flatbed truck had gone missing too.

The fragmented story that Mrs. Cohen had told him was almost too incredible to believe. Yet even if she'd embellished a half-truth, the implications of what Rabbi Cohen had in store for the Ark and the captive 'Messiah' were shocking.

Immediately, Amit broke into a sprint to get back to the car. Midstride, he pulled out his cell phone and hit the send button. The call took three rings to connect. As always, Enoch was heedful about answering his call, no matter what the hour.

'Hey,' he said between heavy breaths.

'Are you having sex?' Enoch joked.

Under better circumstances, Amit would have laughed heartily. 'I need' – *breath* – 'your help. It's critical.'

His tone instantly went serious. 'Tell me.'

'Just a sec,' Amit said as he approached the car, ducked inside, and fumbled for the key. The Fiat's engine turned over with a growl.

'Where are you?'

Amit told him as he threw the car into drive and peeled out along the curved road. He paused to regulate his lungs, then laid out the facts he'd confirmed with the rabbi's wife – the abduction of an American geneticist, the clandestine shipment flown back from Egypt.

'And where's Cohen heading?'

'The Temple Mount.' When Devora had told him this, his heart had almost given out. 'Something to do with the excavation in the Western Wall Tunnel. I'm not sure about that part.'

'What's in the box?' Enoch had to ask.

'Something very dangerous.'

This made Enoch fear the worst, because some hard-core Zionists were considered religious extremists, even terrorists. The Mossad kept a very close eye on the select few considered credible threats. Yet somehow Rabbi Cohen had remained below the radar. 'A bomb?'

Amit liked the way this proposition resonated with Enoch. So he went along with it. 'That or something worse.' If it really was the Ark in that box, he wasn't stretching the truth.

Along the straightaway below the Temple Mount's eastern wall, he gunned the engine to swerve around a Toyota sedan moving sluggishly along Derech Ha'ofel. 'I'm just about there now,' Amit told him. 'You need to get over here immediately – the Western Wall Plaza. And call for backup.'

'All right, Commander,' he said, thinking back to the old days. 'I'm on my way. Give me ten minutes. Just sit tight outside the gate – and don't do anything crazy until I get there.'

Luckily, though Enoch periodically reported to Tel Aviv, he spent three days each week telecommuting from his Jerusalem condominium on Derech Beit Lehem.

Amit pushed the car to its limit as the headlights cut a straight line below the white tombs heaped up along the Temple Mount's eastern wall.

Amit's fears deepened. The Old Testament depicted the Ark of the Covenant as a telephone to heaven – a vessel through which Moses and Aaron communicated with God in the Tabernacle. And it was the Ark that could summon God's essence in the form of a brilliant light – the Shechinah. The Ark's roster of supernatural powers included an ability to levitate and strike down scorpions and dangerous predators with bolts of energy. It could push back rivers and move earth. It could spontaneously combust anyone who came into contact with it.

But what troubled Amit most was the Bible's detailed descriptions of the Ark as antiquity's ultimate weapon of mass destruction, capable of channeling God's wrath to annihilate armies and decimate cities. Could this be what Cohen was really after? And this woman who Joshua had dubbed the Messiah? Well, if this was what Cohen believed, then it stood to reason that he was convinced that the American was meant to usher in a day of reckoning that would reinstate Zion as the epicenter of God's world. He couldn't suppress the images of a decimated Temple Mount and a grand Temple City rising from the ashes.

Scary stuff.

No. *Crazy* stuff.

The man of science and reason in him couldn't believe what he was envisioning. Yet everything in his gut told him it made sense. The second book of the Pentateuch (the Torah), Exodus, described the Ark of the Covenant as a cubit and a half in height and width, two and a half cubits in length. Most believed the cubit God was referring to then probably hadn't been the same one conveyed to Noah for construction of his *seaworthy* ark.

Since Moses was an Egyptian, he'd have employed the Egyptian royal cubit. In modern terms, that put the Ark's proportions at about three quarters of a meter high and wide, and under a meter and a half long.

Indeed, the crate Amit had seen Cohen's cronies wheeling out of the museum could have easily held it.

It took him less than a minute to cut through the Kidron Valley and approach the gate where tour buses entered the Old City to drop their loads outside the security gates – the Dung Gate. Unfortunately, the very short ride from the Rockefeller Museum and the rabbi's significant head start practically guaranteed that he'd already made it inside.

Instead of drawing attention by heading through the gate, Amit hung a left where a brown road sign pointed to the City of David in English and Hebrew. He immediately steered to the curb.

When he got out of the car, a pair of Palestinians huddled on stools over a backgammon board began yelling at him in Arabic, pointing to the car, gesturing in impolite ways for him to move it.

With no time to argue with them, Amit tossed the key ring onto the game board and told them, 'It's yours. Take it.'

Then he set off for the gate.

66.

Rabbi Aaron Cohen's mind was stretched to the limit. Things had gotten very sloppy, and any semblance of his original plan had long since vaporized. The killings were to be expected. Sacrifice was always required. The fact that the assassin assigned to eliminate Amit Mizrachi had not reported back to the museum, however, was deeply troubling. Could the archaeologist still be alive?

Then he thought back to the Muslim who'd snuck into the tunnel and managed to report to someone on the outside about what he'd seen beneath the Temple Mount – the event that put everything into fast-forward. Whom had he called? What would the response entail? Too many possibilities.

But if there was a destiny for the Ark, it certainly was in the Lord's hands now. After so many, many centuries, the Testimony was back in Zion – ready to fulfill the great prophecies put into motion two thousand years earlier by Jesus.

'Unload the truck,' Cohen instructed his foreman.

The man, dressed in a blue Israel Antiquities Authority jumpsuit and white hard hat, looked warily over the rabbi's shoulders at the six IDF guards standing watch at the archway. They were all busy talking and smoking. 'What about the soldiers?'

'Don't worry about them,' Cohen said. 'They're clueless. If they cause any problems, you do whatever it takes to hold them back.'

The anxious foreman had no more questions and began shouting orders to the men gathered around the side of the flatbed truck that had backed in beneath Wilson's Arch.

Cohen watched as another crewman rolled a forklift closer, raised the fork, and eased it under the first pallet. The machine's engine rumbled heavily, its frame groaning under the extreme weight. Then came loud beeping as the machine reversed in a slow arc and maneuvered to set the pallet down on the ground. The process repeated as the second batch of stone was unloaded.

Once the forklift spun back into its parking spot and the engine was shut off, Cohen said to the foreman, 'Unpack them and bring them straight inside, understand?' He pointed to the pallets.

'Right away.'

'I need to get ready. I'll meet you there.'

Pacing over to the white delivery van, Cohen opened the passenger door and retrieved his black garment bag and tote. Then he headed down the steps and into the Western Wall Tunnel.

67.

'Sorry, Commander,' Enoch said, jogging over to Amit outside the Dung Gate with a lit cigarette dangling from his right hand.

'If this was Gaza, I'd have you reported to the *aluf*'s office,' Amit said with a grin. 'But five minutes is a forgivable offense in the civilian world.' He gave his friend a handshake and embraced him. 'I really appreciate your coming.'

'Wouldn't miss this for the world,' he said with a sardonic grin.

The image of Enoch that would be forever stuck in the back of Amit's head – a painfully thin, timid kid – did not match the man who stood before him. At least thirty pounds heavier, and none of it flab, Enoch was an intimidating fellow. In fact, it looked like he could bench-press a car. His face had filled out too – more handsome, yet the same bony nose and undersized chin.

'Still haven't given up on those things?' Amit said, pointing to the cigarette. 'Why kill yourself? You've got a family now.'

Enoch raised his eyebrows, took a final drag, and tossed the butt to the ground. As he stubbed it out with his foot, he replied, 'Living in Jerusalem and working for Israeli intelligence?' He smirked. 'Cigarettes are the least of my worries.'

'Good point. Were you able to call ahead to anyone?' Amit asked. He could sense an apology coming.

'I tried,' he said. 'But I was told that the area is already under heavy supervision. The IDF is working triple-time in there.' His eyes motioned ahead to the Western Wall Plaza.

'You didn't mention the abduction?'

'Of course I did. But according to those guards over there' – he pointed to the service gate left of the tourist depot – 'Cohen just went inside and there was no woman, no crate.'

What?

'So unless we have proof, suffice it to say that the rabbi is untouchable. Your word against his. And I shouldn't even be here with you, because there's an ex-IDF man with a bullet in his neck who was just scooped off the pavement at the Israel Museum.'

Amit's expression turned sour.

'Lots of witnesses there said a big guy with a cargo vest and a goatee downed him. Way to keep a low profile,' he lightly jabbed. 'Bottom line is, you're wanted for questioning. Didn't exactly help me to escalate matters, if you know what I'm saying. You could've told me, you know.'

Now Amit was the apologetic one. 'Sorry about that.'

'No worries. Good shooting, though,' he said. 'You got the guy right in the spine.'

'I was aiming for the chest, but thanks anyway.'

'You still armed?'

Amit flashed David's Beretta, then dropped it back in his deep vest pocket.

Enoch's left eyebrow tipped up. 'It'll have to do. Let's get in there.' He set a brisk pace along the drive leading to the security barrier and turnstiles that cordoned off the plaza.

'You're sure about all this, Amit?' Enoch asked.

'Was I ever wrong in Gaza?'

'No, sir,' he replied with assurance. It still amazed him that Amit hadn't pursued a career with the military. He was a natural leader with a brand of cunning born from instinct, not training. Rumor had it, however, that Amit's proficiency in archaeology was even more impressive. 'So it's just like old times, eh?'

'That's right. Now work your magic with these guys and get us down into that tunnel.'

They slowed when the guards at the main gate saw them coming and stood.

Enoch dipped unthreateningly into his pants pocket for his Mossad ID badge.

68.

Charlotte Hennesey felt like she'd been buried alive. The oxygen inside the pitch-black wooden box she had been folded into was getting thinner by the moment, not to mention that the stale air was a keen reminder that she was in desperate need of a shower. With knees pulled close to her chest, hands bound tight behind her back, and an excessive gag triple-wrapped over her mouth, the muscle cramping had quickly set in again. Though she'd never been claustrophobic before, this could unnerve Houdini himself, she thought.

The rabbi had promised a short drive. That much seemed to be true, because the bouncy truck had come to a stop within minutes. Then she'd heard the muted groaning sounds of a loud engine followed shortly thereafter by a sensation of movement, first up, then down.

But now, things seemed to be getting louder. There was banging and thudding on the crate's front face. Without warning, the wood violently cracked. She jerked her head sideways as splinters showered in on her. The box's entire front face snapped away.

A rush of cool air swept in.

Crystalline voices.

When she looked up again, a dark figure was silhouetted against bright white light – hands reaching in for her, clasping her bound ankles and pulling.

69.

Enoch was trying his best to be patient with the two rookie night-shift police officers posted at the security gate. They'd already confirmed what they'd relayed in an earlier phone inquiry – no sign of a woman, definitely no crate.

'And you inspected the trucks?'

'As best we could,' the taller one confirmed. 'The van came in empty.' He pointed a bony finger to where it sat outside the cordons. 'Just a driver and the rabbi up front. Nothing suspicious about that. Take a look inside it if you don't believe me.'

Ignoring the exchange, Amit's gaze was transfixed on the bright lights under the archway on the plaza's north side. He could see soldiers calmly standing there, but little more. What the hell was happening inside?

'And the truck?'

The guard rolled his eyes and huffed. 'That truck's been in and out of here at least two dozen times over the past month.'

'But you *did* inspect it?' he dug in.

'Just a driver in the front cab. Same as always.'

'And the shipment?' A squeezing sensation came over Enoch's chest, and the cords in his neck stretched tight.

The guards exchanged guilty glances.

'You didn't check it?'

'Stones?' He shrugged. 'What's to check?'

Now Enoch snapped. 'Get out of my way,' he roared, and pushed past them. 'Let's go, Amit.'

The metal detector squelched in turn as each of them passed through.

'Wait!' the tall guard protested, scrambling after them waving a handgun. 'No guns in there!'

Enraged, Enoch spun, eyes like daggers. 'Oh, now you're inspecting things?'

The guard aimed the gun at him. 'I'm serious.'

'Are you kidding me?' he scoffed. Shaking his head, he slapped the gun aside. 'Don't test my patience. You know Mossad are never permitted to give up weapons.'

'But—'

'Call your superior if you have any complaints. I've got a job to do.'

With that, Enoch marched his way across the plaza, Amit trailing close in his wake.

70.

'Everything okay over here?' the female IDF guard said, rifle slung over her knobby right shoulder. The group had sent her over to investigate the loud cracking sounds that had echoed up through the high vaults.

'Fine,' the foreman reported. 'Just fine.' Out of the corner of his eye, he saw the men goading the geneticist down the steps leading into the tunnel.

'What was that noise?' she asked.

'Noise?'

She might have been a novice, but she was no idiot. The guy was playing dumb. 'Yes. Like wood splintering.'

'I don't know what—'

'Hold on,' the woman said, raising a hand to hush him. She moved around the truck's rear, and her curious eyes locked onto the splintered mess near the two pallets. 'What's going on over there?' she asked, moving closer.

The foreman quickly glanced at the other soldiers, who remained at the entrance, chatting away. Then he traipsed to the female soldier.

Eyes pinched in confusion, she studied the hollows in the center of each pallet. Buried underneath the stacked stones were sizable wooden crates, empty. The torn-apart front side of each crate littered the ground. Why would a crate be sealed away inside a stone pile? Unless . . .

She yelled out to the others. 'I need help back here!'

The foreman's eyes went wide. In a panic, he snatched up a shovel propped against the truck's front bumper.

The soldier raced to bring the rifle off her shoulder and pivoted to face the workman. No sooner was her finger on the trigger then a loud clang instantly preceded a sharp pain that exploded through her skull and made her see pure white. Her body dropped limply to the ground, forcing her finger back on the trigger. The stray shot echoed through the vaults like a thunderclap.

Terrified, the foreman ditched the shovel and dashed for the tunnel.

71.

Halfway across the plaza, Amit and Enoch simultaneously registered the resounding gunshot that echoed out from the brightly lit archway adjacent to the Wailing Wall. The soldiers outside the opening reacted quickly, pulling down their machine guns and scrambling for cover.

'Shit,' Enoch grumbled. 'Let me check it out. You stay here for a sec.'

Before Amit could protest, the kid was off and running.

The frenzied guards at the security post began yelling. When Amit looked back at them, they were bickering about what to do. Then the tall one was picking up a phone.

Lights began snapping on in the windows of the residential buildings overlooking the plaza.

Amit swung his gaze back to the soldiers, trying to figure out what Cohen was up to. Why would he bring the American and the Ark into the Western Wall Tunnel? The renovations that had been going on there since the quake first struck had forced the exit onto Via Dolorosa to be closed. The tunnel was a dead end. Made no sense. Unless . . .

His eyes crawled up the Wailing Wall. Backing up a few steps, he saw the peak of the Dome of the Rock's lit-up cupola come into view. He remained transfixed by it for a few seconds, considering a very remote possibility.

Could it be?

As more IDF reinforcements stormed into the plaza, Amit needed to make a move before someone started asking him questions. The tunnel was now officially under siege. Not much use for him down there. And unlike the soldiers, Amit was a much bigger target – who wasn't wearing Kevlar.

He calmly backtracked toward the metal detectors. But just before he reached them, he vaulted over a wooden construction fence and landed on a temporary walkway set atop steel columns, sheathed in plywood, and covered by a corrugated metal roof.

Beneath the raised walkway, the excavations on the Temple Mount's southwest corner had now reached below the Ottoman-period steps and aqueducts to expose a monumental construct of eighth-century-B.C.E. columns, steps, and walls called the Ada Carmi Building. And as he curved up the temporary bridge spanning over it, he couldn't help but think that the site had suffered serious damage during the firefight that had taken place here back in June, when the thieves who'd stolen the ossuary from beneath the Temple Mount had opened fire on Israeli soldiers. Mortar shells had taken down entire walls and Iron Age stonework.

Staying low and moving up the curved walkway, he looked over to the archway where the soldiers were flooding in, Enoch right behind them.

'Go get 'em, kid,' Amit said.

The ramp peaked at Moors Gate, high up on the Western Wall – under normal conditions, the main tourist entrance to the

Temple Mount esplanade. However, the Waqf had kept it closed ever since the restoration work in the Western Wall Tunnel had commenced.

The freshly painted new steel door featured a very modern key lock. Amit was fully prepared to put his lock-picking skills to the test once more. But he figured he'd test the door first. And much to his surprise, it was unlocked.

Open?

Amit slid inside and pulled the door shut.

72.

Now Charlotte's pulse was pounding. The gunshot had thrown Cohen's thugs into high gear and they pulled harder at her arms as they moved her through a huge vaulted hall full of scaffolding. At the base of one of the room's massive stanchions, three men were dismantling a pile of stones to access something covered beneath. Another eight stood close, looking on. She barely glimpsed one of the men emptying the arsenal concealed there – machine guns and other ominous-looking weapons.

They muscled her through an open security door and alongside the huge foundation stones.

The sweaty foreman had just caught up to them. In Hebrew, he rattled off what had transpired. Then he warned them that the soldiers were quickly advancing.

The channel beyond the door was tight, huge rectangular blocks on the right, modern concrete slabs on the left. They'd definitely brought her deep underground. But she still felt completely disoriented. Where in hell were they taking her?

Up ahead there were some stone steps. The handlers were getting antsy, pushing her along, almost forcing her to trip.

On the left side, the passage widened considerably, but the huge blocks on the right were still running along a straight line. Here they met up with seven bearded men dressed in white robes and headdresses. Opposite them were half a dozen others dressed in blue jumpsuits, each armed with a machine gun.

As if that wasn't enough, Cohen was there too, dressed like a snake charmer. The sight of him actually made her stop dead in her tracks. His long sky-blue robe had shiny gold thread woven into its fabric, and tassels dangled from its hem. Tied around the waist was a crimson and red garment that looked like a fancy apron. And his colorful head-wrap was secured by a gold frontlet inscribed with Hebrew letters. The ensemble included a gold breastplate inset with twelve sparkling rectangular gemstones – topaz, emerald, sapphire, and amethyst among them – each with Hebrew inscriptions.

The veiled Egyptian relic had been placed in the center of it all, except this time, it had been fitted with two long wooden carrying poles and it was covered in animal furs.

'Remove the gag,' Cohen said.

One of the handlers cut away the duct tape, taking plenty of hair with it.

For a moment, Cohen stared at her natural, unblemished red curls. 'Your screams won't matter now,' he said. 'So I suggest you not waste your energy.'

She glared at the rabbi's attire. 'Where are we?'

'We are beneath Jerusalem's Temple Mount,' the rabbi coolly replied.

Jerusalem? 'What is going – ?'

His hand snapped up. 'All in good time.'

Given what was brewing outside, Charlotte thought, he seemed remarkably calm, as did the others gathered around him.

What did Cohen have up his sleeve? There was no way he could stay holed up down here. Did he have a death wish?

Cohen spread his hands, signaling for the robed men lined up along the foundation wall to separate.

What Charlotte hadn't seen behind them was a gaping hole that had been pounded through a thick layer of mortar and stone that sealed a soaring archway. She watched four of the robed men each claim a position at a corner of the box. In tandem, they reached down and clasped the closest pole end. Then they hoisted the box smoothly from the floor, like pallbearers.

'What you are about to take part in, Charlotte,' the rabbi said, 'is a ritual that hasn't taken place in almost twenty-five hundred years.'

The rabbi summoned one of the priests from the rear, who hastily brought over a gold cup fitted with a long handle. Charlotte watched as the rabbi took the vessel, closed his eyes, and chanted a prayer over it. Then he dipped his finger into the cup and proceeded to fling a drop of thick red liquid over the darkened threshold.

Is that blood?

He repeated this six more times, while chanting a prayer.

'The sacred blood consecrates the gateway,' Cohen explained to her.

Her eyes went wide as she realized that it was her blood being used for the ritual.

Returning the vessel to the attendant, the rabbi made his way through the dark hole. Two paces ahead, he stopped and crouched low to the ground. There came a metallic click, followed instantly by a bath of white light that washed away the darkness from a grand corridor running straight through the heart of the Temple Mount.

73.

Pacing the Dome of the Rock's wide ambulatory, the Keeper glanced over at the craggy expanse of the rock itself – Sakhrah. In preparation for what was to come, he prayed to the seventy thousand angels who continuously guarded over this spot, beseeching them for strength, begging for a sign should his intentions not please Allah.

Though young Ali had entered the secret tunnel never to return – *peace forever grace him* – he had still managed to confirm Ghalib's suspicions that something devious was taking place beneath the Haram. He'd been surprised when Ali had reported just how ambitious the plan really was.

As he meandered past the balustrade along the rock's southern side, he paused to pay homage to the wide gap that opened into the Well of Souls directly beneath. Islamic legend said that when Muhammad ascended to heaven, the rock had begun to fracture at this spot and rise up beneath him. But the angel Gabriel had held the sacred stone in place. Along the Sakhrah's surface, he could see the indentations left behind by the angel's fingers.

Oh Merciful One, most compassionate and all knowing, Ruler of Judgment Day. Give me guidance. Show me the straight way.

He circled back to the south door, where two Palestinians armed with Uzis awaited him.

'The Evil One is coming. Dajal is in our midst. Soon, brothers,' he told them. 'Very soon.'

'Shall we lock the doors?' one of them asked.

Ghalib shook his head. 'Leave them open.' Then he went outside.

74.

Five soldiers had pushed forward and taken positions close to the unloaded flatbed truck parked near the stairs – the Trojan horse that had passed through the walls of the world's most secure city. Another four soldiers hunkered behind the piles of stone beside it, one crouched low behind the forklift, another using the bell of a portable cement mixer for cover.

Having taken up a post behind them, Enoch noticed that there seemed to be some deliberation as to how to proceed. All focus was on the steps where the gunman had retreated into the Western Wall Tunnel. 'Come on,' he grumbled, losing patience.

If there was going to be more shooting, he wasn't wearing proper safety gear. Best to leave the heavy lifting to the front line. So as not to be confused for the enemy, he made sure to prominently display his blue Mossad armbands showing the agency logo – a menorah set inside a circle. He briefly wondered how Amit might react when the IDF's reinforcements came spilling into the plaza.

Another six soldiers fanned in around Enoch, Galils drawn.

One of them dropped to one knee beside him – a female

wearing the epaulets of a captain. She was young, pretty too. Momentarily, he was taken aback, since during his days with the IDF, women had performed only low-rank duties. The IDF's first female pilot had only earned her wings in 2001.

'What's happening in there?' she asked, eyes forward.

'Rabbi Cohen just carted in an unknown shipment presumed to be a high-powered weapon or bomb. He's also taken an American hostage.' This didn't seem to faze her.

'What does the hostage look like?'

Amit hadn't specified. 'Not sure, but just look for the only woman in plain clothes.'

'How many hostiles are we talking about?'

Anyone's guess, he thought. He shrugged. 'Maybe a dozen. Just assume the worst. And they already shot one of your officers. So assume they're all armed.' No doubt the truck had also been used to smuggle weapons.

'Got it.'

A military jeep came to a rough stop in the plaza, just outside the entry. More soldiers spilled out and immediately dropped a retractable ramp from the jeep's tailgate. One worked a remote transmitter that brought the payload out on its own accord.

'Let's get it up front,' the captain yelled back to them.

Enoch watched as the robot bounced off the ramp on two rotary tracks, looking like a miniature tank or moon rover. The thing sped past him on a beeline for the tunnel stairs, the operator keeping a safe distance, using an LCD on the remote to see through the robot's camera eye.

'We'll get them out,' she assured Enoch.

The robot was just easing to a stop atop the stairs. Its two mechanical bomb-dismantling arms stayed tucked at its sides while a third, equipped with a camera, telescoped out.

'Nothing so far,' the operator said.

'Sit tight,' the captain told Enoch. Then she sprang up and signaled for the operator to follow her.

Enoch watched them move swiftly to take positions behind the robot.

Less than thirty seconds later, when the robot bounced its way down the steps and detected no activity below, the captain signaled the first wave of soldiers into the tunnel.

Thirty seconds after that, Enoch heard the first exchange of gunfire – and it was fierce.

Two soldiers remained behind while the others spilled down into the tunnel.

'Damn it,' Enoch cursed. If the rabbi was planning to put a bomb beneath the Temple Mount, there was little time to spare.

75.

The sides of the wide corridor rose high above, curving to form a continuous arched canopy that tapered far off along a perfect line. The ground had been meticulously cleared and the wide, flat stones that paved the walkway were worn so perfectly smooth that they squeaked underfoot. There was a very distinct smell down here – a pleasant redolence of minerals and earth. Squinting, Charlotte tried in vain to make out what lay at the corridor's other end, but the armed men in blue had taken the lead and obstructed the view. The robed pallbearers were traipsing behind her with the relic shoulder-mounted between them; the other robed men formed the train's caboose.

'A beautiful restoration, wouldn't you say?' Cohen proudly stated.

He explained that this had been the main thoroughfare, used in the first century for visitors coming in from the east gate en route to the marketplace that ran along the Temple Mount's western wall; its roomy dimensions easily accommodated pedestrians, horses, and wagons. Its design was King Herod's, as evidenced by the beveled frames carved into the bedrock to resemble the blocks of the mount's outer walls. To prevent sneak attacks, the underground roadway had been sealed by the Romans immediately after they'd destroyed the second temple in 70 C.E.

While clearing the tunnel, he went on, the workmen had found Roman coins and refuse commingled with the fill – all circa 70 C.E. And most remarkable were the remnants they'd recovered from the original temple buildings – fractured stones inscribed with Greek and Hebrew citations of the Torah, beautiful stone columns that would have supported the porticoes, ornate foundation blocks etched with cherubim and rosettes. He told Charlotte that he'd taken the most beautiful stone and put it on display in his own museum in the Jewish Quarter.

'So you see, Charlotte, the second temple certainly did exist, and we've found all the proof to substantiate it. The Muslims have feared this for centuries. Precisely the reason they so vehemently object to any excavation beneath the Temple Mount.' Which was a partial blessing, he thought, since Jesus's ossuary – strategically buried here by the Essenes just beyond the temple's sacred precincts – had remained protected for so long. 'However, though all of this is very impressive' – he swept his hand in circles over his head to imply the entirety of the Temple Mount – 'it is nothing compared to God's plan. King Herod built the second temple for vanity and pride. In God's eye, it was a mockery. Its destruction should not be lamented.'

Charlotte remained silent, still grappling with all that was happening. Cohen was a lunatic. But there was something about him that commanded respect.

They continued along until they neared the terminus, where a formidable wall sealed the tunnel's east gateway.

'See here what the caliphs had done?' he said, pointing to the stonework. 'They sealed this gate too. And on the other side they heaped up the earth and pushed it against the mount's eastern wall. Then they buried their dead all along it. Out there' – he motioned to what lay beyond the wall – 'you can see the tombs, thousands of them.'

He told her that for the same reason, the Muslims had also bricked up a second double-arched gateway still visible on the eastern wall just above the graves. The Jews called that gate the Golden Gate.

'Do you know why they block the east gates, Charlotte?'

'Enlighten me,' she sarcastically replied.

'The Jewish Messiah who is to redeem Zion is prophesied to return through the East Gate, just as Jesus did. So they eliminated the gates. And when they learned that the Chosen One would become impure by coming into contact with the dead, and thus be forbidden by God to enter the temple precincts, they constructed the graveyard.'

The heaped-up corpses made the security system sound an awful lot like voodoo, she thought.

'As you might imagine,' he continued, 'the Muslims fear the destruction of their sacred shrines, because the return of the Messiah will usher in the building of the third temple – and the Messianic Age.' Then he gave a wry smile. 'But what they miss is that *that* east gate' – he pointed to the bricked-up dead end – 'is *not* the one to which Ezekiel refers. Ezekiel speaks of the entry gate through the temple walls on top of Temple Mount at its center . . . where the Dome of the Rock now stands.'

The far-off patter of automatic gunfire suddenly echoed down the tunnel and caught his attention.

Come and get him, she thought eagerly.

The rabbi scowled when he saw her reaction. 'We must move quickly,' he told his entourage.

Directing his attention to a sweeping arch that opened up on the left wall, Cohen glanced up a wide, high staircase. At the top, his men worked to remove a wooden framework that had stabilized the overhead paving stones.

76.

The plaza on the Temple Mount's southern end was vacant as Amit slipped past the huge circular ablutions fountain set before al-Aqsa Mosque. Seemed odd.

A harvest moon floated above Jerusalem; the air was balmy, lifelessly still.

He turned onto the wide paved walkway leading between the wispy cypress trees surrounding the Dome of the Rock's raised platform. But he quickly ducked for cover when he saw a tall Arab coming in his direction.

As the Arab hastened under the multiarched *qanatir* and down the steps, Amit retreated along the shadowed platform wall until he rounded its corner. He watched the man continue down the path toward al-Aqsa Mosque. The man paused briefly just beyond the fountain, making Amit second-guess whether he'd properly closed the gate. Then Amit realized the Arab was simply listening to the shouting and gunfire emanating up from the Western Wall Plaza. Oddly, the guy didn't seem at all surprised by what he was hearing. Then he calmly proceeded to al-Aqsa Mosque and disappeared inside.

Strange.

That's when something more peculiar caught his attention.

Just beyond the olive trees on the platform's east side, the massive paving stones gritted and scratched, and seemed to shift before his eyes.

'What in God's name . . . ?' He moved closer.

Then, without warning, four of the pavers fell inward, disappearing into a massive hole.

77.

Enoch raced out to the jeep parked in the plaza and retrieved the spare Kevlar vest that one of the soldiers told him would be there. He hoped to see Amit, but there was no sign of him. Where could the commander have gone?

Then he quickly moved back inside and darted forward past the flatbed. There he caught a glimpse of the two crates covered in stone that Cohen had secreted beyond the security post. No doubt the hostage had been inside one of them. The second was large enough to hold just about anything – a harbinger of doom that anguished him. An attack against the Temple Mount could easily spark World War III.

Wasting no more time, he slid on the vest, then scrambled down the metal treads and entered the first leg of the Western Wall Tunnel, the large visitors' hall. Staying close to the wall with his Jericho pistol directed straight ahead, he surveyed the area – or at least the section he could see. Five soldiers had already been taken down, two fatally with gaping head wounds; three others sprawled on the ground with critical wounds to their exposed extremities. Straight ahead, two soldiers had just managed to break open a security door blocking the entrance to the tunnel stretching north from the hall.

The chamber had turned into a shooting gallery, filled with bullets spraying wildly in all directions, the heavy smell of gunpowder, and deafening gun blasts.

Staying low and poking his head around the wall, Enoch could see that Cohen's men had taken secure positions throughout the hall, behind piles of stone. Ten Israelis had them hopelessly pinned down and were tightening their perimeter. Most likely, if they couldn't take them out, they'd certainly avoid explosives down here and start using tear gas to root them out. But Cohen's gunmen weren't letting up and their supply of ammunition seemed limitless.

There was no sign of the rabbi here. Odds were he'd made his way deeper into the tunnel.

Now the bullets started flying in Enoch's direction, making him drop to the floor behind a broad tool chest. But these shots hadn't come from inside the hall – they were strays from the second wave of fighting that had just erupted beyond the breached security door.

The first soldier through the door was already lying in a pool of blood, helmet blown clear off his head. The second had taken some pounding to his chest armor but was able to stumble back for cover before anything worse happened.

Enoch had a straight sight line into the tunnel, and he saw a man in a blue jumpsuit scramble deep into the passage and up some distant steps. To chase after the guy through the narrow channel was risky . . . make that stupid. But that's what needed to be done – fast.

Luckily, the kid who'd taken some deep bruising to the ribs had already caught the attention of three others. He was pointing to the open door.

The three smoothly dropped back from the hall and filed into the tunnel.

The barrage of bullets was riddling the huge foundation stones. And the odds of Enoch catching a few with his brain were high.

But then he had an idea.

Enoch tested the tool chest's wheels by nudging it a few centimeters. The sturdy casters were actually quite smooth. The lumpy stone floor, however, was a problem.

There wasn't going to be a better opportunity than this, Enoch thought.

Snapping his gun into its holster, he opened the chest's middle drawer enough to grip his left hand around the metal frame. He pushed it forward and crab-walked behind it, angling it sideways as he emerged into the hall.

The first rounds thwumped into the casing and clanged off some tools in the top drawer.

Rolling the chest was a much bigger challenge then he'd bargained for – the thing was heavy and clumsy, jerking side to side and jostling the tools inside fiercely enough to drown out the gun blasts.

More bullets pounded through, pushing the chest back into him and sandwiching him against the mount's cold stone base. Then a neat line strafed directly overhead, so close it tousled his hair.

He cursed.

He looked to the security door. Only three meters to go.

Shoving the thing out again, he resumed rolling his makeshift shield, clattering louder than ever. When he'd reached the door, he abandoned the metal hulk.

He unholstered his Jericho and sprinted up the tunnel.

But he quickly slowed when he saw that just up the steps where the blue-suited gunman had fled, the IDF trio was engaged in another shooting match. What confused him was that they were firing through a huge hole in the mount's foundation.

'Holy shit,' Enoch murmured. He cautiously pressed forward.

Then something horrible happened that didn't give the Israelis any hope for escape.

Enoch barely saw it all go down.

It started when they began screaming and throwing themselves away from the hole. A split second later, a rocket-propelled mortar came streaming out at them, hissing as it cut through the opening. When it struck the wall opposite the hole, the entire tunnel came down on top of them.

The pulsing shock wave took Enoch airborne, his body striking a wall with appalling force, and flung him over a second low wall. Suddenly he was falling into blackness. Then a cold sensation crashed over his body.

78.

First the gunmen came up from the hole to secure the area.

Cohen came next, pleased to see that the esplanade was empty. The commotion in the Western Wall Tunnel had brilliantly diverted all attention from the Dome of the Rock. There wasn't a soldier or policeman in sight.

The stairwell opening was situated approximately midway along the esplanade's eastern side. In the first century, this had been the outer confine called the Courtyard of the Gentiles – a public area outside the walls of the sanctified temple complex itself.

The rabbi tried to imagine Herod's Romanesque porticoes running along the outer wall, where, during the Passover festival, Jesus would have challenged the moneychangers for their profiteering and blasphemy. And when the holiday had passed, pagans would have refurnished the temple with their idols and resumed sacrilegious offerings on the Lord's sacred altar.

Oh, how the temple priests had prostituted God's most hallowed sanctuary!

It came as little surprise that God had brought destruction to Jerusalem in 70 C.E. Jesus had tried to warn the people of the Lord's anger, the imminent doom that would befall them should they continue to break the covenant. But as they had done to Isaiah, Amos, Jeremiah, Ezekiel, and all others who had come before Him, the Israelites chose not to listen to Jesus. Like a dark avenger the Roman scourge came down upon the brood of vipers, the den of thieves.

Just as He had with the Babylonian exiles, for whom the prophets promised a return to this land, so too had God mercifully gathered the tribes once more in 1948. Yet even now they did not heed His message. They embraced an impotent, secular government and bowed down to Western culture. Worse yet, they had still failed to retake the Temple Mount – the Lord's most sacred ground. In 1967, the Israeli army had an incredible opportunity to expel the Muslims during the Six-Day War, yet they lacked the faith to follow through.

'Be very careful.' The rabbi intently watched over the priestly attendants as they eased the Ark up the steps, the pair in the rear pressing the poles up above their shoulders to compensate for the sharp angle. It was imperative to keep the vessel level so as not to disturb its hallowed contents.

The rabbi turned his attention up to the Dome of the Rock. Over the three millennia since King David made Jerusalem the Israelite capital, Jews had suffered many setbacks, even expulsion from these holy lands. When God's covenant was ignored, His punishment was without pity. But when the people abided by His laws, His blessings had been limitless.

Though the temple had been destroyed twice, its third incarnation would stand until the very end of time.

For decades, he'd dreamed of this moment. For millennia,

his family had waited. So much preparation. So much sacrifice.

He was close now.

Having safely emerged from the opening, the priests stood beside the rabbi with the Ark raised up. Seconds later, Charlotte was dragged up and out of the hole.

Clasping his hands together, Cohen bowed his head and began praying. Where the true eastern gate of the temple courtyard would once have resided, he sprinkled more blood from the *mizrak*.

Then he slowly made his way to the stairs leading up the dome's platform, the procession following behind him. Once all had reassembled in front of the shrine, the seven priests stepped forward, each wearing a blue satin side pouch.

For a long moment, the rabbi glared at the Dome of the Rock, helplessly captivated by its Arabian tile work and gold-leafed cupola. Up until this day, he'd seen the building only from afar. Standing at its foot was intimidating. Then again, Jericho had once intimidated Joshua.

He motioned to the seven. In unison, each man pulled from his pouch a shofar and brought the twisted ram's horn to his lips. Their guttural bellow filled the air.

Cohen signaled for two of the gunmen to proceed to the shrine's south-facing double door.

The priests lifted the Ark to prepare for a grand entrance.

Then something shocking happened.

The moment the men pulled open the doors to the shrine's darkened interior, they were immediately gunned down in a hail of bullets.

'Protect the Ark!' Cohen yelled. He motioned for them to move away from the door, to take shelter beside the shrine's solid marble wall. 'Bring her immediately!' he said to the priests handling Charlotte.

As they all scrambled for cover, the rabbi's six remaining gunmen raided the shrine.

79.

Two things let Enoch know he hadn't been killed by the blast: the raging pain that shot through his left shoulder, and the frigid bite of the chest-deep water into which he'd plunged.

High overhead, the tunnel glowed orange through a thick haze of dust. On four sides, sheer block walls formed a huge rectangular pit set below a lofty barrel vault.

An ancient cistern.

When he looked around he could see that there were no doors, no stairs, no ladders. Once he'd slogged to the nearest wall, his fingers confirmed that the surface was impossibly slick. The opening to the tunnel was a good five meters up. There'd be no climbing out of this hole.

His teeth were chattering uncontrollably, his body vacillating in the stinging water.

'Hey!' Enoch yelled up through cupped hands. 'Down here!' He repeated a similar SOS multiple times over the next minute.

No response.

There was a good chance he'd pass out from hypothermia before the soldiers would hear his screams and pull him out.

Above, the flickering fire glow taunted.

Unexpectedly, something bumped up against his leg, making him flinch. When he looked down he simultaneously gasped and pushed back in repulsion.

A grisly corpse floated face-up. And there wasn't much face to talk about. The front side of the skull had been reduced to pulp – one eye swollen shut, the other stripped of its fleshy lids so that a single hazy green eye stared up at him. Even the lips had been violently peeled back so that the dead man's few remaining jagged teeth seemed to grimace.

He stretched his leg up high and kicked it away. The corpse went bobbing along a smooth wave to the cistern's opposing wall, leaving a rippling wake in its path.

'Disgusting.'

The orange glow reflected over the top of the water. But along the wall directly below where he'd fallen from the tunnel, a different light caught Enoch's eye – an ever-so-faint outline below the crystal-clear waterline.

Plowing his way through the water, he dipped his hands below the surface to examine the wall. The stones fell away under his fingertips. His numb digits had a tough time transmitting texture, but he had no problem determining that there was an opening there – and it was wide.

A passage? Maybe. But why the light? Had the explosion blown a hole this deep?

Couldn't be. The light wasn't orange. It looked more as if someone was shining a flashlight from deep within – a warm, yellowish light.

So the next question was, just how far in was the light source?

The trembling was getting worse by the second. Still no activity overhead.

He screamed for help several more times, to no avail. Then he came to the desperate realization that the underwater passage was his only hope.

It took a good thirty seconds for him to get up the nerve to immerse himself. But that's what he did.

The water felt like needles against his eyes as he assessed the channel – maybe a meter in height, same in width. It ran straight for about eight meters, then took a slight bend where the light shone brightest. Since the ancients hand-carved these things, there was enough room to pass through them. But what lay beyond?

He sprang his head up from the water, his entire body tight.
Here goes nothing.

He pulled off his sneakers and socks, then stripped off the heavy Kevlar vest riddled with shrapnel that would have otherwise minced his chest. Filling his lungs to the limit, he dropped back below the water and kicked his way through the opening. A combination of foot-flipping and hand-grappling the smooth walls propelled him forward at a healthy clip. But if the light source wasn't indicating a way out, he'd never be able to reverse course without first running out of oxygen.

This was a one-way trip. And it terrified him.

Up ahead, the passage got tight – *really* tight.

Now his eyes felt like glass on the verge of shattering.

The constricted bend came up quickly. He was forced to squirm through it sideways.

The light instantly brightened so that he could see its source up ahead, another ten meters or so away. With his limbs offering little response, he gave it everything he had, kicking off the stone wall for one final forward thrust.

Now he could actually make out the shimmering surface of

the water. If the light was dropping down some kind of vertical shaft, like a well, he thought, he might have an opportunity to draw more air. But if he wasn't able to climb it . . .

Two meters.

'*Gaaah!*' he screamed as his head broke through the surface of the water. He gasped for air. But he needed to hold his eyes shut and rub them for a minute before he could see where fate had delivered him.

When his eyes finally began to adjust and the blur gave way to discernible dimensions, he liked what he could make out so far. The water tunnel hadn't ended in a vertical shaft. It actually continued up a sharp rise.

The light was very bright now, about four meters up the grade. On his elbows, Enoch began dragging himself up and out of the water until his slightly bent knees could be of assistance. As he crept higher, his vision became crisper, so that now he could make out the substantial metal grate that blocked his exit.

80.

Cohen and his men anxiously waited for the gunfire inside the shrine to cease. When it finally did, only two of the six who'd stormed the building emerged, and one of them was bleeding profusely from a wound to the thigh.

It was then that the rabbi first heard the sounds coming from the east. Gazing up into the night sky, he could see lights approaching, the whopping of rotor blades echoing through the valley.

'Quickly!' he instructed.

One of the men went ahead and found the lights.

At the shrine's door, the rabbi paused to study what lay beyond. He'd heard much about the exquisite Arabian décor inside the Dome of the Rock. On one occasion, he'd even happened upon some pictures of its interior. But all that did little justice to its true magnificence. Punishing himself for this unwilling admiration – this evil enticement – he cast his eyes straight ahead to the open area that sat directly beneath the cupola. He proceeded into the ambulatory.

If it wasn't the first step, it was the second when his senses immediately registered an overpowering presence here. It was as if he felt a supernatural aura wrapping around him. Faltering midstride, he struggled to conceal his alarm. He froze. But as quickly as it had come, the sensation dissipated. *Something atmospheric, perhaps?* he tried to convince himself. *Calm yourself. Let God guide you.*

Cautiously, the rabbi – the high priest, the *kohen gadol*, he reminded himself – eased deeper into the shrine. Cutting a straight line across the ambulatory's rich red Persian carpeting, he ignored the two dead Muslims who had been pulled off to the side and gave a reverential glance at his brave men who'd fallen close to the entrance.

The Ark was paraded in behind him, followed by the men handling Charlotte and the surviving two gunmen.

'Close the doors!' Cohen ordered.

He stopped along the ornate railing bordering the Foundation Stone. The emotions that came over him were overwhelming as he laid eyes upon the most sanctified ground on Earth.

Here God had made Adam and all creation. Here was the exact spot Abraham had come to sacrifice Isaac. And here, as told in Genesis 28, God promised Jacob the land of Israel . . .

A stairway was set on the ground with its top reaching heaven, and God's angels were going up and down it. The Lord was standing there above it, saying, 'I am the Lord, the God of your father Abraham and the God of Isaac. I will give you and your offspring the land that you are now sleeping on. Your offspring will be like the dust of the earth, and you will spread out toward the west, the east, the north, and the south. All the peoples on earth will be blessed through you and your offspring. I am with you and will watch over you wherever you go. I will bring you back

to this land, for I will not leave you until I have done what I have prom-
ised you.

When Jacob awoke from his sleep, he said, 'Surely the Lord is in this
place, and I did not know it.' He was afraid and said, 'What an awe-
some place this is! This is none other than the house of God. This is the
gate of Heaven.'

Now his legs could barely keep him standing, and the rabbi
struggled desperately to overcome his elation. Upon this rock
the Holy of Holies had been erected by King Solomon's masons
for one purpose: to permanently house the Ark of the Covenant.
And now it would stand here again.

The gate of heaven would open once more.

81.

At the top of the water passage, Enoch turned onto his back and grabbed at the grate with his shaky blue fingers. Then he gave the thing a good shove.

Nothing happened.

He fought the desperation. *It's not like they used screws in the old days*, he reminded himself. It simply had to be rusted or stuck.

Another shove. Then some intense pounding with fists. The warm air blowing down from above was making his thawing skin itchy.

Come on! Damn it!

He wasn't about to go back into that cistern.

Grunting, he tried a bench-press motion – steady, even pressure.

Something on the right side let out a gritty *snap* and the grate popped up lopsidedly.

'Hah!' Enoch jubilantly yelled out.

The rest of the job was much easier as he bent back the rusty hinges on the grate's opposite side.

One threat gone, another taking its place.

He remained perfectly still and listened. Nothing.

Cautiously, Enoch poked his head up from the hole, praying that a bullet wouldn't split his noggin. That's when he saw that he was in a long tunnel that was easily wide enough to drive a truck through.

Enoch felt completely disoriented as he pulled himself up and out of the hole.

In one direction, the overhead string of work lights led far off to what appeared to be a dead end. There were seven or eight bodies intermittently strewn along the passage in thick puddles of blood. But behind him, only a few meters back, was the flaming rubble where the Western Wall Tunnel had collapsed.

That's when it hit him.

Cohen had dug his way beneath the Temple Mount to access this ancient tunnel. And the water passage Enoch had just crawled up had most likely been intended as one of its sewer drains.

It didn't take a map for Enoch to realize that this tunnel made a beeline beneath the Dome of the Rock. 'M-m-my G-G-God,' he said with trembling lips, teeth clicking like a keyboard.

The air was cool, but it was a huge improvement over the water. And from the far end of the passage, a subtle breeze was wafting over his dripping face.

Keep moving.

He began with a fast, sloppy trot that forced blood back to his legs. Then he quickened the pace, his bare feet slapping rhythmically along the ancient paving stones. As he passed the downed men wearing blue jumpsuits, he snatched up three abandoned machine guns to replace his waterlogged Jericho.

Within two minutes, he'd reached the spot where the breeze was blowing strongest – a staircase leading up to a swath of night sky.

82.

Charlotte watched the robed priests set down the box dead center on the huge, flat stone that was the shrine's focal point. The carrying poles were slid out from the box's corner loops and set aside. While they stripped off the animal furs laid over its blue veil, Cohen stood close to them, praying intently. When only the blue shroud remained – the final protective layer – the Ark's sharp contours and double-humped lid were more pronounced.

Cohen stretched his hands to heaven and pronounced Isaiah's prophecy: "'And it shall come to pass in the last days, that the mountain of the Lord's house shall be established in the top of the mountains and shall be exalted above the hills; and all nations shall flow unto it. And many people shall go and say, come ye, and let us go up to the mountain of the Lord, to the house of the God of Jacob; and he will teach us of His ways, and we will walk in his paths: for out of Zion shall go forth the law, and the word of the Lord from Jerusalem.'"

Four priests surrounded the Ark, each claiming a corner of the shroud. They took much care not to come into contact with what lay beneath it. With hands outstretched, Cohen signaled for them to proceed. Pulling the sides up and drawing the shroud tight, the priests raised it up, then shuffled sideways until the overhead lights splashed over the gleaming gold lid.

'The Ark of the Covenant, Charlotte. Behold the world's most coveted relic, the vessel of God's essence.'

83.

Charlotte's mix of grief and rage was temporarily trumped by intrigue. What little she knew about the Ark of the Covenant began cycling through her thoughts – tales of an all-powerful weapon that directly channeled God's wrath. An ancient lockbox for Moses's Ten Commandments. Of course, there was also Charlton Heston and that whole Indiana Jones thing.

Nonetheless, the box's beauty was awe inspiring – even more impressive than Spielberg's best-guess Hollywood mock-up. The workmanship was incredible, particularly the fine detail that went into the unfolded feathered wings of the lid's two lifelike angel figurines, which knelt with heads bowed. All the box's edges were covered with ornate braiding. Could it really be the fabled Ark of the Covenant? That could certainly help to explain the strange energy coursing through the thing.

'I thought the Ark was lost,' Charlotte said.

'Only in the movies and in legends,' Cohen said. 'Never lost, but hidden for a very, very long time.'

'By who?'

He smiled. 'Me, my father, my grandfather – my ancestors. An unbroken chain of men who were the custodians of the Lord's covenant.'

Studying him for a moment, she could see that he was serious – dead serious. 'So why bring it out now? You're just going to leave it here? In a Muslim shrine?'

He answered with a question. 'See this stone beneath your feet?'

Charlotte glanced down at it. Surely it had significance or the Muslims wouldn't have built around it. She couldn't remember much about Islam, but she could recall from a college class she'd taken on world religions what this place was meant to commemorate. 'Where Muhammad rose to heaven.'

This immediately made the rabbi's face contort.

'That is a fabrication made up by zealous Muslim caliphs who'd have used any excuse to expand their empire,' he growled. 'Now listen to what I say to you.' Pacing over to her, he began circling like an animal of prey. 'This is the Foundation Stone,' he said, sweeping his hands out as if presenting it to her as a gift, 'where God created the world and breathed life into Adam. It is the place where Abraham built an altar to sacrifice his own son to God. And it is where Jacob saw the gateway to God's eternal domain – to the Light.'

'And what does the Ark have to do with all that?' The question seemed to disappoint him.

'Everything,' he answered with utmost passion. 'Around this very stone, Solomon erected his temple, as instructed by God. Where you now stand, the walls of its most sacred sanctuary would once have protected the Foundation Stone. And when Zion was first established as a nation, there was one thing that held it together.' He motioned to the Ark.

'A box?'

'The Ark isn't just a box, Charlotte. Don't test Him with blasphemy,' he warned, pointing heavenward. 'The Ark is a direct link to God. In it, his covenant has been preserved, awaiting atonement . . . awaiting the Chosen One to bring its divine powers back to Zion. And everything you see here' – his broad hand gestures indicated not only the shrine, but everything around it – 'will all be taken down. Not a stone unturned. Just as Jesus foretold. A new temple will rise up according to God's plan – an earthly kingdom built to honor Him, so that all nations will worship in peace and harmony.'

'Sounds like a plan,' she scoffed. 'But I don't think the Muslims are going to appreciate that.'

'They don't belong here,' he soberly replied. 'Their shrine is a mockery of God. Their place is in Mecca – eight hundred miles from here. When God passes his judgment, these Muslims can return to their homeland, or they will perish.'

The sound of helicopters sweeping overhead drew the rabbi's eyes up to the cupola. 'Free her hands and bring her to me,' he ordered, moving to within a meter of the Ark.

The priests sliced away Charlotte's bindings and brought her beside him.

'Now, Charlotte,' he said with more urgency. 'We are going to open the Ark. You and I. We're going to restore the Testimony so that a new covenant will be made. Then it will be up to God to determine the fate of this place.' He spread his hands and rolled his eyes up to the cupola.

'It can't be that easy.'

'Wait and see,' he promised.

84.

From the shadows, Amit had watched as Cohen and his men hurried into the Dome of the Rock with the Ark and the female hostage, then pulled the doors closed.

He'd been tempted to pick off the remaining two gunmen with the Beretta. But the short-barreled pistol wasn't suited for long-distance shooting. There was also the option of rushing them, trying to take them by surprise. But the gap was wide, the pistol was no match for a machine gun, and Amit was no small target. Not to mention that the choppers were quickly closing in. And if the Israelis confused him for the enemy, he'd be gunned down on sight.

'Amit!' a voice suddenly called.

He spun around. It was Enoch . . . coming up through the hole the rabbi's men had burrowed beneath the Temple Mount.

'What took you so long?' Amit said with open arms.

Keeping a careful eye on the choppers zigzagging overhead, Enoch ran over to him. 'What the hell is going on up here? Are we too late?'

'Not sure,' Amit said, eyeing his friend curiously. Enoch was barefoot and soaked to the bone. His pale face, tinted blue, had him looking like the walking dead. Under his right arm were three Galils. 'What in God's name happened to you?'

'Long story,' he glibly replied, preoccupied with that fact that Amit had actually considered taking on the enemy with his puny handgun. 'Get rid of that peashooter and take one of these.' He tossed a Galil to Amit.

'Much appreciated,' he said, catching it smoothly with his left hand.

'They're in the shrine, aren't they?' Enoch ejected the magazine from the third Galil before abandoning it in the flower garden.

'Afraid so,' Amit gloomily replied.

'The rabbi and how many others?' he asked, pocketing the magazine.

'Nine left. I think only two or three with weapons.'

'Better odds than Gaza.'

'Much better.'

'And the woman?'

'Still alive.'

'Right.' He took a deep breath. The icicles in his lungs were starting to thaw. 'You have your mobile with you?' Thanks to the cistern, Enoch's own phone had fizzled out the moment he tried to power it on.

'Yeah,' Amit said, pulling it out of his pocket.

Enoch put a call in to Mossad headquarters, and after providing his agent ID number, he informed the desk that Cohen and his crew had already made it inside the Dome of the Rock with an unidentified procurement and a hostage. He didn't need to insist on backup or provide instruction. Necessary protocols had already begun.

'We can't wait for backup,' Amit said. 'If Cohen hears them coming—'

'I know,' Enoch replied. He handed the phone back. 'I have no intention of dying in there. So let's make it count. Shall we?'

'We shall,' Amit proudly replied. How the kid had grown. Not exactly like old times.

The two raced up the steps and across the platform. There was a double door centered on the lower marble-clad tier of the shrine's wall. As in the other seven walls, there were seven stained-glass windows positioned in line above the doors, where the wall's marble cladding gave way to magnificent Arabian tiles. So there wasn't much concern about anyone on the inside seeing them coming.

Once they reached the wall, Enoch immediately raised his machine gun to blow out the doors' center lock. But Amit quickly waved it away and dug into his pocket for his trusty lock-picking set.

85.

Standing over the Ark, Charlotte was surprised by its robust dimensions. She could easily curl up inside it. Dominating the front of the box was a cartouche set above a large engraved disk with lines radiating down, each connecting to an ankh – no doubt a depiction of the sun. Small ideograms in neat columns covered the remainder of the front side, as well as the Ark's side panels. She guessed the rear panel was similarly engraved. The designs could have come from only one place. 'These Egyptian symbols and hieroglyphs,' she said. 'Why are they . . .' Her voice trailed off.

The rabbi smiled knowingly. 'Long ago, Egypt had been the dwelling place of the inexplicable life force the Egyptians called *ka*, the source of ultimate power attributed to the sun and the eternal light. Ancient Egyptians worshipped hundreds of gods, but the sun god *always* reigned supreme. Their entire society embodied it – from buildings to funerary rituals. And their secrets had been encoded in stone for thousands of years, in temples, tombs, pyramids. Through the centuries, they'd given it many, many names: Ra, Atum, Amun, Aten. But a single visionary pharaoh understood it best.'

Cohen went on to explain that around 1350 B.C.E., Egypt's first and only monotheistic ruler, Akhenaton, came to power and commanded that a new capital be constructed on the Nile's east bank, set between the power centers of Memphis in the north and Thebes in the south – a city entirely dedicated to a single supreme god and creator. In the process, the pharaoh had completely abandoned the traditional polytheistic temple system, which had brought tremendous wealth and power to the centuries-old Egyptian priesthood, the priests of Amen.

'Akhenaton made many enemies,' Cohen continued. 'So when terrible plagues befell Egypt during his reign, the priests of Amen expeditiously blamed the misfortune on Akhenaton's religious digressions. They claimed that the pharaoh had tampered with *Ma'at* – the spiritual bonds uniting all elements in the universe. Hence a rebellion began brewing throughout the land, fueled by the pharaoh's increasing number of political dissenters. Fearing not only assassination and reprisals against his family but destruction of his new capital, Akhenaton entrusted the clandestine export of his most powerful relics to his closest vizier.' *Just like in 154 B.C.E., when Onias fled the rogue Sanhedrin in Jerusalem, took the Ark from its hiding place in Qumran, and brought it to safety in Heliopolis,* Cohen thought. 'The vizier was a virtuous man who had mastered the ancient secrets during his tenure as high priest in Akhenaton's temple. His name was Moses.'

'*The* Moses?'

'That's right,' Cohen replied.

Cohen was on the verge of ranting – a man teetering on the precipice of a lifetime's endeavors all coalescing in a single event. Charlotte could tell that Cohen needed to tell his story, almost as if to ensure that should his ambitious plan fail, his secret knowledge (perhaps even his justification for his actions) might be passed on. And she wanted to encourage him, because if she could keep him talking, stall him a little longer, perhaps the Israelis might get to him before anything worse could happen.

'Luckily, Moses did agree to Akhenaton's request. But Moses feared an even more calamitous reprisal against those who'd always believed in the one true god: an industrious and mysterious group of Semitic tribes tens of thousands strong who had lived in the Nile Delta for over four centuries.'

'The Israelites?' Charlotte said.

'Very good,' he said approvingly. 'After secreting the temple relics north and preparing them for transport across the Sinai, Moses secretly went to the elders of the Israelite tribes. He knew that their ancestral beliefs traced back to a great patriarch named Abraham, who legend told had been the first to speak with the one god. Legend also told that the one god had promised Abraham's progeny a return to their tribal lands in the north. So Moses convinced the elders that the time of the prophecy had arrived. And under the cover of darkness, the Israelites abandoned their villages and rendezvoused with Moses at the Sinai.'

'And the exodus began,' she muttered.

Cohen nodded and his nervous eyes began scouting the shrine. He waved a couple of the robed men closer.

Keep him occupied! Charlotte thought. Frantic, she tried to remember the biblical account of the exodus. But at the forefront of her brain was the film adaptation produced in the 1950s with Charlton Heston raising a magical staff to part the sea for the Israelites, the Egyptians giving chase, the waters crashing down upon them. 'So then why did the pharaoh send his armies after Moses? Did he change his mind?'

Cohen managed to chuckle. 'Those were not Akhenaton's armies that pursued Moses and the Israelites. Those soldiers were dispatched from Memphis by Akhenaton's coregent, Smenkhkare – a malevolent schemer who supported the priests of Amun, a snake who had even had an affair with Akhenaton's wife, Nefertiti, and fathered her son.'

'*The* Nefertiti?' she asked. This exodus story was fast becoming a who's who of Egypt.

'That's right. But that beautiful, iconic Egyptian queen was a very treacherous woman.' His eyes pinched tight. 'With six daughters and no heir to his throne, Akhenaton had been so elated to have a son, he never suspected his wife's infidelity.'

Cohen considered stopping here but felt compelled to finish the story. After all, the woman deserved to understand the necessity of what was to happen next.

'But Nefertiti's ambitions had only just begun,' said Cohen. 'After Moses successfully fled Egypt, Nefertiti conspired with Smenkhkare to kill her husband by poisoning. Smenkhkare then attempted to erase Akhenaton's name from dynastic history – the deepest insult to an Egyptian pharaoh. For in the remembrance of the name, the spirit lived on. Akhenaton's new capital city was abandoned, his cartouches scratched off temples and tombs . . .' He sighed. 'And to honor Smenkhkare and restore honor to the priests of Amun, Nefertiti changed her son's name from Tutankhaten, "the living image of Aten," to Tutankhamun, "the living image of Amun."'

This took a moment to sink in. 'Wait. You mean King Tut?'

Cohen nodded. 'And only a year after murdering her husband, Nefertiti poisoned Smenkhkare too, so that Tut's true paternity would remain a secret. Naturally the boy inherited the throne in Thebes. Then Tut became Nefertiti's pawn,' he scoffed. 'God's retribution eventually did come, though it took almost a decade. The priests of Amun turned against Tut and his manipulative mother. Both were assassinated. An ironic twist of fate, wouldn't you say?'

Charlotte didn't answer, though the story was indeed reminiscent of a Sophoclean tragedy.

'Without the treasures of Aten, however, even the priests of Amun could never return the kingdom to its past glory. Egypt was never to rise again.'

'And how do you know all this?' she had to ask.

'The most profound knowledge is not found in books, Charlotte. That is why legacies are so vital to humanity. The written word deceives. The most awesome truths – the most *fearsome* truths – are those handed down through the righteous words of our most trusted ancestors. There is much to learn from history. Yet people forget. Pride. Vanity. Complacency . . .'

Now she was sensing that Cohen's patience had run out. But she needed to try to keep up the charade. She pointed to the glyphs. 'And what does all this say?'

'That is the story of God,' he reluctantly replied, more abrupt now. 'The origins of the universe and creation. It is also a warning given by Moses about what resides within the Ark, how it should be feared and respected. And see there?' Centered on the Ark's front side, he pointed to glyphs representing a feather, sun disks, water, and an ibis – all framed within an oval outline. 'That is Akhenaton's royal cartouche. His seal.' Charlotte regarded the Ark with equal doses of fear, reverence, and skepticism.

Another low-flying helicopter made the cupola rattle. Cohen's anxiety visibly deepened.

Eyeing the Ark again, she fished for another question. 'And the two angels on the lid? What are they?'

His reply was curt: 'Each is a depiction of the winged female goddess that embodied the harmony of creation: Ma'at. But that is enough, Charlotte. It is time to proceed. Kneel before the Ark,' Cohen urged her in an appeasing tone. 'Then I want you to remove the lid.'

She took a step back and held up her hands. 'You're a good storyteller. I'll give you that. But I'm not on board with this whole end-of-times thing you've got going on here—'

'I'd hate to have to drug you and pull your hands like a puppet,' he soberly replied. 'After all that we have gone through to get here . . .' He pursed his lips and shook his head. 'One way or another, the Ark is going to be opened,' he flatly stated. 'After all that you've sacrificed, and after all the hidden truths I've just shared with you, wouldn't you like to be awake to see with your own eyes the secrets of the universe? Wouldn't you like to see what Moses carried off from the Egyptians? Don't you long to know that everything that has happened to you has had a purpose – a divine design? Do you think God is in you by accident?'

She didn't know what to say. Her reluctance was starting to dissolve.

'You must be very curious as to what we've protected for so many centuries, no?'

Perhaps he was right, but she could tell that his curiosity easily trumped hers. The guy was practically jumping out of his skin. If this was the real deal . . .

Then, as she looked back at the lid, a plan began unfolding in her mind. 'Fine. Let's open it.' Now she was the one going all-in at the poker table. However, the real question loomed large: was *he* bluffing?

Cohen's face softened with a smile. 'Handle it carefully,' he reminded her.

This wasn't the first time she'd been asked to open Pandora's box. Granted, the Vatican's approach had been more pragmatic. As she eased down onto her knees before the Ark, her heart was jackhammering behind her breastbone. Now she began a silent prayer of her own. She could feel the rabbi drawing close behind her to watch over the ritual, and the final part of her plan fell into place. 'Won't this be too heavy?' she asked, hesitating and eyeing the lid. 'It's gold, right?'

'A thin gold sheathing covering acacia wood. A purposeful design, since the Israelite priests would've been incapable of carrying a solid gold box of this size. You'll have no problems.'

Charlotte looked around for any opportunity to escape, but the two surviving gunmen were posted on opposing sides of the shrine, behind the rock's cordons. And they were watching vigilantly.

'I beseech You, O Lord,' Cohen chanted in Hebrew, raising his hands up. 'Grant atonement for the sins, iniquities, and transgressions that the entire house of Israel has committed against You. As it is written in the books of your servants Moses and Jesus, atonement shall be made for You on this day to purify all sins. Before the Lord shall we be purified.'

The priests unanimously responded with 'Blessed be the Name of His glorious kingdom, forever and ever.'

Charlotte reached out and positioned both hands on the short sides of the lid, the tingling sensation coursing up through her fingers.

Cohen watched in astonishment as Charlotte's hands spread over the elaborate lid – the *Kaporet* ('atonement piece') or Mercy Seat. His focus homed in on the void beneath the outstretched wings of the gilded cherubim. For there, God's presence, the

Shechinah, would begin to converge to reign over Abraham's altar, to judge and purify – to speak to humankind and provide guidance and law.

Curling her fingers tight under the lid's braided rim, Charlotte took a deep breath and applied pressure.

86.

At first, the Ark's lid resisted.

Charlotte dug her fingers in tighter until they turned white.

Then came a muffled *pop*, followed by the hissing sound of escaping gas. The sound immediately brought a flashback of her and Dr. Giovanni Bersei's opening Jesus's ossuary in the Vatican Museums.

Another incredibly preserved ancient seal had just been breached.

As the lid unseated from the Ark, Charlotte could already detect a faint glow emanating from deep within, forming a rectangular halo around the lid. At the same time, the tingling sensations had quickly migrated up her arms and spread into her chest. Now her curiosity was giving way to a raw, primordial terror that signaled danger.

Her eyes went wide as the void beneath the wings of the cherubim began to noticeably change – the distortion she'd detected the first time she'd touched the Ark. Like a tiny, gathering cloud, something was forming there. Mist? Smoke?

The rabbi's excitement built with the Ark's response. 'Few

have ever laid eyes upon this wonder. Moses, David, Solomon . . . Behold!'

Eyes fixated on the opaque orb, Charlotte detected a brilliant white glow at its core – a pinpoint of light that burned with the blinding intensity of a welder's torch.

An electrostatic energy began to build, lifting short strands along her hairline. The atmosphere was changing. *Impossible.* Adrenaline poured through her system, threatening panic. But the tingling that had spread through her entire body brought forth a sudden transformation – an inexplicable calm.

'Now see what is inside,' Cohen urged her.

Tearing her attention from the orb, she reared up on her haunches to see what she'd uncovered, carefully resting the lid upon her lap.

On the right of the Ark's interior were indeed neatly piled stone tablets – though it appeared to be hieroglyphs that covered them, not some form of ancient Hebrew as legend suggested. Laid atop them was a beautiful gold, gem-encrusted scepter in the shape of a serpent, its tail straightened along the short staff and coiling near the top to its fanged head, an ankh between its eyes.

But Charlotte was transfixed by the source of the most unearthly luminescence being generated on the Ark's interior left half – a neatly packed human skeleton. And the eye sockets of its smooth skull were glaring directly up at her.

87.

'*Moshe*,' Cohen gasped in vindication. 'Moses,' he repeated for Charlotte's benefit.

Could it be? Charlotte wondered.

He began reciting Deuteronomy 34: '"Then Moses went up from the plains of Moab to Mount Nebo and the Lord showed him all the land ... saying: 'This is the land I promised Abraham, Isaac, and Jacob when I said, "I will give it to your descendants." I have let you see it with your own eyes, but you will not cross into it.' So Moses died there as the Lord had said. God buried him in the valley and no one to this day knows where his grave is. Moses was one hundred and twenty years old when he died; his eyes were not weak, and his vitality had not left him."'

She stared at the bones during his utterance. 'So God interred Moses in the Ark?'

'Yes, Charlotte,' he replied, remaining behind her. 'But notice in the words I just spoke that the Torah states that Moses did not die from physical ailment. He was a perfectly healthy one-hun-dred-and-twenty-year-old with the body of a young man.'

'So either he killed himself,' she surmised, 'or . . . God killed him?'

'God *sacrificed* Moses's body to free his spirit for the next realm,' he said in a soft tone. 'The covenant – the *Testimony* – isn't just the laws written on those tablets. It is an elevation of the human spirit to a boundless existence. These remains left behind – Moses's *bones*,' he said, pointing inside the Ark, 'are a physical connection to the most sacred legacy. The bones are the vessel through which the Testimony had been passed on to the next Messiah.'

'Jesus?'

He nodded. 'And when the Spirit passed into Jesus, he preached the Lord's word, then sacrificed himself atop Golgotha to seal the covenant God had spoken through Him – the Second Covenant. Or if you prefer, the New Testament.'

'I don't remember Jesus willingly killing himself,' Charlotte countered. 'Judas betrayed Him.' There was that whole story about Gethsemane when soldiers came to arrest him.

Cohen smiled. 'Misinterpretation,' he sternly replied. 'Judas was an Essene, certainly no traitor. Jesus sent him to the Sanhedrin to facilitate the final sacrifice.'

'That can't be right,' she insisted.

'Oh?' He tilted his head. 'I ask you, then: when Jesus named his betrayer at the final meal, did the other disciples try to stop Judas?'

Good point, she thought. 'No.'

'In fact, they all went to the Mount of Olives to await the Temple Authority, just as Jesus had planned. The words are there, yet the truth is missed,' he said. 'Another reason why the oral legacy is so vital.' He made a ball of his fist. 'If one reads the texts according to their historical context, the Bible tells a most remarkable story of human existence, an evolution of spirituality that shifted from metaphorical rituals of animal sacrifice in the First Covenant to the slaughter of our own egos and pride that God taught through Jesus in His Second Covenant – the metaphors transformed into parables. Now we herald a Third Covenant.' He spread his hands over her head to indicate the glowing orb.

Charlotte watched as one of the priests presented something to Cohen – shiny, long.

'But like each of its predecessors, the New Covenant begins with blood. Sacred blood.'

88.

Enoch snapped some bullets out of the spare magazine to fill the empty slots in Amit's Galil and flipped the safeties off. He then insisted on going through the door first. His rationale was sound: 'I'm a much smaller target,' he told Amit. 'Standard protocol.'

Point taken. 'Fine. I've got the right,' Amit said.

'Okay.'

'Just don't shoot the hostage this time,' Amit teased. During one of the Gaza raids, Enoch had planted three rounds in the buttocks of an Israeli diplomat.

'Funny,' he grunted.

'You scared?'

'Scared shitless,' he responded with a big smile.

'Godspeed, my friend,' Amit said, clasping his friend's hand.

Since there were no exterior handles or knobs, Amit wedged his fingertips under the left door's vertical stop and squeezed slightly to lever the door just enough to confirm that the lock was indeed breached.

In a sideways stance, Enoch was a meter from the door,

weapon raised to his sodden right shoulder. His left hand stabilized the muzzle along his sight line, and his right index finger was hooked at the ready on the trigger – hunt-and-scope mode. Rolling his neck, he drew breath, held it, and signaled to Amit.

89.

Before Charlotte could turn to get a better look at what Cohen had in his right hand, the fingers of his left hand had snaked through her hair and cranked her head back. A knee simultaneously jammed into her spine.

'Before the Lord shall we be purified!' he declared, his bestial eyes riveted to the bare flesh of her neck.

Now she had an upside-down view of the meaty gold blade Cohen was bringing down over her throat in preparation for a broad slice.

Just as her fingers clutched the glowing Mercy Seat, there came a loud disturbance from behind, immediately followed by gunfire.

The rabbi's face showed surprise, but his gaze did not falter. He bared his teeth and prepared to cut her to the bone, to seal the covenant – at any cost.

But Charlotte had a different plan. As he crouched deeper to position the blade for a long, sweeping slash, she swung the Ark's lid up into his face. It was unavoidable that the blade would cut her. How deep was the only uncertainty.

The sharp-edged wings of the gilded angels caught him below the chin. Crackling tendrils spat across the sphere's surface and webbed over his face. Instinctively, he dropped the dagger mid-pull as his hands went for the lid.

Charlotte rolled out from under him, clutching at the blood spewing from the left side of her neck.

Grasping both sides of the lid like a serving tray, Cohen tried to throw the thing away, but the light held him steady between the angels, physically grasping at him, pulling his face forward. Shrieking in pain, he tried shaking his head free, but to no avail. The beard, earlocks, and hair sizzled away almost instantly. Then the light turned on the flesh, unfastening it, stretching it from the bones of his face, tearing it away in wet slabs.

More agonizing screams; tremors shaking the body . . .

Simultaneously, Cohen's hands succumbed to the fury, the flesh rising up into horrid boils that blackened and split to release the ghastly red-brown ooze beneath. He fell to his knees before the Ark, pitching forward so that the lid fell back into place on the Ark's base. Beneath the vestments, the entirety of his body was roasted within seconds, his organs bursting.

Then the robes went up in flames.

The light did not relinquish its hold until Cohen's entire body had burned so fiercely that the gold frontlet and breastplate had melted into his blackened bones. Only then did the blinding glow subside and let the hideous remains slide onto the rock.

The fetid stench of burnt hair and flesh had Charlotte gagging as she scrambled away on hands and knees, blood trailing beneath her in splotches. The room seemed to be spinning as she struggled for air. How deep had Cohen cut her?

When she lifted her eyes and tried to get to her feet, her spotty vision captured one of the blue-suited gunmen in triplicate. He was pinned down behind one of the huge marble columns supporting the cupola. He swung his machine gun at her, his face snarling with hate. In that instant, she knew that her luck had run out.

She hoped that Cohen had been right – that God did have a plan for everything, that her life had meant something or had some divine destiny. Perhaps, as Donovan had suggested, in death there'd be another realm where the spirit would defy the flesh and roam free . . .

Knowing she'd cheated death one too many times, Charlotte Hennesey shut her eyes in peaceful surrender, just before she heard the gun let loose its fury.

90.

After taking down one of the gunmen, Enoch rounded the ambulatory. That's when seven robed men came charging across the rock, screaming like banshees. As far as he could tell, they weren't armed. But he needed to get below the shrine immediately, which meant there was no time to negotiate. The best he could do was show some civility by shooting them low.

Enoch made three sweeps with the Galil, strafing the marauders below the knees, dropping six of them onto the rock. The seventh man managed to hobble even closer and gripped the railing to vault himself over it. A nasty shot to the groin put an end to those ambitions, and the man crumpled back onto the rock, screaming in agony.

Enoch went directly for the steps descending beneath an elaborate marble arch ornamented with gold Arabic text – the access way to the cave below the rock called the Well of Souls. He knew it to be a mystical realm where, according to legend, the voices of the dead could be heard. Running purely on adrenaline, he needed to remind himself not to be foolish and turn *himself* into one of the dead down there.

Ducking low, he peeked at the bottom of the steps. What little of the space below he could make out was brightly lit. There didn't seem to be any shadows moving across the ornate Persian rugs covering the ground. It was also evident that there was nothing that would provide cover. If another gunman were hunkered down at the bottom of the stairs, he'd be a fish in a bowl. And this time, no Kevlar vest, either. Down there, at close range, head shots would be easy.

But if Cohen had secreted a bomb into the building, the cave would be the most logical place to position it: right where a strong explosion could be amplified enough to take down Islam's sacred rock, right along with the foundation supporting the shrine's walls.

And it all came tumbling down.

Taking a deep breath, he pressed forward, weapon at the ready on his shoulder, trying his best to keep his muscles loose and his trigger finger flexible.

The marble treads were like ice against his bare feet. He crouched low and dashed down the steps. Two thirds of the way to the bottom, he jumped and immediately did a tuck and roll when his feet connected with the ground. Heroism aside, he knew he stood a better chance moving abruptly and unevenly. Better than getting his legs shot out from under him.

One controlled tumble and Enoch rolled up into a well-executed crouch. He immediately depressed the Galil's trigger and emptied a third of the clip in a wide sweep.

The biggest danger was the wild ricochets. One deflected round managed to graze his left shoulder.

The cave was empty. No hidden gunmen.

No bomb either.

Heart pounding, Enoch exhaled and pulled himself together.

That's when he noticed the stark white angular casing of a newly installed security camera mounted high up the cave wall just beneath the stairs. And if he didn't know any better, he'd swear that its lens winked in the light to tighten in on him.

'Crap.'

91.

'Rumor has it you're the next messiah,' a deep voice said.

Amazed that she was still alive, Charlotte eased her eyes open. There was a broad-shouldered guy with a goatee standing over her, smiling.

'Amit Mizrachi,' he said, introducing himself. He slung his machine gun over his shoulder and maneuvered to help her to her feet.

Dazed, Charlotte glanced over at the column, where, just beyond the railing, Cohen's last gunman was facedown and spread-eagle, soaked with blood.

'Your throat all right?' He tried to see where the blood was coming from but couldn't make out anything.

Probing it with her fingers, she found that the four-inch gash that had been there just seconds ago had already smoothed over. 'Yeah. It . . . it is,' she said. 'Thank you. I don't know what I would have done if . . .'

'Looks like you handled yourself just fine without us,' Amit said, giving the rabbi's charred corpse a sideways glance.

'Us?' Charlotte could see only dead bodies.

The rumble of rotor blades was shaking the cupola again, much closer now.

Then the second man materialized through an archway to her left. When he saw that Amit had secured the area, he slung his Galil over his shoulder and let out a whistle. 'All clear below.'

As Enoch hopped the rail onto the rock and made his way over, a repulsed look twisted his face when he saw what had happened to Cohen. Despite the grotesqueness of it all, he found himself moving closer to inspect the body, and more important the magnificent glimmering relic looming over it. 'What in hell—'

'Don't touch the box!' Amit yelled over to him.

Startled, Enoch immediately fell back a step and held up his hands. 'What the—?'

'Sorry,' Amit softly replied. 'It's just that . . . well, you can see what it did to the rabbi.' He'd barely glimpsed the rabbi go up in flames upon contact with the Ark's lid.

'Gotcha.' He cringed again. It appeared to Enoch that the rabbi might have been the victim of intense radiation burn. His eyes suddenly went wide and he pointed to the Ark. 'Is it nuclear?'

'Something like that,' Amit said. 'But if you don't touch it, you've got nothing to worry about.' That piece of Ark legend certainly seemed true. 'Right, Charlotte?'

She pictured the glowing bones inside the Ark. Moses? Her eyes went back to Cohen's charred corpse. Shaking her head, she didn't quite know how to respond.

'Ah. There's one up here too,' Enoch blurted, pointing to the cupola's base where his gaze happened upon another discreetly mounted security camera. 'Have a look.'

Taking two steps closer, Amit craned his head until he saw the device's tiny lens glinting in the light. 'Well, that should make things a bit more interesting.' If the camera wasn't just for show, the Muslims were sure to have a field day with the footage.

'A camera downstairs got a great shot of me shooting up the Well of Souls, too,' Enoch confessed. 'That can't be good.'

Both Amit and Charlotte looked at him and cringed.

'What were you shooting at?' Amit said.

Enoch's cheeks immediately reddened. He shrugged, saying: 'It was a precaution.'

Amit's eyebrows tipped up. *A stupendous mess.* And the Israelis were going to have one helluva a time spinning it all. Striding to the Rock's edge and clambering over the railing, he inspected the walls above the ambulatory. Immediately he spotted another camera glaring down about three meters behind the Arab he'd riddled with bullets. He groaned in frustration.

'Another one?' Enoch yelled over.

'Yep,' he sighed.

'You did what you had to do,' Charlotte said. 'If you hadn't stopped him . . .' She motioned to the rabbi's remains and the Israeli's eyes followed. 'Can you imagine what might have happened?'

'I suppose.' Slouching on the railing, Amit momentarily transfixed on the Ark. Did Cohen really believe that by returning the legendary relic to the Foundation Stone he'd invoke God's retribution upon the Muslims? Did he expect legions of angels to come liberate Zion? Then again, what if Cohen *had* actually fulfilled his ambitions? Suddenly sensing the enormous weight of the death spread about him, Amit felt a cold chill come over him.

He knew the maelstrom had only just begun.

92.

Amit and Enoch immediately collected the weapons from the two dead Palestinians and Cohen's six guards and piled them in a faraway corner. Confirming that the seven robed men were all immobile and posed no threat (thanks to Enoch's crafty shooting), they tossed their own weapons on the pile too. Then they sat beside Charlotte, in clear view of the shrine's open doorway.

'Best to raise our hands so they don't confuse us with the bad guys,' Enoch suggested.

They all raised their hands high.

A minute later, the rover bot came treading over the threshold and squeaked to a stop three meters from the door. Its camera arm telescoped out and panned side to side, then settled on the three survivors.

'Wave hello,' Enoch said. He waved and flashed a thumbs-up. Then he loudly reported his name and rank for the bot's microphone. 'All clear in here,' he added.

Within seconds, soldiers began funneling into the shrine with weapons drawn, fanning out along the ambulatory.

'Just don't touch that big gold box over there!' Amit yelled to them as they passed by.

Charlotte conveyed instructions to the Israeli commanders on how Cohen's men had safely covered and transported the Ark. Then Amit assisted her out of the shrine, holding her by the arm.

Amit was still buzzing with excitement. This night had far and away surpassed the raw excitement of any raid in Gaza. And having beheld firsthand the Ark of the Covenant was the ultimate archaeological dream come true.

The scene outside was chaotic: helicopters set down on the Dome of the Rock's raised platform and Israeli troops as far as the eye could see. And Enoch was at the center of it all, taking quick drags on a bummed cigarette between sentences. Encircled by IDF commanders, he was recounting in great detail what had transpired inside the dome.

Charlotte looked up at Amit. 'Do you really believe that's the Ark of the Covenant in there?'

The question surprised Amit. 'You saw what it did to Cohen. Absolutely, I'd say it's the real thing.'

'And how about me being a messiah?' she jested.

He paused to consider this. 'Rabbi Cohen might have been a bit crazy. But if *he* believed you were . . .' He shrugged.

'Hey!' a female voice yelled over to Amit.

Glancing up, Amit was surprised to see Jules tottering over to him, shirt tied below her chest and clutching a bandage taped to her left side. Grinning widely, he stopped in his tracks.

'What is this?' Jules said with pretend offense. 'I'm gone only an hour and you're already in the arms of another woman? Haven't you learned your lesson?'

Amit shook his head. 'You've got chutzpah, I'll give you that.'

Jules threw her arms around him and held him tight for five seconds. 'God, I was worried sick about you.'

'How did you – ?'

'The police got to me before the ambulance arrived. When I told them what happened, they were kind enough to share their first aid kit and give me a ride here.'

'Good to see that chivalry is still alive and well,' Amit said.

'After all you told me about the temple and the Ark, I knew they'd find you here.'

'Clever.'

'Thanks.'

Amit formally introduced Charlotte.

Jules had been so focused on Amit that she hadn't noticed the woman's neck was covered in blood. Alarmed, she said, 'My goodness, Charlotte . . . Are you all right?' Gently cradling Charlotte's chin, she tried to find the wound. 'Is this your blood?'

'Yes, but—'

'Where are you hurt? We need to take care of this.'

'Actually I'm fine, Julie. It's a bit complicated. But thank you. How about you?' Cringing, Charlotte pointed to her bandaged stomach.

'I'll get to the hospital later. It's just a graze.'

'Actually, maybe I can help you with that.'

93.

THREE DAYS LATER

As Ghalib had hoped, the Israeli prime minister and president were claiming no responsibility for the events that had taken place at Temple Mount. Naturally, they were having great difficulty explaining why the Israeli army had laid siege to the site, and why an underground tunnel had been secretly excavated beneath the site by a fundamentalist rabbi who'd been a former member of the Knesset. The firefight that had erupted inside the Dome of the Rock, however, proved most difficult to spin.

'An attack upon Islam's third-holiest shrine will not be taken lightly,' Ghalib's delegate promised the prime minister.

Finally, a clear line had been drawn in the sand – the tipping point.

What Ghalib's eyes had seen over the closed-circuit cameras he'd installed in the shrine had been astounding. He'd played silent witness to the uncovering of a most profound relic. Islamic legend told that the Ark of the Covenant heralded the coming of the true Messiah – and the beginning of the Last Judgment. He'd witnessed the woman open the box. He'd witnessed how it so horribly burned the rabbi alive in mere seconds.

Shortly thereafter, he'd watched the IDF secure the building. The goateed Israeli and the woman whom Cohen had taken hostage had coached the IDF commanders on how to safely remove the relic, how to cover it first with the blue cloth and animal furs. The audio feed had crisply recorded the entire conversation.

Less than an hour after the Israelis had locked down the shrine, the relic had been ferried outside by a team of men in blue jumpsuits, heavily guarded. They'd brought it down to the Western Wall Plaza and loaded it onto a truck.

Outside, Ghalib had used his digital camcorder to secretly shoot video of that too.

All that remained now was to compile the recordings onto a single DVD, carefully edit the footage, then have a courier deliver the video to Ghalib's contact at al-Jazeera.

Soon the world would witness firsthand the savagery of the Israelis: the carnage, the desecration, the defilement. The audacity of it all. The Islamic outcry would be deafening.

This would breathe new life into the intifada and force the Arab nations to formulate a response to the Jewish nation's growing threat to the region. No doubt, the coalition would grow by the day as the entirety of the Middle East would be forced to take a stance – to choose a side.

His tired caramel eyes gazed out at the Dome of the Rock's cupola, which shimmered like liquid gold against the morning sun.

'*Allahu Akbar*,' he whispered. '*Taqwa.*' Fear God.

'Sorry I am late,' a breathless voice said from the doorway. 'I came as fast as I could.'

Ghalib turned to the bearded Palestinian toting a laptop bag – the Waqf's lead IT specialist, who managed the council's Internet sites, telecommunications, and press releases. 'You are forgiven, Bilaal,' he said with a crooked grin, waving the young man inside. 'Come. I am anxious to finish this.'

While Bilaal settled in at the conference table and powered up his laptop, Ghalib set beside him the mini DVD from his digital camcorder and the slim removable hard drive from the Dome of the Rock's surveillance system.

'I need both of these on one disc – this one first,' Ghalib instructed him, pointing to the hard drive. 'You can splice the videos, yes?'

'I can do anything you want,' he assured Ghalib.

Standing with arms folded tight, Ghalib watched over the tech's shoulder.

Bilaal fished a USB cable from his bag and used it to connect the hard drive to his laptop. Then he activated a video editing program and accessed the files on Ghalib's hard drive. 'We'll run through the video first. Then you tell me what you want to do.'

'Remember, Bilaal. You are not to tell anyone about this. Do you understand?' Ghalib warned him.

As he looked up at the Keeper's baleful expression, an uneasy feeling came over Bilaal. 'You have my word.'

Back on the screen, nine video clips simultaneously came to life in a neat three-by-three grid. The tech immediately recognized the various vantage points – all interior shots of the Dome of the Rock. He tried to recall if he'd ever seen cameras inside the shrine, but nothing came to mind.

Bilaal initiated playback.

On-screen, two plainclothes Palestinians anxiously paced the shrine's dim ambulatory with semiautomatic machine guns, slipping out of one camera frame and into another. On the audio tracks, all was silent except for their bare feet plodding along the ornate Persian carpet and their heavy breathing. Camera nine provided an unchanging view of the empty cave beneath the rock – the Well of Souls.

When Bilaal studied the tiny date stamp and running clock in the lower right corner of each video window, his muscles went rigid. These were the minutes preceding the nasty firefight that had taken place at the shrine only three days ago. He'd only heard shocking rumors about the siege. But none included these armed men – these Muslims – being inside the shrine just before it all went down.

Ghalib bent and whispered, 'We'll need to delete these scenes. Understand?'

'I understand,' he tremulously replied.

'Now move it ahead about twenty minutes.'

With shaking fingers, Bilaal sent the recordings into fast-forward.

The video counter spun wildly for a few seconds. 'Ah! There! Stop there.'

Bilaal clicked on the play button. The two gunmen were now screaming back and forth to one another, agreeing to immediately begin shooting the moment anyone entered the shrine. They shouted out blessings to one another as well as praise for being chosen as martyrs. Seconds later, creaking hinges made the two gunmen retreat and take positions with their weapons trained on the shrine's southern doors.

'Now watch, Bilaal.' Grinning, Ghalib eased back and folded his arms. 'We begin here.' Ghalib tapped the images captured by camera one: doors slowly parting, moonlight spilling in through the opening.

Bilaal leaned closer to try to discern the dark silhouettes that appeared in the shrine's doorway, but he couldn't make out any of it. Then something completely unexpected happened. In chorus, all nine video frames filled with static as the feeds went off-line.

'What the—'

'What did you do there?' Ghalib snapped. 'Fix that.'

As he shrank in his chair, Bilaal's fingers worked feverishly at the keyboard, rewinding, fast-forwarding. Ghalib's sharp chin was practically resting on his left shoulder, so close he could feel the Keeper's hot breath on his neck.

After the fourth attempt, the static still came back.

'What did you do?' he hissed, nostrils flaring.

'I – I—' Bilaal was shaking his head in bewilderment, holding his hands out at the screen. 'Nothing. I swear. It's the recordings. They just . . . They stop.'

'Impossible! I watched it all happen! I watched everything through those cameras!' Ghalib slammed a hand down on the table beside him. 'Did you erase the files?' Crazed, he jabbed an index finger at the tech's face. 'Tell me you didn't erase them, Bilaal!'

He cowered in his chair. 'This isn't something I could've done. You've been watching me this whole time. I could not have . . .' He kept shaking his head. 'I erased nothing – I swear it!'

Over the next hour, Ghalib kept at it with Bilaal, going over the corrupted footage again and again . . . and again. Bilaal adjusted settings, tested the connection, swapped cables, ran diagnostics on the hard drive. Yet each time, at the very moment the shrine's doors opened, the static would take over. For good measure, Bilaal went through the entire process again using a second laptop that was his backup.

Same thing. Static.

Finally, dripping with sweat and pale as goat's milk, Bilaal tried to play back the footage Ghalib had shot with his own camcorder. That's when something even more astounding appeared – more static. The entire disc had been wiped out.

'What are you doing!' Ghalib erupted. 'See what you've done now! What have you done!'

But after he saw the inexplicable fate of the second disc, Bilaal's demeanor had changed dramatically. The man was spooked. 'What happened to these videos,' he calmly replied, shaking his head slowly and steadily, 'I cannot explain it. I can only take your word that there were videos here. But if there *were* pictures on these discs . . . and now they have been erased without explanation . . .,' he weakly replied. 'Then with all respect, I must ask something of you, Ghalib. Perhaps the same question Allah might ask.'

'What might that be?' Ghalib growled.

'What have *you* done?'

94.

ROME

The sterile corridors of the Agostino Gemelli University Polyclinic were a stark reminder of an alternate fate that might have befallen Charlotte Hennesey. Behind every door of the critical care wing, Death was patiently waiting.

Knowing that she'd been endowed with the ability to change the fate of so many was overwhelming. There was no guarantee that she could reverse the damage of every malady. But ALS would certainly be considered one of the toughest, and she'd handled that one swimmingly. According to the Gospels, the laundry list of Jesus's healings included the lame, the crippled, the paralyzed, lepers, the deaf, the mute, and the blind. Of course, there were His multiple exorcisms too. Not to mention the granddaddy of them all: raising the dead. What was Charlotte Hennesey supposed to do about that one? How dead was dead? Was there a limited window of time to repair the effects of death? Regardless, it was already too late for Evan. His body had been cremated the same morning her abductors had flown her to Israel.

'*Permesso!*' a loud voice called from behind.

Startled, Charlotte immediately quickstepped to the wall.

389

'Sorry.' A quintet of paramedics and doctors sped past with a stretcher between them. Their neat formation – two on each side, one at the rear – brought to mind Olympic bobsledders. The poor man laid out on the cushion, bare from the waist up, had suffered terrible burns to the chest, arms, and face. His eyes were wide open in shock, limbs twitching.

The tremendous urge to stop them, to intervene, to lay her hands on the poor man, was agonizing. Breathless, she watched the triage unit disappear behind the burn unit's mechanized double door at the end of the corridor.

The raw emotions tugging at her made her feel like a drug addict undergoing withdrawal. It got her thinking about how Jesus came to cope with all this. Had he been scared too? Had he had doubts that he was worthy of such a thing? After all, though God may have touched Him, He still had been human. Did He also feel lonely, lost, and confused? How did Jesus choose who to heal, how many to heal?

Such power could provoke so many different responses, from full-blown magnanimity to runaway misanthropy – perhaps even delusional mania. No doubt she needed guidance, temperance . . . faith. But where was she supposed to find the right answers? This wasn't exactly suitable material for psychoanalysis.

That's when she knew that the best place to begin was here, in Rome.

Get it together.

A young woman in sky-blue scrubs came over from the nurse's station. The garments' color had Charlotte flashing back to the robe that had once covered the egomaniacal misanthrope who'd been reduced to ashes at the foot of the Ark of the Covenant.

A quick glance at Charlotte's YMCA duffel bag confirmed the nurse's hunch that Charlotte was a fellow American.

'Are you all right?' the nurse said in English with a heavy New England accent.

'Yes.' Charlotte took a deep breath. 'Thank you.'

'Sorry you had to see that,' she said, motioning with her eyes to the burn unit. 'The toughest cases come through these doors. Takes some getting used to.'

'Think he'll make it?'

The nurse's head tipped sideways. 'We have to believe he will. Sometimes, when you think there's no hope' – she shrugged and smiled – 'you get a surprise.'

The nurse's eyes went down to the yellow laminated visitor's pass Charlotte was holding.

'Who are you here to see?'

'Patrick Donovan.'

'Ah,' she said. 'He's one of mine. I thought he had no family.'

'He does now,' Charlotte gently replied.

'Really nice of you to visit. Come, he's just down the hall. I'll take you to him.'

Charlotte walked beside the nurse.

'How is he?'

The nurse's sorrowful gaze turned to her.

'Not so well, I'm afraid. Lots of trauma to the chest. If he makes it through the next few days, he stands a good chance of pulling through. He's a real fighter.' She flashed an encouraging smile and said, 'I have a feeling he'll surprise us.'

Suddenly, she pulled Charlotte to the wall as a cardiac team came racing around the corner pushing a defibrillator. Another race against time and flesh. She could feel Death grinning.

'Sorry,' the nurse said. 'There's another reason we call them "crash carts."'

They continued down the corridor.

'You might not like what you're going to see,' the nurse apologetically explained. 'Since he's not breathing on his own, we've got him on a ventilator. Lots of tubes in his chest and throat. For the time being, we have him under heavy sedation.'

Hearing this, Charlotte got choked up, and tears spilled down her cheeks. 'Okay.'

They walked by two more rooms that had clear glass walls. Inside the third, Charlotte spotted Donovan propped up in a bed. With so many tubes taped over his mouth and nose, he was identifiable only by his hairless scalp and drooping eyebrows.

'Here we are.' The nurse stopped outside the door. 'You may want to say a prayer for him.' She placed a consoling hand on Charlotte's shoulder. 'I truly believe it helps. If you need anything or have questions, my name is Maryanne.'

'I really appreciate everything you've done. Thank you, Maryanne.'

The nurse made her way back to the triage station.

For a long moment, Charlotte stood by the door, frozen in place. Finally she made her way to his bedside, pulled a chair close, and sat beside him facing the door. The tears came harder, and when she brushed them away, she stared long and hard at her glistening fingertips, thinking how the healing powers in her DNA had so easily transferred to Cohen's son. But she kept wondering: would the boy's genome have completely recoded to resemble her own . . . and Jesus's? It couldn't be that simple, or Joshua would've had no trouble coming into contact with the Ark.

At the genetic level, something has to be different inside me.

But how could such a distinction, such a genetic selection, be made? The concept set myriad scientific principles on end. The rabbi's proposition seemed impossible – that she'd been among the 'chosen.' But how could a box filled with stone tablets, a scepter, and bones distinguish her from any other? Then again, those were no ordinary bones, the way they glowed like moon rocks. And that incredible light on the Ark's lid . . .

The all-powerful eternal light.

The idea that the ancient Egyptians had somehow stumbled upon the secrets of creation and God seemed far-fetched. Even modern genetic study couldn't come close to unlocking those mysteries. But what if there was some truth to what Cohen had told her? Moses's exodus. One supreme god somehow embodied in light?

Carefully, she placed her hand on Donovan's forearm and studied the clear intravenous tubes snaking into his hand.

He felt cold, so cold.

From her bag, she pulled a small syringe one-third filled with her blood and uncapped it. She glanced back through the glass partition to verify that no one was watching. Concealing the syringe in her hand, she pierced the needle through the IV's injection port. Uttering a silent prayer, she depressed the plunger with steady pressure until the cylinder emptied.

Another anxious glance at the corridor. No one watching.

She withdrew the syringe, capped it, and slipped it back into her purse.

Studying Donovan with hopeful anticipation, she found it hard to imagine what was happening inside him at the genetic level. Recoding of genes? Cells repairing themselves? But one thing was certain: the damage was being undone – dare she think, *miraculously*?

'You're going to feel some tingling,' she whispered, stroking his arm.

Epilogue
BELFAST

Charlotte ambled beside Father Donovan, her hiking shoes swishing through Milltown Cemetery's dewy grass. A chilly breeze rustled some yellow-tinted leaves off an oak tree's branches, portending autumn's early arrival. The sloping hillside provided a dramatic panorama of the city, just beyond the A501 motorway bordering the property. Lively jazz music echoed up from the Cathedral Quarter, where the Belfast Music Festival was kicking off its second day.

Donovan was wrapping up a very important call that he'd received on his mobile just as they'd gotten out of the car. Smiling, he slipped his cell phone into his pocket, then glanced over at her and flicked his eyebrows.

'So?' She swept her red curls back from her face. A bulky Blarney Woollen Mills sweater kept her warm.

'The Swiss Guard apprehended him last night as he tried to leave Vatican City.'

'What will happen to him?'

'Nothing good, that's for sure. Father Martin falsified documentation to allow those two men in . . . the deskman was killed, you were abducted—'

'And you were left for dead.'

'That too,' he humbly replied. 'Being an accomplice to these things . . .' He shook his head gravely. 'Some serious charges. The *commandante* told me there'll be a trial in a few weeks. We'll both need to testify, of course.'

'Of course.'

'And when will you be returning to Israel?'

'A few days, maybe. Told them I'm still recuperating.'

'But you will do it?' he asked with insistent eyes.

She sighed. 'I'd be a fool not to. Besides, they seem to be having trouble opening it. And when they found out I have the magic touch . . .' A playful shrug.

He smiled. 'I must admit I'm quite envious. To be able to study the Ark of the Covenant?' It was difficult for him to grasp the profundity of the story she'd told him about the events following her abduction from Vatican City. But the very notion that she'd likely touched the Bible's most legendary relic? He shook his head in disbelief. 'An incredible opportunity.'

'You know, if I agree to this, I will be needing some help – theologically and otherwise. I've already made a couple friends in Israel – an archaeologist and an Egyptologist. I recruited them for the project. But I was thinking, if you have some time, maybe you can accompany me . . . lend some support?'

Beaming, Donovan eagerly replied, 'You think the Israelis will allow it? I mean, I don't suppose they'll fancy me being a Catholic priest and all.'

'As I see it, if they want these puppies to open that box' – she splayed out all her fingers and wiggled them – 'they won't have much choice now, will they?'

Donovan chuckled. 'I suppose you're right. Well then, I am honored and you can count on me.'

'I knew I could.'

He led her through a maze of gravestones and monuments dominated by tall crucifixes – traditional and Celtic alike – crafted from marble and granite.

'I don't remember much after I hit the floor,' Donovan explained to Charlotte. 'But I had a strange vision of this place right before I went unconscious.'

'It's beautiful,' Charlotte said, looking out to the distant rolling hills.

It wasn't the view he was referring to. 'There's a quarter million souls buried beneath us,' he said. 'Barely any space left for newcomers. But luckily, some years back, my mother convinced my father to buy a couple of plots. He wasn't keen on it, of course,' Donovan said with a smile. 'The man celebrated life, didn't want to speak a word about death. Though I remember he'd toast the old-timers at the pub by saying, "May you be in heaven a half hour before the Devil knows you're dead."'

Charlotte laughed.

'Right over here,' he said, pointing to a humble cross-shaped gravestone. 'You would have gotten on marvelously with my parents, Charlotte. Good people with big hearts. Now see here.' He pointed to the symbol etched in his father's gravestone:

'Do you know what this symbol stands for?'

Growing up Catholic, she had seen the overlapping P and X many times before – mainly on priests' chasubles and on altar linens. But its meaning escaped her. She shook her head.

'Chi and rho are the first two letters of the Greek word for "Christ" – X and P. But as they're pronounced, they correspond to C and H in our alphabet. Christ,' he repeated. '"The anointed one," or "the chosen one."' Now he looked at her and smiled.

Stunned, Charlotte looked down at the new grass that had sprung up from the plot. 'Jesus's bones are *here*?'

Donovan smiled and nodded. He explained how his father's oversize casket included a smaller coffin inside it – an ossuary. 'The safest place I could think of. So now you know. Just you, me, and Him.'

She was speechless.

'There's something else you'll need now.'

Charlotte watched him dip into his pocket and pull out some very old-looking paper sealed in clear plastic.

'Remember our discussion about how the Gospel of Mark originally ended with the empty tomb, how the ending had been amended?'

She nodded.

'Here's the real ending,' he said. 'The world's only copy. Taken from the first Gospel, written by Joseph of Arimathea – the man who interred Jesus's body in that ossuary you studied.' He'd cut the shocking epilogue from the journal of secrets just before shipping it back to Jerusalem.

She accepted it. 'Why are you giving this to me?'

'I don't think it's a coincidence that your initials are C-H.' He tipped his head back toward the gravestone. 'I believe you were meant to have it.'

Acknowledgments

Special thanks to my wife, Caroline, my fountain of inspiration. To D. Michael Driscoll's keen eye. Once again, my hat goes off to Doug Grad for his incomparable editorial skills. To my friend and agent, Charlie Viney, for his unwavering encouragement and market savvy. Thanks, Julie Wright, Ian Chapman, and everyone at S&S UK. And cheers to the fabulous team at ILA – Nicki Kennedy, Sam Edenborough, Mary Esdaile, Jenny Robson, and Katherine West – for enabling me to share my stories in so many languages.

The Sacred Bones and *The Sacred Blood* feature hardy infusions of theology, science, and history. Since I'm a control freak when it comes to research, I take full responsibility for any unintended errors.

Multiple manuscripts of the oldest known gospel, Mark (circa 60–70 C.E.), did indeed close with the empty tomb. The confusion and disappointment this presented for Christianity's early pagan converts is believed to have spawned Mark's multiple addendums. Most scholars contend that Mark is the common source – aka the *Quelle* or Q – for the synoptic gospels of Matthew and Luke. Some also suggest that Q is comprised of both Mark and an even earlier undiscovered gospel – the 'lost gospel.' I've fictionalized this lost gospel's discovery, what the text might tell us, and its authorship by Joseph of Arimathea – in my estimation, the only likely broker for procuring Jesus's body from the cross.

I've stretched the current parameters of genetic research, though only time will tell if a more refined genome might be discovered or engineered. The ethical issues surrounding these breakthroughs should prove challenging for religion and humanity. Though I strongly believe that faith itself will remain strong, as it always has.

The religious squabbling and bloodletting over Jerusalem's Temple Mount is scarily real, as it has been since King Solomon supposedly laid its first cornerstone over three millennia ago. In its modern incarnation, this bitter turf war exemplifies Israeli and Palestinian discord over land rights and national sovereignty. Though the Mount resides wholly within Israel's borders, it is tacitly controlled by a Muslim trust, or *waqf*. Therefore, an act of terrorism committed there could easily ignite a third world war.

Josephus and Philo provide the most definitive accounts of the highly secretive Jewish community, the Essenes, who inhabited Qumran. The Essenes' obsession with the purity of body and soul present many tantalizing parallels to Christ's ministry and the emergence of Christianity. Most intriguing are their elaborate and ambitious plans for reshaping Jerusalem into a grand temple city that would herald the earthly Messianic Age. Many scholars credit the Essenes for transcribing and preserving the world's oldest copies of the Old Testament and Jewish apocryphal texts, collectively known as the Dead Sea Scrolls. The hunt for more scrolls is still under way.

Theories abound as to the fate of the Ark of the Covenant, most maintaining that a foreign empire invaded Jerusalem and claimed it as booty. In antiquity, however, sieges against heavily fortified cities like Jerusalem took months – not hours or days. So suffice it to say that the temple priests would have hidden the Ark – the centerpiece of Jewish faith, the relic that symbolized the Israelite nation – well before any combatant could have pillaged the temple. Once in hiding, the vulnerable Ark would likely have been clandestinely moved around. Inevitably, the safest hiding place would have been within a fortress's keep, behind walls, and protected by an army. Enter Josephus's chronicling of Onias's Jewish temple city in ancient Egypt's Heliopolis, complete with a homegrown army . . . and imagine the possibilities.

Finally, on navigating the minefield of the three Judaic religions . . . I recently met a very wise and pious Muslim who attributed his impressive optimism in the fate of all things to 'The Higher Power.' I sensed that he avoided a more decisive label so as not to create a barrier between us. I must confess that I liked his approach. Because though most religions seek to build community based on rigid – many times, exclusionary – doctrine, *faith* is a very personal journey that reflects a universal need in each one of us to connect with the mysterious, indefinable power(s) responsible for our world and our mortality – in other words, something bigger, or 'higher,' than ourselves. In my stories, I explore the various paths along which this most remarkable quest might take us.

MICHAEL BYRNES

†HE SACRED B⊕NES

Jerusalem is a ticking time bomb . . .

An ancient artifact is stolen from beneath Temple Mount. With thirteen Israeli soldiers dead, and the Palestinians outraged over the desecration of the sacred ground, tensions are running high. Detectives must work against the clock to identify the stolen relic and the thieves, before civil unrest escalates to deadly proportions.

Meanwhile, in Vatican City, American scientist Charlotte Hennesey and Italian anthropologist Giovanni Bersei have been secretly summoned to analyse a mysterious discovery that could prove to be history's darkest secret: a human skeleton, approximately 2,000 years old, and bearing the unmistakeable marks of crucifixion . . .

With the malevolent eye of Vatican security expert Salvatore Conte watching her every move, Charlotte must work against the clock to uncover an astonishing truth that threatens the very foundations of belief. And there's a more immediate question to face: whether the Vatican will allow this information – and Charlotte – to see the light of day . . .

ISBN 978-1-84739-012-7
PRICE £6.99